Evolution of Gestalt Series
Volume III

CONTACT AND CONTEXT: New Directions in Gestalt Coaching

Editors:
Ty Francis PhD
Malcolm Parlett PhD

A GestaltPress Book

Published and distributed by Routledge, Taylor & Francis Group Ltd., London and New York

302 Moore Street
Santa Cruz, CA 95060 USA
and
165 Cranberry Highway
Orleans, MA 02653 USA

Published and distributed by Routledge, Taylor & Francis Group Ltd.

Library of Congress Cataloging-in-publishing Data
1. Coaching; 2. Gestalt; 3. Organizational Development; 4. Ty Francis; 5. Malcolm Parlett

ISBN: 978-0-415-30000-1 (hbk)
ISBN: 978-0-415-37089-9 (pbk)
ISBN: 978-1-315-22897-6 (ebk)

Ty Francis: To my Gestalt teachers – those therapists, academics, workshop leaders, clients, colleagues and friends whose work has contributed so much to my own.

and

Malcolm Parlett: To Rosemary and Beth, and to those whom I never met – Harry, Margaret, and David.

Contents

Acknowledgements

First, we would like to thank colleagues and contributors whose work is featured here. We have enjoyed working with you and are grateful for your patience in bringing this book to publication.

Chapter 2, by Sally Denham-Vaughan and Mark Gawlinski, and Chapter 8, by Catherine Carlson and Robert Kolodny, appeared in pre-publication versions in the British Gestalt Journal, with the ready cooperation of Christine Stevens, Editor of the BGJ. Our thanks to her.

We thank Karin Groet, for her help in translating some of Georges Wollants' notes from Flemish to English, and in liaising more widely with us on his behalf.

We are grateful to Robert Rhead for the cover photograph and cover design, and to Piers Parlett for the book's page design and typesetting.

Finally, we acknowledge the seminal contribution of Gordon Wheeler, as the President of the Esalen Institute in California, and host of the conference series that gave birth to this book. Deborah Ullman of GestaltPress has also been centrally involved in this venture from the beginning. We are aware of the obstacles that have delayed publication, and celebrate that these have been surmounted through our working together. Our thanks to them.

Preface

The origin of this book has its roots in an international study conference in 2009 on Coaching, one of a series of conferences on The Evolution of Gestalt, at the Esalen Institute in California. The conference explored the potential of Gestalt theory and practice to connect to more diverse levels of social and organisational systems; and to support a deeper dialogue about Gestalt approaches and other perspectives and methodologies.

Most of the chapter contributors of this book were attendees at this conference. As consultants, coaches, therapists, teachers, activists, academics, artists, entrepreneurs and managers, we came together to explore what we understood by 'Gestalt Coaching'; as well as to develop theory and expand our practice-choices.

This book is a bridge between the rich dialogues and 'creative experiments' we engaged in at that conference, and people in the wider world of organisational coaching and Gestalt therapy, who are also interested in the qualities and contributions of contemporary Gestalt at work.

This book is therefore written with three kinds of readers in mind: 1) for organisational coaches who do not currently employ a Gestalt approach, but who might benefit from exploring what Gestalt Coaching has to offer their own practice; 2) for Gestalt practitioners already providing 'Gestalt Coaching' who will benefit from some clear articulations of how others apply Gestalt principles; 3) for psychotherapists with an active interest in Gestalt theory and practice, who would like to understand coaching and its relationship to their clinical work.

As editors, we have tried to do justice to the diversity of contributions we have received: so for example, this volume includes practice-guides, action-research accounts, interviews, opinion-pieces and articles; and reflections on delivering coaching as well as on coach training and supervision. Each shines a unique light on the practicalities and possibilities of Gestalt coaching. Taken together, the chapters also illuminate a key characteristic of Gestalt that often perplexes newcomers to the field – that there is no 'standard' practice, no 'cookie-cutter' approach, no convenient formula to recommend: Gestalt is powerful precisely because it is exquisitely relational – its core principles are brought alive differently by each practitioner, and applied differently in each situation.

We have also tried to keep our editing 'light' and not force people into a rigid framework. This is especially evident, perhaps, in the way we have celebrated the use of *both* the British-English *and* the American-English spellings and idioms of the writers – so, as a reader, you can discern the national identity of each contributor by their sentence construction (there is one exception here, where we have liaised with a Belgian contributor and translated his thinking into British English – something that seemed most honest for two British editors!).

One of the things that excites us about bringing together these accounts of organisational Gestalt coaching, is that there has been so little published about a specifically Gestalt approach in the vast coaching literature that is available – even though there are many writers who have integrated features of Gestalt thinking and practices into their work. Perhaps this tide is turning, with a shift taking place both in the wider recognition of Gestalt coaching as a distinctive contribution to organisational life, and also in the readiness of those steeped in Gestalt coaching to write about their theory of practice for those both inside and outside the Gestalt specialist field. Earlier this year, our colleague John Leary-Joyce published a welcome practical handbook about the application of Gestalt to coaching (*The Fertile Void*), and this volume is a further contribution to what we hope will be a continuing trend.

Ty Francis and Malcolm Parlett
Editors

August 2015

1

Introduction

Ty Francis PhD and Malcolm Parlett PhD

Coaching is an expanding field of professional practice – and possibly the fastest-growing arena of applied psychology in organisations today. Increasingly, leaders, managers, consultants and other clients are exploring issues of meaning, purpose, and identity that arise at the complex intersections of work and life. Contemporary coaches no longer simply focus on 'straightforward' issues of performance improvement. The role of the coach is thus changing, but the focus on organisational issues remains paramount: coaching is not a substitute for therapy, nor for management.

This book is specifically about *Gestalt* coaching. Many readers may be asking – *what is Gestalt?* Or *what does Gestalt coaching offer that is distinctive?* The purpose of the book is to respond to these questions, through presenting a range of accounts from organisational coaches describing how they ground their practice in Gestalt theory and methods; how they apply the basic principles in their coaching relationships; and how they are working creatively within the broad scope of this versatile and powerful approach. We hope that these varied practitioners' tales will demonstrate the breadth and depth of organisational Gestalt coaching, and inspire readers to re-examine their own coaching practice in the light of what they discover here.

The chapters of *Contact and Context* reveal a signature feature of Gestalt – that there is no standard coaching template that we draw on – no generic model of Gestalt coaching that provides a uniform and convenient 'how to…' answer. It is a strength of the Gestalt approach that it is a 'bespoke' product, tailoring what is done to the combination of people, environments and conditions presented in different client situations. This is precisely why we describe Gestalt as a 'relational' approach, sensitive to the unique construction and demands of each setting. Gestalt coaches 'creatively adjust' their stance and methodology to the conditions and defined needs that are present, while at the same time remaining authentic and dialogic – both hallmark capacities of an experienced Gestalt coach.

Why is this approach so relevant to the climate of today? Because the complexity of contemporary organisational life and the demands it makes on us, both personally and professionally, frequently call for more than conventional consultancy and coaching techniques: simplistic frameworks and change models are altogether insufficient. Rather than prescribe techniques or protocols, Gestalt suggests that we focus on illuminating two dominant themes in particular – one, about *contact,* or the ways we turn up in relationships; and the other, about *context,* the physical, psychological, and organisational environments that influence the quality of relating and handling of differences.

However, the exquisite responsiveness of Gestalt – while a strength – is also problematic. It is not always easy to pin down 'the Gestalt brand' so that it is easily communicated nor to teach a single Gestalt orientation. However, we believe the accounts of coaching practice within this volume will help demystify Gestalt and demonstrate the range of contemporary Gestalt thinking. For readers who are less familiar with this increasingly popular modality, we offer here some further explication of the philosophy.

Some Gestalt principles

The German word *gestalt* doesn't translate well: but roughly speaking means a 'whole configuration'. Gestalt can be seen, therefore, as an approach that preferences 'seeing wholes' and working with 'wholeness'. Thus, if we look down on a village from the top of a mountain, we see the village as a whole, not the individual buildings and roads that we put together *in order to* see the village as a whole: we see it at once as a totality, as a *gestalt*. Similarly, when a client brings an issue for exploration to a Gestalt coach, the coach does not focus on the problem in isolation, but considers it as arising from, and being in relationship to, the complexity of the client's whole situation. As Kurt Lewin – one of the founders of Gestalt – once explained, $B = f\,(P,E)$; behaviour is a function of *both* the person *and* their environment. Without this 'bigger picture' consideration, any solution is likely to be piecemeal and result in difficulties elsewhere for our clients or others.

Gestalt coaches therefore lean in the opposite direction to splitting things up into their parts – the way in which reductionist approaches to management proceed, with their attention to elements, cells, variables, identified causes, results, and marketing data points. Gestalt coaches stay as close as possible to how human beings experience their reality, which is in the form of complex and meaningful configurations of experience that are changing all the time. Drawing upon Kurt Lewin's ideas, we call this organised experience the person's 'field' – a term that readers will find widely used in this book.

In attending to our client's field – their whole construction of experience, or the 'world' in which they exist – the complexity of possibilities could obviously be overwhelming. How do we know where to begin, or what to pay attention to? Well, there is a brilliant Gestalt discovery and method that enables some of the complex patterning of experience to be revealed in a very straightforward way. At any point in time, there is something which Gestaltists call the 'figure' – something which stands out from the rest of the field (which we call the 'ground') – and attending to this relationship between figure and ground shows how the client's field as a whole is presently organised. Thus, if hungry, we notice restaurants: they stand out as figural; when we have eaten lunch, they no longer do so; when a conflict arises within a team and interrupts workflow, resolving the breakdown in the relationship assumes importance: when harmony is restored, the team can attend to other matters. Our field reorganises around a different figure when a different need arises.

So the Gestalt coach tends to begin from what is 'figural' for the client at the time of meeting: it may have to do with the meeting itself, especially in the beginning of the coaching relationship when everything is novel and uncertain. In time, the meeting with the coach is likely to become something which moves in to the background – relied upon as a supportive resource; when this occurs, work issues of many different kinds can then surface as figural, each one revealing a preoccupation, concern, or source of excitement that is 'organising the client's experience' – even when they had not always realised it was doing so in advance of the coaching session.

The extraordinary diversity of what is possible to explore is part of what makes Gestalt coaching satisfying, instructive, and unforced. It is a way of tapping into a person's (or team's) *actual* concerns and priorities, rather than what they 'should' be thinking about, as defined by others. This does not mean ignoring key concerns for the organisation, but these are approached 'phenomenologically' – that is, through how the client is actually experiencing them: perhaps ignoring them, or thinking about them rationally, or reacting to them with some personal agenda.

Given the huge possibilities of how each coaching session could unfold, each can seem an adventure in its own right. However, usually key themes as well as patterns of relating tend to surface repeatedly, and these can provide more of a long-term focus for inquiry. Refining the 'bespoke' experience is part of the excitement and power of the Gestalt approach, as clients experience it – and which keeps coaches themselves at their creative edge.

Because we take a view of the *whole situation* of which our clients are a part, the Gestalt coach has a quite particular perspective on the subject of change and how it comes about:

- We reject the role of 'Change Agent' and don't try to change anything! Instead, we bring greater awareness to the realities of how our clients (individuals, teams and whole enterprises) actually function. While this can seem at odds with organisational imperatives to meet short-term goals and targets, the sometimes dramatic nature of outcomes that *do* arise often surprises clients in their apt relevance! A classic Gestalt stance is one of 'creative indifference' to outcomes – of holding an energised interest in what our clients are attempting, while not investing too heavily in any preferred solutions and results: instead, staying scrupulously close to what is actually happening between us as coach and client. Our focus is the present experience of people as they engage in work and life tasks.

- Change happens in the here-and-now, so we use the coaching relationship as a microcosm of how the client relates and interacts elsewhere in his or her work life. So, changes in our ways of relating as coach and client can ripple out, although not necessarily in a simple cause/effect manner. Our experience of clients' behaviours, assumptions, unconscious habits and patterns of interaction that we encounter as coaches can be shared selectively with our client; equally, we can use our own 'presence' to provide different ways of responding than might be expected by our client. Frank exchanges help to disturb familiar ways of thinking, and challenge ingrained patterns of behaviour. However, this works both ways – the client is also invited to heighten contact by sharing his or her experiences of the coach. The whole approach emphasises dialogue, with a 'horizontal' relationship more than a 'vertical' one in which the client becomes over-dependent on the coach. This models openness and appreciation of authenticity, although it is not always comfortable for either party!

- Change comes about organically, influenced by the quality of contact we have with ourselves (for example, how aware and 'in touch' we are regarding our needs, feelings, concerns, assumptions and so on) as well as at the 'contact boundary' with others – the intersection between our self, colleagues, significant others and the different environments we find ourselves in. As Gestaltists we believe that growth and development occur at this intersection of the known and unknown. One of the ways in which we work to enable change at this contact boundary is through a method called 'the creative experiment'. This is a suggestion to do something differently – to take an action either in the room or later, and to explore what emerges. The purpose of a creative experiment is to provide heightened awareness and insight through trying out something different from what is more familiar. Creative experiments are jointly-created, novel experiences that are influential in disturbing the *status quo:* they are not techniques that are cut-and-pasted between different client encounters, but original suggestions arising in the here-and-now of the relationship, often challenging the client's patterns of behaviour.

- Gestalt coaches recognise that all change requires us to contend with multiple realities. In doing so, the first imperative is to surface the different realities so that change happens with fewest 'drag factors'. For instance, there are *institutional* realities (things accepted throughout the organisation); *sub-system* realities (marketers see client entertainment as an investment; accountants see it is as an overhead cost; engineers may see it is unnecessary and inefficient...); and *individual* realities (each person's construction of his or her world). In most change efforts, resistance is seen by those driving change as an opposing and deviant reality. Significant and lasting change for Gestaltists is accomplished by dealing with multiple realities in a way that produces a joining around a new, shared understanding (a new 'figure'). This involves recognising that other views exist and must be surfaced, accommodated and engaged with openly (which is core in the outlook of phenomenology that is so central to Gestalt inquiry: there is no 'reality' that cannot be re-conceived). Change is an attempt to alter what people experience as reality – not just a matter of redefining work structures, processes or methods. It involves shifting people's consciousness of how they experience themselves and others. Consequently changes sometimes lead to painful disturbances of the 'taken-for-granted' realm and to raising questions of values and even of identity, calling for additional support.

- Change is made in direct relationship to the amount of 'support' available for that change. While support is needed at all times – 'support is that which enables…' – the nature of support requires fine-tuning: what one person might find supportive would be off-putting or even disrespectful to another.

- There are dangers in introducing changes that undermine people's sources of support. People resist change because it threatens their self-support. The Paradoxical Theory of Change (Beisser, 1970) suggests that rather than intentionally pushing for changes, people need to deepen their sense of themselves and their current reality – an approach that is more about revitalising than re-engineering.

No short account of Gestalt principles can do this subject justice. In the rest of this book, a much fuller picture can be assembled: each reader can 'gestalt' their own understanding of the approach, drawing on what they already know, and according to their interests, needs, priorities, and values, add to it to gain a fuller picture.

Overview of chapters

While it is possible to 'dip in' to this book randomly, and approach each chapter according to which topics and writers you feel drawn to, it is also possible to read it in a more structured way. We have arranged the flow of chapters in a way that might help readers who are less acquainted with Gestalt theory, methods and practice.

The first three chapters not only lay out more extensively the principles of Gestalt coaching; they also invite experienced Gestalt practitioners to rethink the application of Gestalt in important new ways. Sally Denham-Vaughan and Mark Gawlinski describe their attempts to teach rapidly a set of Gestalt-based coaching skills, to large numbers of managers and clinicians in a one-day training environment; Malcolm Parlett reframes Gestalt practice as seeking to enhance five dimensions of 'whole intelligence' through pursuit of different 'explorations' – of practical use for both coach and client – in ways he describes; and Frances Johnston's chapter describes a personal research project undertaken to account for the success of a faculty of Gestalt-influenced coaches who delivered a programme over several years for a major global corporation. Each of these chapters identifies and elaborates key elements of a Gestalt coaching orientation.

The next four chapters explore the application of Gestalt coaching to leadership, management and team development. Mark Fairfield and Maggie Shelton tell the story of 'insider coaching' – where Mark (as founder and Executive Director of a non-profit organisation) engaged Maggie (as a staff member) to coach him through some leadership challenges on a series of difficult change projects; Sue Congram amplifies a view held by all contributors – that leadership is an emergent relational practice, rather than an individual skill or ability, and she describes how using imagery and engaging the imagination enables her to work in depth with her clients; Rob Farrands substantiates his claim that coaching provides the best developmental process available to managers, through presenting a parallel exploration of both coaching and managing; and Catherine Carlson and Robert Kolodny describe how their coaching of groups has been challenged and changed by embracing a relational Gestalt approach.

The final three chapters provide some even more radical and personal perspectives on Gestalt coaching. The interview with Georges Wollants challenges us to take seriously the place of embodiment in coaching and to approach coaching from a less individualist, cause-and-effect set of assumptions. Wollants also, controversially, substantiates his view that it is no use asking questions in coaching! Seán Gaffney's chapter has a distinctively personal note as he shifts our attention from what we do and how we do it as coaches, to *how we can be* in our practice; finally, Ty Francis explores the transformational micro-moments of the client encounter: he encourages us not only to pay attention to our 'felt sense' of when a moment is alive with significance and therefore the potential for change, but also believes that we can be more proactive as coaches in creating the conditions for breakthrough and transformation.

Conclusion

As editors, we are proud to present these varied chapters, and think they will stimulate thought and be interesting and useful to read both for organisational coaches interested in Gestalt, and also for Gestalt practitioners who do not have experience of working in organisational settings. While satisfied with how the collection has come together, we are also aware that there are certain themes and topics which are missing – for instance, the issues of virtual coaching, including by phone or Skype; and team coaching. However, had we included even more topics and chapters, it would have perhaps become a different kind of book – longer and maybe 'heavier' – so we are happy with how it has turned out to be, and now warmly invite you to read on...

References

Beisser, A. (1970). The Paradoxical Theory of Change. Fagan J. & Shepherd, I. (eds) *Gestalt Therapy Now*, Penguin, London.

2

Field-Relational Coaching for Gestalt Beginners: The PAIR Model

Sally Denham-Vaughan DPsych & Mark Gawlinski

To date, a number of Gestalt coaching models have been developed. Principally, they focus on activities occurring within a relatively formal coach/coachee interaction. So far, most of these tend to require the coach, and sometimes the coachee, to have extensive specialist training in Gestalt psychotherapy theory and organisational skills (see Denham-Vaughan and Chidiac, 2009, for further discussion).

Our aim in this project was to focus instead on the organisational field/culture and existing relationships *per se*: to develop a coaching process that would leverage the quality of *all* interactions occurring in the situation and be easy for people without specialist Gestalt training to understand and use. Here, we offer the PAIR coaching model as a process that can be rapidly delivered in a wide range of organisational settings where people lack pre-existing explicit Gestalt psychotherapy or organisational Gestalt knowledge or expertise.

Introduction

Working as Gestalt-informed coaches, supervisors, and coaching trainers in a range of organisational cultures and contexts, we often experience two particular tensions. The first is working in a 'field-relational', emergent and responsive way, *versus* our clients' (and sometimes our own) desire for tools, techniques as well as models providing reassuring pre-set anchor points, and sense of agency. The second is related, and is the tension between giving ample time and space for 'good enough' contact to emerge, *versus* the pressures of operational requirements and organisational cultures leading people to 'barcode' their daily schedules.

In our experience, both of these tensions point to foundational cultural differences and competing drivers – between a classic 'Gestalt' orientated environment (privileging relationships), and that of corporate and organisational life (favouring products/ tasks). We make sense of these tensions with reference to the dialectic identified by Denham-Vaughan (2005), when discussing Gestalt psychotherapy theory, between 'will' (directed action) and 'grace' (field-relational emergence). In organisational contexts, 'will' can be associated with tools, techniques, tasks, products, and time-focused action; and 'grace' with staying present and supporting co-emergence in relationship within the current situation.

As two authors, we have both noticed how difficult it can sometimes be to explain and teach these complex aspects of a field-relational 'grace-biased' Gestalt approach within more 'will-orientated' organisations. As Gestalt organisational practitioners we often find ourselves within cultures that privilege the machine metaphor (Morgan, 1986); 'cause-and-effect' psychology, and the individualised, Cartesian, medical model of change. Here, the very word 'Gestalt', with its alien sounding consonants and mysterious, elusive meanings, can turn some people off – since it (quite accurately in our opinion) conveys something hard to define and impossible to pin down. Indeed, we recognise that due to complexity in both theory and praxis, Gestalt takes many years to learn and finesse: years that most managers, employees, and leaders in organisations may not wish – or be resourced – to invest in. Our joint aim in this project, therefore, has been to spread the benefits of a Gestalt-based approach as widely as possible: to help ensure that it does not become marginalised as an elitist, 'luxury good', only available to a selected few at the top of well-resourced organisations, or reserved as a 'remedial tool' for under-performers.

Of course, in aspiring to broaden the reach of a Gestalt-based approach to work settings, we recognise the pioneering work of Burke (1980), Latner (1983), and Nevis (1987), all of whom saw linkages between a field-theoretical Gestalt approach, systems theory, and organisational behaviour. These writers pointed to the power of Gestalt interventions to affect 'total organismic functioning' (Nevis, 1987, p.18), through awareness and phenomenological exploration of the key principle of creative adjustment within changing environments.

While there has been a huge increase in coaching activity, the overarching impact of the prevailing toxic field and culture are well-described by Cavicchia (2009), who brilliantly articulates the ongoing costs of the increasing pressure of organisational life. In particular, he draws attention to coachees' awareness that 'failures to examine the complex field of intersubjectivity and interactions that contribute to, and perpetuate, familiar problems and counterproductive behaviours' (p.53) are often responsible for individual dips in performance.

In other words, and as relational Gestalt theory predicts, an individual's work performance is inextricably linked to, and emergent from, the web of interactions and relationships that surround them. As Maurer (2005) succinctly stated when discussing organisational/ large system work, 'we are *of* the field, not just in it' (p.241).

In view of this, and with the various challenges of time-pressured culture, ongoing individualism, relational interdependence and complexity in mind, we ambitiously aimed to develop a process-based, synthetic model for teaching and delivering field-relational Gestalt coaching in one day. We wanted a model that did not perpetuate the 'Lone Ranger' myth that Magerman and Leahy (2009) had pointed to, but that aimed instead to attend to and optimise key relational supports already existent in the working situation.

Specifically therefore, within this particular chapter, we will describe our seven-hour 'real-world coaching' course designed for National Health Service (NHS) leaders in the UK. This is a culture where the 'machine' metaphor, productivity, and individual heroics are still figural, and field-relational self-emergence is generally unrecognised in the dominant epistemology. As such, none of the course participants are expected to have any prior knowledge of Gestalt theory or praxis. What they do share, however, are aspirations to develop coaching style interventions that change the ethos of their working culture and that support people to flourish and work at their best.

The coaching context

As has already been stated, coaching is an increasingly popular intervention in organisations and the NHS organisations we were working with already had a successful one-day coaching training programme in place. This training is based around the popular 'GROW' model, developed by John Whitmore and colleagues (Whitmore, 2002) from the Inner Game theory of coaching, devised by Timothy Gallway (Gallway, 1986) for use in sports coaching. 'GROW' stands for Goal, Reality, Options, Will. It is usually taught with reference to particular questions that a coach can use to help their client through each stage of the process, such as: What do you want to achieve? (Goal); Where are you in relation to your goal? (Reality); What could you do? (Options); and What will you do now – and when? (Will).

Some of the ideas of Inner Game theory will be familiar to Gestalt practitioners: they place an emphasis on awareness, relaxed focus of attention, and fulfilling potential. Others, however, are far more alien to contemporary field-relational Gestalt practice and perhaps closer to a more individualised approach. In particular, there is a strong emphasis on overcoming obstacles in order to reach a goal – including seeing fear, self-doubt, and lapses of focus as interferences to the coachees' full potential.

One way we account for the success of the GROW model (in addition to its heavy reliance on the notion of a sole hero conquering adversity, which fits many organisational cultures), is that the model is *very* easy to understand, learn and use. We therefore kept these latter features as figural concerns when developing our own Gestalt-based model. Specifically, we wanted to create something as *equally appealing and accessible* as GROW, yet retain our epistemological base in the complex, field-relational, process orientation of high quality, theoretically informed Gestalt interventions. In this, we drew inspiration from the work of Leahy and Magerman (2009), who acknowledge that 'Gestalt therapy was never intended to be able to be captured in three bullets' but nonetheless continue to ask 'how we take what might be esoteric and make it more widely available'? (p.135).

Developing the model

As we clarified and discussed our aims, we found that we orientated ourselves to five inquiry topics and key questions. On examination, these proved to be our attempts to 'translate' the complex language game of field-relational Gestalt psychotherapy principles (see Yontef, 1993; Hycner and Jacobs, 1995, 2009, among others), into more easily accessible frames and language.

Key Principle 1: *Change occurs in the present moment, not at some future point identified in a goal.*
Key question: What do we need to teach participants in order to transform all spontaneously occurring interactions within the organisation into useful 'coaching' conversations?

Key Principle 2: *Change occurs in the current situation.*
Key question: How do we design and deliver coaching *within* a culture rather than taking individuals 'out of ' the culture to be coached?

Key Principle 3: *Change emerges within existing relational contexts.*
Key question: How can we improve (leverage) the quality of existing relationships and 'role-based' meetings as opposed to creating more/separate relational structures?

Key Principle 4: *Honour what exists, not what you might wish for.*
Key question: What is realistic for participants, who are leaders in

the NHS, to learn and then implement from one day of training presupposing no prior Gestalt knowledge or experience?

Key Principle 5: *Each person is a reservoir of strengths, abilities and talents which can be supported to create a coaching ethos and field.*
Key question: How can we help people draw on their inherent relational skills and personal strengths and bring them forward in the service of this task?

We will spare readers details of our many hours of discussion, debate, construction, and revision that took place as we attended to answering these questions and slowly created our model together that, appropriately, we call 'PAIR.'

The PAIR process model
As Wheeler (2006) reminds us, we are 'born to be scenario-planners, to look for a pattern fit, a solution, a prediction, as a basis for action' (p. 31). Accordingly, in any context, we are always and already making meaning of both what exists and what to do about it. We are forming gestalts that inform our action practices. Classically, within Gestalt psychotherapy theory, this phenomenological process was referred to as the 'Cycle (or wave) of Experience' (see, for example, Clarkson, 1989, for further discussion). Indeed, this aspect of theory has been used extensively by Gestalt coaches with individuals, teams, and whole organisations, with reported excellent outcomes, (e.g. Bluckert, 2006; Allan and Whybrow, 2007; Rousseau, 2009).

Recently however, Denham-Vaughan (2010) revisited this particular theoretical map to emphasise that this ongoing process of figure formation and action imperative always emerges from a context; a field that is both comprised of and activated by the relational constituents of a situation. As such, any Gestalt-based coaching model lends itself to being both field-relational and process-orientated, always embedded in the context and employing awareness of the total situation to plan action. It is these theoretical premises, comprising responses to some of our key questions outlined earlier, that we used to develop our four-phase PAIR process model.

Four phases forming a whole: Gestalt as narrative in action

The four phases of the PAIR model are: P: Presence; A: Agreement; I: Intervention; R: Review

As we have said earlier, the PAIR model aims to be a field-relational Gestalt model of coaching that is suitable for beginners to Gestalt and for use in a wide variety of organisational contexts. In particular, we aspire to use *all* existing relationships and situations within the organisation, wherever and whenever they arise, as opportunities for coaching interventions to occur. We believe that by this process we can transform an organisational ethos and culture, without specifically targeting interventions at the team or group level.

To this end, *we define coaching within our approach as a collaborative process of enabling others to experience their situation from a fresh perspective.* We believe this emphasis on collaboration (similar to 'relational', but a more commonly used and valued organisational term), both reflects and confirms the relational nature of our Gestalt approach. Similarly, the emphasis on 'fresh perspective' reflects our emergent field-theoretical orientation, wherein we do not plan in advance what the precise goal or outcome of any coaching session/meeting will be.

In practice, we envisage the model as an iterative loop that can have a fractal or recursive quality. In other words, it can be used in a step-by-step order (P, A, I then R) but also, within any one stage of the process, a coach may follow a mini-PAIR process, paying attention to any one of the stages, or all of the stages, simultaneously. In this way, we believe the model reflects the hermeneutic process[1] that we believe is necessary for all genuinely emergent process of dialogue, where both equality and active reciprocity are essential (see Orange, 2011, for full explication).

In order to simplify the description of the model, and reflect our teaching and delivery, we will now explain each individual element separately. We will then emphasise how this linear presentation works together as a whole gestalt in practice to form an emergent, field-relational, process-based Gestalt coaching model.

Element One: Presence

One of the first things that aspiring Gestalt practitioners are taught is how to become 'present' in the here and now: to 'bring all of herself to the meeting' (Joyce and Sills, 2010, p.45). Indeed, this quality was emphasised by Nevis (1987), in his seminal work *Organisational Consulting*, as being a cornerstone of the Gestalt approach, crucial to successful practice and the means by which omissions in the current situation are 'manifest, symbolised or implied' (p. 69). Nevis thus emphasised from the outset that presence has two specific qualities: turning up, and then, what you do when you have arrived. The first is a necessary precondition for anything that follows.

In practice, a number of 'action practices' can help in becoming present: sitting with one's feet firmly on the ground, paying attention to the other (including the conversation at hand), focussing on different elements in the environment and scanning inner, middle, and outer zones of awareness. (See Joyce and Sills, 2010, p.46, for further details.) In so much of organisational life, however, people find themselves flitting from meeting to meeting often finding themselves juggling multiple tasks and agendas. The result is frequently that people are distracted and pulled in multiple directions (a kind of half-distracted presence) that we believe, does not make for a productive coaching conversation.

The basic skills of turning up/becoming present are, therefore, very relevant and essential to good quality field-relational coaching conversations in organisations: not much of value for the field can emerge if you are not present within the field.

To help teach these skills we draw on Chidiac and Denham-Vaughan's (2007) definition of presence as 'energetic availability and fluid responsiveness'. We explain this as 'bringing all of yourself and your potential to this moment' and emphasise the three strands of 'paying attention to self, other, and the situation.'

We help participants to experience what impact *not* doing this can have by asking them to coach another person while planning, in detail, their dinner menu for that evening! This generates a thoroughly unpleasant experience that rapidly leads to the coachee becoming speechless when faced with the coach's poor quality and distracted presence. We follow this with the same exercise but replace the dinner distraction with our 'SOS' protocol for becoming present; where 'SOS' stands for:

1. *S*: Stick your feet on the ground; 2. *O*: Observe their eyes; 3. *S*: Slowly breathe out.

By doing this, the coach actively pays attention to the situation (noticing feet on the ground), the other (by looking at the coachee's eyes), and to self (by becoming aware of breathing). We lightly describe this as 'listening to me as if I am someone you love' and find the 'SOS' mnemonic, with its association of 'a cry for help', to be both easily remembered and associated with being of service.

This simply-taught action practice leads, in our experience so far, to delegates registering and reporting a transformational difference in experience. In addition, and consistent with the field-relational and emergent model of self arising in each moment in our relational field (Philippson, 2009), people being coached also report a radical change. Participants report that they are more able to talk, feel more supported and behaviourally enabled because of the change in the quality of the coaches' listening as they attempt to be present.

We in no way want to suggest that the complexity and multi-dimensional nature of presence – as, for instance, developed from Martin Buber's philosophy (1958/1984) – can be mastered in one day (or even in a lifetime). However, we do believe the simple teaching and practice of 'SOS' conveys some of the essence of field-relational Gestalt theory: we emerge *together* as a function of the current field, so my talking depends on the quality of your listening. In true hermeneutic spirit, we also acknowledge the converse to be true and refer to this as creating the core ingredients to have a 'good quality coaching conversation or dialogue.'

Element Two: Agreement

We begin this teaching element with the simple question: 'Have you ever been offered advice that you didn't really want? Or felt that someone who is trying to help you has missed what is really important about the issue for you?' Unsurprisingly, most course participants are easily able to offer examples.

We formulate these common experiences as 'Relational Ruptures' (Tobin, 1982). We believe these moments are inevitable consequences of differing perspectives that have a high impact on ongoing relatedness. It is one thing to be misunderstood; it is quite another to have no opportunity for dialogue about the misunderstanding. As such, while our course does not attempt to teach dialogue/psychotherapy skills (indeed, it may be risky and/or counter-productive to attempt this), we nonetheless believe we need to attend to these moments due to their impact on the relational field.

We therefore frame ruptures as being most frequently a consequence of poor quality of contact and/or lack of a working alliance/agreement. We suggest that the most common reason for this can be lack of presence (turning up and attending) on the coach's part, but that another common problem is failure to agree on the aim, task or style of the coaching conversation. There is thus no mutual or shared understanding of the process and, accordingly, there can be no surrendering to, or running with, the process. Interestingly, this was the experience of other coaching approaches that some participants reported to us; leading to us coining the phrase 'Coaching by Stealth'. This referred to a practice of leaders/managers approaching their staff and starting to coach them without ever agreeing to the process. We concluded that in some cases, enthusiasm to coach had clearly outflanked the need for coaching.

While we see the potential dangers of this lack of agreement, we nonetheless teach – subject to certain core conditions being in place – the agreement between the coach and coachee does not necessarily need to be stated explicitly by the coach. Our experience is that, with sufficient presence and contact in relationship, agreement regarding what happens and what is helpful in relationship is apparent and can be phenomenologically observed in the coachee's responses, both verbal and embodied.

The key question we ask people to consider, therefore, is *not* whether they have explicitly agreed to a goal or aim with the coachee. Rather, we ask coaches explicitly to ask themselves how confident they are that they are being helpful to the coachee. Paradoxically, positioning this question as a figural concern for the coach leads to greater verbal exploration of the agreements that are being made and more frequent exploration of this with coachees. In our training we support this frequent 'temperature testing' of the agreement process and further support this by our use of reviews (see element 4). Furthermore, we explicitly discuss with coaches the various down-to-earth ways of checking agreement that do not jar the conversation (and therefore the relationship).

Our personal experience of the GROW model is that the questions suggested are designed to be used in quite formal contexts and, therefore, can sound strange when used day-to-day. They may evoke a response of 'what was that question about?', or worse, 'what is this person trying to *do to* me with that question?'. The latter response can create a strong sense of objectification that potentially ruptures the relationship and risks extreme shame for both parties. (See Carlson and Kolodny, 2009, for a full exploration of shame in the coaching context.) Contrast, for example, the following two types of questions:

GROW goal-checking examples:
"What do you want?"
"What are you hoping to achieve?"

PAIR model agreement-checking examples:
"How about I…?"
"Is there anything you would like from me?"
"Would it be useful if I…?"
"I get a sense that it would be good if we…"

Our intention is that the latter generate an altogether lighter, looser, and more collaborative and relational form of being together than the rather individualised and potentially objectifying language of the former.

Indeed, some participants in the GROW training running in the NHS sometimes reported that not being able to state clearly at the start of the coaching process what they wanted or hoped to achieve had led to the process stalling and/or an intense sense of failure. Many participants stated that they wanted coaching in order to become clearer *about* their goals, as opposed to getting clearer about ways to action and achieve them.

Element Three: Intervention
A novice coach on a course is usually presented with a bewildering choice of potential interventions to use at different, often prescribed, points in the process. However, when uncertainty and anxiety levels increase in a conversation, people's access to creative choices tends to reduce dramatically. At worst, there is a kind of tunnel vision where people see limited or no options and the coaching process runs out of steam.

Our experience is that the tonic for this is *not* in presenting people with lots more options: in many conversations less is more. Instead, at least in the context of a one-day course, we believe that a coach increasing their awareness of their habitual/figural style of intervention and recognising that they have at least one other option is hugely and pragmatically helpful. Furthermore, when an individual's awareness of their habitual style of intervention is framed as them playing to their strengths in a conversation, they are more likely to feel the kind of relaxed, fluid responsiveness that we know opens up new possibilities in relationship.

In this spirit, we determined to utilise a four-part minimal structure model devised by Denham-Vaughan to support 'helpful' conversations. This model is called the 4As and refers to four forms of commonly occurring, easily recognisable and rapidly accessible intervention styles: Ask, Advise, re-Assure and Action. We will now briefly describe our presentation of these styles:

1. Ask

'Ask' involves a process of inquiry aimed at deepening both parties' understanding of the issue and people involved. This is similar to the reality and options part of the GROW model and is generally supported by using open questions such as 'what' and 'how' that lead to descriptive, as opposed to yes/no answers.

We know from our experience as Gestalt psychotherapists employing phenomenological inquiry and from our experience with inquiry-based organisational change approaches – for example, Appreciative Inquiry (Cooperrider and Srivastva, 1987) – that asking good questions stimulates a deepening of awareness and spontaneously evokes change. Indeed, leadership writer Keith Grint (2005) says that what he defines as 'wicked problems' (problems that are messy, complex, and uncertain) are best approached using a collaborative and inquiring stance. In simply taught and easily learnt terms, we define this as 'Asking.'

2. Advise

Although acknowledging more and more 'wicked problems' in organisations, Grint also says that one person's wicked problem is another's tame problem. A tame problem is one where the causes are known and where a known solution is likely to work. We often learn how to deal with these kinds of problems through experience and thus may well have useful advice about ways forward.

In terms of the coaching dyad, it is sometimes the case that experienced leaders are coaching less experienced colleagues or that someone with specialist experience is coaching someone without that experience. In our experience, one of the big disadvantages of traditional coaching approaches is that they are often accompanied by a strong message that coaches 'never give advice'.

This is, no doubt, in reaction to the tendency of some coaches to jump in with advice before they have become present, reached an agreement or listened to what the coachee is actually saying. However, the 'no advice' should-ism has been so strongly introjected by people on coaching training courses that, when we began to wonder out loud in the training whether advice could occasionally be useful, we had many incredulous responses!

In fact, our advice to coaches in these situations is *not* to hold back their experience; to do so is often to retroflect that element of self that could be most helpful to the coachee and to deny the very real field-relational supports available. For example, if I fall out of a boat into a fast flowing river (a not uncommon sensation in organisational life), I'd prefer to be rescued before being instructed to swim. The former recognises the collaborative team spirit often present and available in the ground of corporate life, despite rugged individual heroics being promoted as figural. Accordingly, we suggest to coaches that if they are starting to feel that advice might be useful and they have checked out (with themselves and through agreement with their clients) that it could be well placed, they are best advised to offer it. Indeed, it might be exactly what the coachee wants and needs – and holding back can sometimes be experienced at the implicit level by the coachee as inauthentic, disingenuous, or downright annoying.

3. re-Assure

Many people in organisations and organisational cultures *per se*, are afraid of and guard against emotions, particularly anger and sadness. Some people are also afraid of coaching slipping into becoming 'therapy'. In the Gestalt world this issue is starting to be more widely explored. Some senior coaching trainers thus warn of the dangers of coaches working with or evoking emotion without very clear contracts and good-enough training in dealing with them. (See Gillie and Shackleton, 2009, for full discussion.) We agree, of course, that there can be very real dangers of coaches deliberately evoking emotions or of coaches not being able to deal with sudden emotional reactions from coachees. However, our experience in organisations is also that huge support, soothing and re-assurance can be provided by simply 'being' in relationship: listening and acknowledging what is going on for the other person. Indeed, we observe that this is often one of the most powerful things a coach can do and, sometimes just out of awareness, is what coachees would most value.

Sadly, however, more instrumental, task- and goal-focused coaching approaches seem to deny, mask, and actively discourage this *via* an emphasis on independence, agency, and individual achievement. In our training therefore, we aim to help coaches become more aware of their own attitudes to emotion being displayed (by self and others) and gently to challenge and change those patterns when helpful. Provision of simple information regarding the roles of emotion in formulating and asking good questions, energising action and releasing unhelpful patterns supports this element as participants gain a sense that emotions are functional, as well as distressing.

We revisit the 'Presence' (element 1) aspect of the course to emphasise that either too much or too little emotion can radically detract from people's ability to be fully present, focused and concentrated in the moment. We therefore emphasise a mutually shared 'corporate responsibility' to manage our own and support others' emotions within a helpful range. Obviously, we do not attempt to describe or prescribe what this range should be for the organisation. Participants do, however, report finding it very helpful to have a facilitated discussion about the positive role of emotions and that this mitigates against the pervasive 'all or nothing' attitude – whereby staff feel they must suppress all emotion until they 'explode' into tears or temper. Our hope is that these rudimentary discussions provide a supportive platform for enhancing relationships and changing the work ethos to one that is generally more supportive.

It is also worth noting, with the groups we have worked with to date, that there appeared to be very little danger that people would attempt potentially unhelpful therapy-type interventions beyond their capability levels. Indeed, the danger of avoiding and or shutting down any emotional expression seemed far greater. We were, however, always vigilant in demonstrating strategies appropriate for our brief introductory level training and of also raising the need to seek supervision, support and guidance as required.

4. Action
Action involves encouraging agency towards a task or future orientation in the coachee. This may happen near the end of a session with a view to suggesting an experiment at work and it is therefore a vital element of moving the conversation into the wider context and achieving the cultural change to which we aspire. We also found ourselves suggesting 'action' as a specific task when faced with the 'real world' situation of limited time (for instance, a coach being approached at the drinks machine while on the way to another meeting) and finding it difficult to be fully present. At this point, an action intervention can be used to suggest postponing to another time or moving to a more suitable location.

In the British health service context, we developed this specific task for 'real world' use as some leaders found postponing or refusing a request to provide coaching very challenging. Many health service leaders have the expectation that they should be almost constantly available to others, especially members of their team. However, we point out that forcing themselves to provide coaching when there are other priorities competing that cannot be deflected from, rarely enables good presence or conversation. This is thus another example of how attending to one's own ability to be present provides a way of regulating and managing unrealistic expectations and demands on time.

Guidelines for intervening
The key with all four of the 4As, in the context of a short course, is not that participants become masters of every type of intervention. Rather, we hope that they will build confidence

and ability in becoming more aware of their predominant and automatic choice or choices of existing relational style: and will experiment with both the familiar and the novel.

We focus, therefore, on different ways of helping people become aware of their patterns – and then to experience and experiment with catching themselves in the moment, becoming present, and possibly exploring a different route. Here we use the concepts of habit and stretch. 'Habit', we explain, is an individual's dominant pattern of intervention. 'Stretch' is taking a different option. Experience shows that individuals with no prior experience can quickly learn to spot their own preferred intervention style as well as that of others.

At this stage in the training we ask participants to work a lot in groups of three, with one coach, one coachee and one observer, to discuss and experience the pros and cons of each intervention option. In this way, we believe we are aligning ourselves with Hawkins and Smith's (2006, p.130) guidelines for coach development which focus on building on and extending existing abilities within facilitated peer groups. Certainly, our experience of using this format, wherein coachees present real-life, pre-prepared scenarios on which they want coaching, and novice coaches practise with support/supervision from trainers and feedback from all, is that both confidence and skills in application are rapidly increased.

For example, a manager of a health service IT department discovered, through feedback in the course, that he almost always jumped into either advising actions or inquiring about actions and next steps. Using this insight in the context of recognising it as a strength that may, nonetheless, be over-used in some circumstances, he was able to practise staying with and providing a reassuring presence to others – *before* moving into action. This very simple and easily effected change made a radical shift in his presence and the feedback he gained from coachees.

Furthermore, we invite participants to think of all their interventions in an experimental and iterative way – as part of an ongoing process of checking agreement, suggesting an intervention and then reviewing impact. We ask that they 'hold lightly' to their interventions, in order to stay present to the co-emerging process and not get locked into a fixed objective, outcome, or way of doing things. In this way, we aim to introduce the ethos of 'creative indifference' to the developing coaching culture and begin to question the idea that there is only one right way to do business. We instead assert a very pragmatic approach of 'going with what works', defined as what energises the coachee, maintains the dialogue and holds your own interest. Participants report finding this a very useful concept theoretically and are surprised to see that, by using skills learnt in the review phase, they can easily identify more 'successful' coaching conversations, sessions and interventions.

Element Four: Review

The final stage of the PAIR process is 'R' for review. We believe that dialogic coaching conversations should be reviewed continuously throughout, as well as towards the end of the conversation. We emphasise that by 'review' we mean checking how the conversation has impacted the coachee and the meaning they have made of it. It is similar to the work of assimilation and integration in Gestalt psychotherapy, utilises the hermeneutical model of dialogue previously referred to above and is modelled by us throughout the coaching delivery training day.

We state from the outset that the time for course participants to ask for something, or to give us feedback, is now; not on the feedback sheets at the end of the day. By doing this, we believe we are demonstrating and 'going live' with our five key principles that underpin the PAIR course design (present moment, current situation, relational context, existential 'reality', and motivating to fulfil potential). We therefore believe that through this simple practice we are, in an additional way, also modelling the process of present centred, field-relational, organisational Gestalt practice.

In a similar way to that already described when discussing element 2, 'Agreement', we propose that 'Reviews' can occur at both an explicit or implicit level. We therefore teach and demonstrate both processes on the course, sometimes asking explicit review questions such as: "How do you feel about what we've discussed?" "What's your thinking now?" "How are you about all this?" "On a scale of 1–10, how confident are you about this?"

Alternatively, we point out to coaches the various implicit ways we might deduce how people are responding from their embodiment: for instance, breathing faster, flushing, looking away, fidgeting, moving back, etc. We find that, generally, most leaders have few difficulties in agreeing whether embodied signals indicate either 'this is going well' or 'I don't like this'. We emphasise that we are hard-wired to make these sorts of judgements and interpretations and, in fact, use them all the time as leaders. We also emphasise that staying present makes it much more likely that we can accurately pick up signals from the other; but also that all interpretations should be 'held lightly' and explicitly checked out on a regular basis. Again, we model this during the course and give specific examples of instances when we are 'reading embodied signals' both accurately and inaccurately.

Our experience is that it is especially important to signal the *high* chances of such interpretations being wrong; but that nonetheless, utilising embodied information to support explicit reviews is vital to improving the quality of coaching conversations. We emphasise that being present both to register and respond to such signals, at the very least improves the quality of overall listening to the other.

We thereby teach coaches that paying attention to their own felt body sense, or shifts in the coachees' or the coaches' sense of the relationship during a conversation, may be enough to highlight that a coaching session has achieved its aim. Indeed, we use Gendlin's (1981) concept of 'felt shifts' to help explain to delegates that sometimes, although change is unspoken and implicit, it can be experienced in an immediately obvious way by attending to their own and the coachee's embodied process. Certainly, practice in groups of three supports this statement, with coachees reporting a dramatic improvement in their sense of being listened to and responded to when the coach factors in attention to body process. Of course, for Gestalt psychotherapists and organisational practitioners, this will come as no surprise.

Summary

In developing and teaching the PAIR process model we ambitiously aimed to develop a process-based, synthetic model for teaching and delivering field-relational Gestalt coaching in one day. We also hoped to help participants in the course leverage the quality of *all* interactions occurring in their situations – not just those occurring within the context of relatively formal coach/coachee interactions.

We believe therefore that we have succeeded in designing a Gestalt-immersed approach that achieves the principles of being time-focused, culturally-responsive and field-relational, while working with the strengths and talents that people already possess. We have now run a number of courses and found it to be possible to train Gestalt beginners to work as individual coaches and deliver Gestalt-based coaching interventions.

Follow-up action learning sets and supervision clinics have shown that individuals are keen to continue to use skills, find the frame easy to use and appreciate the relative informality of the format. Costs are kept low through being able to use internal, pre-existing relationships and coach *in situ* rather than at a distance.

There has also been feedback and comment that coachees find local knowledge and intelligence (for example, knowledge of policies, procedures, or compliance arrangements), very useful in both supporting action and avoiding time-wasting suggestions of field-inappropriate actions/experiments. In this way, we would suggest that PAIR utilises existing technical competencies and local knowledge to 'bridge the gap between individual and community' (Spagnuolo Lobb, Salonia and Sichera, 1996). *Via* the frame of the PAIR process individual coachees are supported in their relational webs at work.

With reference to this latter point, we are also satisfied that the PAIR model offers a beginning frame as a field-based intervention that supports a whole organisation to generate more positive and helpful interactions as it goes about its daily business. In this way, PAIR is situationally focused and offers up real possibilities for changing organisational ethos.

Anecdotal evidence gained from feedback at senior meetings indicates that the PAIR process has been particularly supportive during current times of high organisational uncertainty and change. Colleagues would seem to have coached each other, frequently and quite informally, with a focus on providing relational support and encouragement for actions. In view of Leahy and Magerman's (2009) summary statement that 'A trusted, intimate other is essential for deconstructing, reconstructing and making a choice' (p.140), this is perhaps unsurprising.

Indeed, we have been moved and humbled by the depth of relationship that colleagues working together in difficult and challenging circumstances reported experiencing. Consolidating, supporting and enhancing this 'supportive net' would seem to be a high priority, and an alternative to constructing individual heroes who can single-handedly save the day. We would formulate this as leaning into and developing the 'grace-biased', feminine polarity of organisational life and see development of this specific area of work as a priority for Gestalt-based coaches and organisational practitioners.

We are, however, keen not to polarise, and wish to recognise the strengths of PAIR that are more 'will-biased' and masculine: the productivity gains accruing from the brevity of training, the acknowledgement of pre-existing strengths, the recognition of daily organisational realities/constraints and the reliance on field-relational principles. We believe these factors mean that the PAIR model of Gestalt field-relational coaching is thus highly accessible for all organisations; not just highly-paid executives or well-resourced corporations able to invest in lengthy development programmes and/or highly priced external coaches.

As such, we propose that PAIR offers a bridge across the cultural tension between will and grace that can preclude Gestalt-based coaching from many less-advantaged settings. It is a way of bringing the supposedly esoteric and feminine field-relational style successfully into pressurised organisational life. In this, we see PAIR supporting the application of a genuinely phenomenological attitude to work based situations. As Wollants (2007) states,

> *The focus is on the concrete situation, the totality of relations of the person and his world, his bodily being in the world, his being with others and his experience of the givens of the present situation.* (p.158)

We believe that to have addressed this wide range of key field-relational Gestalt principles and have incorporated them in a one-day coach training event that has been so well received, is a step forward for Gestalt coaching. Our early feedback leaves us delighted to have achieved our aim of offering Gestalt-based coaching to a very wide, Gestalt-naïve audience. We also look forward to further, longer-term research in a wider range of organisations in order to explore fully the impact of PAIR on the ethos of a variety of cultures.

Notes

[1] The hermeneutic process is a process of interpretation arrived at through iterative conversation.

References

Allan, J. & Whybrow, A. (2007). Gestalt coaching. Palmer, S. & Whybrow, A. (eds), *Handbook of Coaching Psychology*, Sussex UK: Routledge.

Barber, P. (2002). Gestalt in coaching and consulting: A dialogue with holism and the soul. *Gestalt in Action*, http:// www.Gestaltinaction.com/ (Accessed 13 March 2011).

Bluckert, P. (2006). *Psychological Dimensions of Executive Coaching.* London: Open University Press.

Buber, M. (1958/1984). *I and Thou*. Edinburgh: T.&T. Clark.

Burke, W.W. (1980). Systems theory, Gestalt therapy and organization development. Cummings, T.G. (ed.), *Systems Theory for Organisation Development*. London: Wiley.

Carlson, C. & Kolodny, R. (2009). Have we been missing something fundamental to our work? Ullman, D. & Wheeler, G. (eds.), *CoCreating the Field: Intention and Practice in the Age of Complexity*. Santa Cruz CA: Gestalt Press.

Cavicchia, S. (2009). Towards a relational approach to coaching. *International Gestalt Journal*, 32, (1) 49–80.

Chidiac, M.A. (2008). A Gestalt perspective of coaching: A case for being more yourself. *Development and Learning in Organizations*, 22, 15–16.

Chidiac, M.A. and Denham-Vaughan, S. (2007). The process of presence. *British Gestalt Journal*, 16, (1) 9–19.

Clarkson, P. (1989). *Gestalt Counselling in Action*. London: Sage Publications.

Cooperrider, D.L. & Srivastva, S. (1987). Appreciative Inquiry in organizational life. Woodman, R. & Pasmore, W. (eds.), *Research in Organizational Change and Development: Volume 1*, 129–169. Greenwich CT: JAI Press.

Critchley, B. (2007). Short stories about working with a Gestalt perspective. Critchley, B., King, K. & Higgins, J. (eds), *Organisational Consulting: A Relational Perspective*. London: Middlesex University Press.

Denham-Vaughan, S. (2005). Will and grace: the integrative dialectic in Gestalt psychotherapy theory and practice. *British Gestalt Journal*, 14, (1) 5–14.

Denham-Vaughan, S. (2010). The liminal space and twelve action practices for gracious living. *British Gestalt Journal*, 19, (2) 34–45.

Denham-Vaughan, S. & Chidiac, M.A. (2009). Dialogue goes to work: relational oganisational Gestalt. Jacobs, L. & Hycner, R. (eds), *Relational Approaches in Gestalt Therapy.* Santa Cruz CA: Gestalt Press.

Gallway, T. (1986). *The Inner Game of Tennis*. London: Pan Books.

Gendlin, E.T. (1981). *Focusing*. New York: Everest House.

Gillie, M. & Shackleton, M. (2009). Gestalt coaching or Gestalt therapy: ethical and professional considerations on entering the emotional world of the coaching client. *International Gestalt Journal*, 32, (1) 173–196.

Grint, K. (2005). Problems, problems, problems: the social construction of leadership. In *Human Relations*, 58, 467–1494.

Hawkins, P. & Smith, N. (2006). *Coaching, Mentoring and Organisational Consultancy*. Berkshire: Open University Press.

Hycner, R. & Jacobs, L. (1995). *The Healing Relationship in Gestalt Therapy*. Highland, NY: Gestalt Journal Press.

Jacobs, L. (2009). Attunement and Responsiveness. Jacobs, L. & Hycner, R. (eds.), *Relational Approaches in Gestalt Therapy*. Santa Cruz, CA: Gestalt Press.

Joyce, P. & Sills, C. (2010). *Skills in Gestalt Counselling and Psychotherapy*. London: Sage Publications.

Latner, J. (1983). This is the speed of light: Field and Systems theories in Gestalt therapy. *The Gestalt Journal*, 6, (22) 71–90.

Leahy, M. & Magerman, M. (2009). Awareness, immediacy and intimacy: the experience of coaching as heard in the voices of Gestalt coaches and their clients. *International Gestalt Journal*, 32, (1) 81–144.

Magerman, M. & Leahy, M. (2009). Introduction: the lone ranger is dying: Gestalt coaching as support and challenge. *International Gestalt Journal*, 32, (1) 3–16.

Maurer, R. (2005). Gestalt approaches with organizations and large systems. Woldt, A.L. & Toman, S.M. (eds.), *Gestalt Therapy: History, Theory and Practice*. Thousand Oaks CA: Sage Publications.

Morgan, G. (1986). *Images of Organization*. Newbury Park, CA: Sage Publications.

Nevis, E.C. (1987). *Organizational Consulting: A Gestalt Approach*. Santa Cruz, CA: Gestalt Institute of Cleveland Press.

Orange, D. (2011). *The Suffering Stranger: Hermeneutics for Everyday Clinical Practice*. New York: Routledge.

Philippson, P. (2009). *The Emergent Self*. London: Karnac Books.

Rousseau, B. (2009). Coaching and the Gestalt perspective. *International Gestalt Journal*, 32, (1) 35–47.

Siminovitch, D. and Van Eron, A. (2006). The pragmatics of magic: the work of Gestalt coaching. *OD Practitioner*, 38, 50–55.

Simon, S.N. (2009). Applying Gestalt theory to coaching. *Gestalt Review*, 13, (3) 230–240.

Spagnuolo Lobb, M., Salonia, G. & Sichera, A. (1996). From the discomfort of civilisation to creative adjustment: the relationship between individual and community in psychotherapy in the third millennium. *International Journal of Psychotherapy*, 1, 45–53.

Stevenson, H. (2005). Gestalt coaching. *OD Practitioner*, 37, (4) 35–40.

Tobin, S. (1982). Self disorders, Gestalt therapy and self-psychology. *Gestalt Journal*, 11, (2) 5–24.

Wheeler, G. (2006). New directions in Gestalt therapy. *International Gestalt Journal*, 29, (1) 9–41.

Whitmore, J. (2002). *Coaching for Performance*. London: Nicholas Brealey.

Wollants, G. (2007). *Gestalt Therapy: Therapy of the Situation*. Koninklijke Wohrman, Netherlands: Zutphen.

Yontef, G. (1993). *Awareness, Dialogue and Process: Essays on Gestalt Therapy*. Highland: Gestalt Journal Press, Highland.

Acknowledgements
We would like to acknowledge the senior NHS leaders in Suffolk and Norfolk who participated in the training days and the Suffolk and Norfolk NHS Leadership Academy for supporting the design and delivery of the training.

Editors' Note

Asked by the Editors to review this book before publication, John Leary-Joyce expressed concern about the use of the word 'Advise' in one part of the authors' PAIR model, and its potential impact on new coaches, who might wrongly assume that Gestalt coaching endorses 'advising' clients. In dialogue with the authors – Sally Denham-Vaughan and Mark Gawlinski – the authors acknowledged John Leary-Joyce's concern. What became apparent was that there were two Gestalt value-sets that needed to be differentiated and both of them honoured. One value-set is that the coach's task is to enable the client to make choices on their own, without giving the client anything approaching advice. The second value-set underlines the importance of coaching clients in relation to their current reality, and challenging introjects that stand in the way. As Editors, we see both coaching tasks as valid and important. We also understand that experienced Gestalt coaches and coach trainers do not take fixed positions but rather make decisions based on their understanding of *what the situation requires*. As a result of participating in the dialogue with John Leary-Joyce, the authors have considered changing 'Advise' to 'Alternatives' in future iterations of their model, while still holding the view that advice-giving by a coach, in some exceptional circumstances, is a possible and legitimate 'alternative'.

3

'Whole Intelligence' in Coaching

Malcolm Parlett PhD

I arrive early. I enter the grand building in the City of London and introduce myself to the uniformed functionary who checks me in. I sit down in the entrance hall for the half an hour or so ahead of meeting Alexander for our first coaching session, and look around. People are turning up at work in a steady stream. I watch closely, notice their walks, varied expressions, and what they are 'bodying forth' – the way they are physically manifesting themselves and communicating their 'presence' as they enter their place of work and start a new day. I notice the human variation, the inevitable differences in appearance and gait, and their awareness of their surroundings – some are fixated on forward motion and getting to the elevators; others are a little slower and seem as if they are getting ready to talk to others.

I am already working, gathering background impressions as anybody does who enters a new environment. I am doing it with deliberate, focused attention, knowing from experience that first impressions are often so valuable, and that in my coaching relationship with Alexander – whom I have already met for an informal meeting when we contracted to work together – I am treading onto 'his patch', entering 'his world', breathing the air and ambience of the building he has spent many years within, and in which he has climbed the ladder now to almost the topmost rung – with a formidable reputation as the ultimate insider, expert in the field, and indispensable to the CEO.

Now I shift to 'soft focus' observing, allowing particulars to take second place: I allow overall, almost blurred impressions and feelings to come to me, a deliberate accessing of more holistic perception. As the impressions land, and as I notice the feelings and sensations arising within me, I begin to generate preliminary hypotheses or questions which interest me regarding the ambience, the kind of shared organisational milieu that exists here – and which, in some real way, Alexander will have helped form – and/or will have been formed by.

My basic starting point is that people never exist in isolation: as much as Alexander's problems, management style, ease with exercising power, work-life balance, and what are generally considered 'personality characteristics' may become foreground matters in the coaching to come, the core fact is that I am going to be working with Alexander-in-THIS-organisation. I am not meeting Alexander-in-the bosom-of-his-family, although (who knows?) this may become an important element in the co-created inquiry, but we are not setting out from there.

Both professionally and personally I am a long-standing people-watcher, and also in my earlier days, a researcher of organisations. I have not worked in *this* organisation before, and this time of sitting in the lobby helps to provide an observational background and 'feel' of the organisation. I notice it is different from others I've experienced. The difference is very difficult to pin down but words which are suggestive are: 'directed', 'informal', 'secure': it is not frenetic, ultra-stressed, and a considerable number of the people arriving look as if they are looking forward to the day.

Soon I shall be collected and taken to the top floor of the building to meet with Alexander. I am excited. I feel 'in my element'. I experience coaching as something that combines two work traditions in my career: *first*, organisational research – with its attention to such questions as: What kind of organisation is it? What are its taken-for-granted rules and prohibitions? What are its values and priorities, its history and character, its overall functioning, purposes, and problems?; and *second*, the methodology and thinking which characterise the Gestalt discipline to coaching, therapy, and consultation.

Whole intelligence

In this chapter, I describe my approach to coaching, which has been influenced by both of the above strands in my working history, and which has acquired in recent years a distinctive and central priority. Both in the co-created reality of the coaching process itself, and in the long-term development of the person (or team) who is being coached, I regard my aim as being to promote and support the development of 'whole intelligence' (Parlett, 2015).

By adding the word 'whole' I am distancing myself from conceptions of intelligence that are simply about mental gymnastics. Whole intelligence is a way of talking about more integrated competence, to include people's *overall maturity, high-functioning effectiveness, and emotional intelligence.* Greater exercise of whole intelligence is reflected in enhanced wellbeing and systemic good practice, in making sound judgements, in sensitive appreciation of situations, and in recognising the wisdom of the heart. These qualities need to be integrated and validated – whether they correlate with IQ or not.

I am holding as a beginning proposition that there needs to be a lot more whole intelligence in circulation – both in the organisational settings in which we coach, and in world affairs generally; and that *the coaching itself should espouse and model whole intelligence in action.*

In the past I focused on the acquisition of five high-level skills or areas of general competence, which I called 'abilities', (Parlett 2000, 2003). I listed them as follows: *Interrelating, Responding to the Situation, Embodying, Experimenting,* and *Self-Recognising*. Later, I decided that the term 'five abilities' was probably ill-advised: 'abilities' suggested they were like personal properties located somewhere inside an individual body. This very common 'solo psychology' model of human beings is one that Gestalt thinkers rightly question: we know that human beings never exist independently from their systems, traditions, and cultures.

So progressively I stopped using 'abilities' and began to think of them as *dimensions of a more unified pattern of development* – now termed 'whole intelligence'. Each is necessary for the others to emerge; each facilitates the others; each deepening of understanding in one dimension helps towards the overall developmental process.

I was also registering that each needed to be lived rather than just read about: so I began to think of the five dimensions as five 'explorations', each of them an immersion in the behaviours, values, and characteristic features of the five dimensions of whole intelligence – including of *the context in which these behaviours and styles of engagement are allowed or dis-allowed, encouraged or ignored.* I describe this model more fully elsewhere (Parlett 2015). Here, my intention is specifically how the ideas have penetrated my approach to coaching practice.

I also want to mention a second line of thought, acknowledging James Kepner's insight that:

> *The core of what is healing in the Gestalt approach is our contextual, relational and experiential orientation to create the experiential conditions that make for growth.... This notion of creating fields of experience is perhaps the most significant contribution of Gestalt therapy to the pragmatics of psychotherapy and understanding human experience, yet it is virtually an undeveloped concept in our approach'.* (Kepner, 2003, p8, emphasis in original).

Combining Kepner's seminal insight with my preoccupation concerning whole intelligence leads to the question I hold all the time when coaching: *How to create 'fields of experience' which support discovery and development of the five dimensions?* Acquiring facility with each dimension of whole intelligence involves a particular form of participation in learning and practising. Moving between the different explorations offers a succession of different perspectives, a range of outlooks or 'entry points' to investigating 'the whole'. Calling them 'explorations' again underlines the importance of 'walking in them' rather than 'talking about them': the need for practice, familiarity, and repetition is akin to learning a language.

Thus, now, as I wait to see Alexander, my intention and preoccupation will be to develop a robust and stimulating coaching relationship that will be productive, relevant, and also educative for my client. In terms of the explorations, I want to engage with the person (or team) being coached in five ways:

- Through *interrelating* in a lively, respectful, attentive, dialogic way with the client;
- Through actively engaging with the client's work or life issues as they present them, thus *responding to the situation* – both the client's working situation and our joint situation of coach and client exploring together;
- Through my *embodying* Gestalt principles and values – thus, for instance, setting up an experiential field in which bodily sensations, emotions, and intuitions have a recognised place, and so that we recognise the reality that there are two bodies in the room;
- Through finding and stimulating generative, creative processes so that the client is actively *experimenting* with different frames and possible solutions;
- Through both parties engaging in a reflective process to accompany the activities – promoting and deepening a process of *self-recognising*.

These five explorations provide a framework for *thinking about* and *conducting* coaching, and they also help ensure that all five dimensions are included in the work. As I prepare to begin with Alexander, I am therefore already 'primed' to make sure that the five dimensions all have a place: I have come to rely on them, as reminders and organisers of my approach to coaching, at the same time as not becoming enslaved by them. For me, they are like 'Gestalt universals' but not edicts carved in stone: they are more like friendly guidelines and helpful prompts. They make their presence felt by my living them and applying them; they can be communicated by multiple means – ranging from 'talking about' to direct transmission; they can be thought about conceptually;

and through direct participation and experiment they can be discovered, tried out, tested, and reflected upon, as a whole process. In short, they provide aids to learning through total 'field immersion' – providing the kind of context for multidimensional change.

Working with Alexander: A compilation of relevant notes

What follows in this chapter are brief introductions to the five explorations of whole intelligence, as I thought about them before, during, and after my coaching Alexander. In this main section of the chapter, I am reflecting on them as I look back on the coaching we did together. Up to this point in the chapter I have described *preparing for the coaching before it began*, and now I am fast-forwarding to the end of the coaching to *reflect on the coaching from a position of hindsight.*

I present the notes in the form of a composite summary listing of key points, reflecting my approach to coaching. They are arranged dimension by dimension. A reminder: any listing carries the danger of sounding prescriptive, so it is important to emphasise a cardinal Gestalt principle – namely, that in Gestalt coaching there is 'never a standard way', and fine-tuning them is obviously necessary for each client-situation and each client-hour. I offer these lists of notes both as brief encapsulations of my own thinking, and also to assist readers in thinking through and perhaps compiling their own working 'check-list'.

Interrelating

As I prepared for my meeting with Alexander – and as described earlier – I was aware of the importance of creating an experiential field which was mutually satisfying, and where interrelating was of the highest order. Gestalt has always placed emphasis on the quality of communication between people, and on the central place of dialogue. From the beginning of the meetings with Alexander, I was concerned about how we were connecting, how we communicated and understood one another – and sometimes failed to do so, for instance, when one or both of us misinterpreted the other's meaning or wishes for the session.

The notes below were all important in establishing a good working relationship with Alexander.

(i) *Getting the basics right.* The two parties need to be clear regarding mutual expectations, anticipating problems, and arranging ongoing monitoring of the coaching process. Establishing a stable, known, and agreed framework for the work together pays dividends. Agreeing contractual arrangements – especially around preserving confidentiality while honouring the need to attend to the needs of employers or sponsors – takes time and trouble, but is well spent. The client needs to grasp rapidly that they are well listened to and understood. Openness and straightforwardness between coach and client provides a necessary foundation. If mutual rapport is not apparent, this needs to be recognised and the relationship may not proceed. There needs to be recognition that while some subject matters are easily talked about, some are more 'difficult': for instance, acknowledging the needs, longings, and purposes which are *not being* met in the coaching. While coaches need to be mindful of allowing the client freedom to talk about what they want, they need also to communicate their own willingness to go further afield if the client so desires.

(ii) *Taking in the other person's context.* Related to the last point is that coaches need always to remember *to see the 'other' as a function of their context* – often, without realising it, being a 'carrier' of the organisational thinking and taken-for-granted modes of relating, and operating in ways that are in response to powerful forces within the organisation. What subject matters are appropriate and relevant to talk about is necessary to find out: some secret histories need to be kept secret, to safeguard the client's privacy and to prevent (or offset) a strong shame reaction when the client reflects on a session in retrospect and may have felt s/he went 'way too far' in self-disclosure.

(iii) *Acknowledging the inevitability of 'awkward moments'.* Exploring contact and relationship is straightforward if both parties are working together productively and enjoyably, but often difficulties can arise: and it's important to continue exploring interrelating, for instance through acknowledging misunderstandings, confusions, inhibitions, and unintentional breaks of trust. They often turn out to be profound turning points, and opportunities for mutual learning between the parties. However, I have learned the need for balance – neither ignoring 'breaks of contact', nor over-exaggerating them. The coach can acknowledge that conflict is a fact of existence, and does not have to be destructive of connection and mutual trust; and by modelling staying with 'difficult' or demanding relational moments, there is great learning. The more understanding there is – for instance, that a troubling disagreement has arisen through the two parties having different perspectives, or loyalty to different values – the more the protagonists can shift to a non-blaming 'meta' point of view, standing outside the dispute, seeing it in a broader context, and respecting each other's point of view.

(iv) *Knowing how to recognise and handle shame issues.* As coaches, we need to attend with sensitivity to the almost inevitable presence of shame issues – as a continuum between mild embarrassment and feelings of humiliation. Though statistically a normal phenomenon, shame is often the great 'un-talked about' experience – and shameful to admit to in many business contexts. Often coaches can model openness to the 'normality' of shame by speaking of their own experiences of embarrassment or shame. We need also to remember that some shame reactions may be appropriate and 'educative', and may appear alongside guilt – for instance, if someone is cheating, or breaking a confidence; so not all shame needs to be dispersed. Some overcome their shame with a carapace of 'shamelessness'. Altogether, shame reactions, and fear of shame, are some of the most difficult of coaching issues, and yet cannot be avoided: they are also often the greatest brakes on people's spontaneity and effectiveness.

(v) *'Teaching' interrelating.* The coach can introduce new insights, outlooks, or key ideas when necessary. Thus, we can explore issues of membership, affiliation, and loyalties (conflicting or otherwise), which are often hidden or taken-for-granted influences on how people relate to others, take sides, or act in apparently inconsistent ways. These tangled field connections can sometimes be investigated best by constellation methods (Whittington, 2012) where seemingly inexplicable interpersonal dynamics are sometimes revealed to make sense in terms of the field as a whole and the 'players' sense of loyalties to certain values and causes. Clients can also speak of field 'atmospherics' as they apply to key working relationships or to the relationship with the coach. Relations may be characterised as mutual or rather one-sided, forthright or defensive, plain-speaking or artificial, effective or 'going through the motions'. Attention to the qualities of the shared relational field that has been set up and which exists between the two parties is another way to underline the connectivity between people, their mutual dependence on one another, and the importance of being able to view the organisation as a complex community of different specialist 'tribes' that need to collaborate, not compete against each other. Coaches can articulate and model the principle of 'radically transforming the quality of our day-to-day conversations, whether in team meetings, by telephone, in the corridor or in more structured formal coaching sessions.' (Hawkins, 2012, p.178).

Alexander and Interrelating

I found my relationship with Alexander was relatively straightforward, though it required that I was ready to 'flow with him' rather more than I had anticipated in advance. He did not respond well to being challenged, so I had to present some of my feedback to him with great care. The theme of his relating with others, however, was a key aspect of the work: while I was willing and able largely to 'manage' the relational field we needed for a productive collaboration, some of his colleagues were clearly either unable or unwilling to be so accommodating and sensitive to his needs. So Alexander had some history of difficulties, especially with certain colleagues, that suggested he had significant learning to do in this realm. I was able, by feeding back to him some of my own reactions, to bring clearer attention to where problems might arise in working relationships. To some extent he was aware of the problems, but the idea that it was partly a matter of a co-created 'dance' between two people was not something that had occurred to him before.

Responding to the situation

I knew from my initial conversation with Alexander that the second area of exploration would be central in our work together. I knew that his wanting coaching had arisen as a major work crisis knocked him off balance – and that he did not feel he was 'responding to his situation' in a way that was going to be effective – either for his own interests or the health of the business.

There are a number of words – including 'situation' – that Gestalt writers use which have two meanings: one meaning relates to a common use of the word in ordinary conversation, while the other one has a specialist Gestalt use that is complex to define in formal terms. With 'situation' there is obviously an element of place involved, of being *in situ*. But in coaching (as well as more generally – see Wollants, 2012) it has additional meanings beside physical place. In describing their 'overall situation' clients may well include their relationships with colleagues, career aspirations, and other features of their overall context. In other words, it refers to the totality of their 'world' as it appears to the person speaking. 'Describe the situation here…' is a request that is familiar in the first sessions of coaching. As coaches, we may then notice – in the client's reply – what is excluded, underlined, asserted forcibly, or only referred to in passing, which already can begin to throw light upon their overall experience of their workplace and their place within it – the client's construction of his or her reality.

A potential confusion can arise through speaking of 'responding to the situation', almost as if the situation arrives first and stimulates the person to make a response to it. This linear, cause-effect mode of thinking is considered grossly over-simple in Gestalt, because what people experience as their situation is infused with personal involvement and meaning. To separate responses from situations is to cut with a conceptual knife something that is experientially indivisible: *so the responding and the situation need to be understood together as a complex integrated unity*. The situation is inevitably 'subjective' but this does not mean that the coach and her or his client can afford to overlook other, supposedly more 'objective' or shared accounts – and simply fasten on to personal views instead. An organisation is full of personal little worlds, but there *are* also elements within the overall system or environment that command broad agreement as well. Too much respect for idiosyncratic, subjective 'truth' can be as lop-sided as trying to promote a single so-called 'objective' truth that ignores or overrides the individual meanings and experiences of participants.

In coaching, contexts cry out to be inquired into, not least to explore the important issues of 'fit': does the client feel as if s/he fits in the organisation, and if so how? For instance, does a manager fully 'involve herself' (or 'evolve' in?) an organisation, or some project within it, or not? This is exactly the kind of question that a situational emphasis raises to prominence. In Alexander's case, his involvement and command of work-related issues were not remotely in question: there were other features of his situation which were paramount – his shifting interests in his work, the changed 'atmosphere' following a re-organisation, his impact on key stakeholders. These all entailed investigations of the responding dimension. The *subtle interplay between personal and contextual elements of the situation* lies at the heart of what most coaching attends to – and was notably a factor in Alexander's case. Coaching work in organisations is often at this border of person and workplace, with the client being, at the same time, both part of an organisation and thus *affected by it*, and also, as a presence and force, *affecting the organisation*, not least by how they act and position themselves in relation to its core purposes. This inter-involvement is central in the coaching purpose, recognising the client as a 'carrier' of the organisation as well as a co-creating 'player' and influencer.

In the following notes, I want to capture how a coach can go about creating an experiential field that supports situational awareness and understanding, and thereby assists in 'growing' the capacity of the client to respond – for instance, with insight, resilience, and 'response-ability'. Some suggestions follow.

(i) *Investigating the coaching situation itself.* The coach needs to attend to presuppositions, attitudes, background expectations, hopes, and fears surrounding the 'coach-and-client situation' they are now in together. This may entail recollections of previous experiences of coaching which may be affecting their responses now; and appraising whether there is an overall supportive culture for coaching in the organisation.

(ii) *Communicating a 'situational perspective'.* The coach may (or may not) feel the need to communicate explicitly that clients cannot regard anything in their world as wholly 'other', because they construct or 'gloss' their perceptions of it, and are an intrinsic part of it – thus helping to form, maintain, comply with, or change the situation they are in and of which they are part. This notion may be easily grasped, but some will strongly resist it as an idea that seems bizarre and unfathomable.

(iii) *Exploring the client's experience in its systemic complexity.* The coach needs to remain mindful of the multiplicity of situations – the fields within fields, frames within frames – and be open to exploring relations between levels. There are both superordinate and more inclusive framings, models, and ideas that are widely shared; and the sub-fields, subordinate realities, and local peculiarities that are more differentiated but still subsumed in the greater whole. Alexander was already skilled in thinking along these lines, but others are not.

(iv) *Identifying where energy rises – or diminishes – in the coached person or group.* Attending to personal or collective vitality can indicate emerging trends or indications of change, as well as those factors or elements and those which carry little charge. For example, I have often noticed that people are often 'turned off' by management blueprints, systems diagrams, and lists of objectives and values produced in times past – unless, of course, they are writing them anew themselves; they are more excited by what is 'live' and 'actual' in their present circumstances – something which they directly encounter and experience, rather than focusing on representations that are 'theoretical' or abstract.

(v) *Recognising that each situation is meaningful or organised around a need or purpose.* Engaging with a client requires careful attention to what his specific situation is, and the coach needs not to lose sight of this. This is the *principle of organisation*: nothing exists in a person's or group's experience that is purely random or inconsequential. (For a fuller description of the various field theory principles mentioned in this and the next note, see Parlett, 1991). There are long-standing features of our clients' worlds, along with habitual patterns of responding and of explaining their situation to themselves, that are – again – organised and patterned. Coaches need to attend to the client's or the organisation's habitual patterns of perceiving, stereotyping, problem-solving, data gathering, avoiding difficult issues, and other ways of sense-making (Ancona, 2012) that appear to be automatic and unquestioned; and to raise these into more general awareness. Whole organisations, too, can be affected by any number of different influencing factors – such as changing local circumstances, or distant economic pressures – which may alter the organisational field, as well as personally known situations. In coaching sessions any of these 'conditioners' may become prominent (*principle of possible relevance*): so no theme or subject matter can be ruled out in advance as 'inherently irrelevant'.

(vi) *Acknowledging that every situation is unique***.** What may be a wonderful coaching style in one setting will not be so in another – this is the *principle of singularity.* We are always, as coaches, approaching something never encountered exactly the same as any other situation. Moreover, situations change; they are never static or unchanging: *the principle of changing process* underlines that one cannot presume, in coaching month-by-month, that either 'situation' or responses will be experienced the same as before, even if the buildings, legal frameworks, and formal operations appear unchangeable. This means that as coaches we need to be engaged with 'the now', (the *principle of contemporaneity*).

(vii) *Recognising that responding to the situation is inevitable.* A person or group can never 'not respond': thus, non-attendance, non-voting, or staying silent in a discussion meeting, for instance, are still responses. People are never just victims of circumstances; there is a part that each person or group plays, and there are many different ways of exercising influence on what happens, whether through being an active 'agent/ initiator', or through 'participating in' or 'partnering with' something which someone else has proposed; or through doing nothing. The coach can help decipher what influences the client in one or another direction, when (for example) making a proposal, resigning, stopping an initiative, promoting somebody. The coach needs to recognise how issues of power, wider institutional structures, and societal conventions and ideologies can easily frame unquestioningly what is regarded as 'possible' or 'impossible'.

(viii) *Becoming sensitised to 'invisible' features of the situation.* The coach needs to remain open to realising when a response is *not* happening which 'should' be, and when a response is happening which 'should *not*' be happening, and be prepared to investigate the circumstances whereby there is missing support (support defined as 'that which enables') for what is 'right'. If unethical, unintelligent, or otherwise perverse practices are in operation, then what are the hidden supports that 'en-able' these to happen – or, often more accurately, 'dis-able' a more enlightened response from being chosen? In each instance, there is a need to examine critically the judgements being made – including both the client's and one's own criteria regarding what 'should' or 'should not' be happening. Discovering some of the 'invisible' organisers of Alexander's situation took him into an extensive examination of his priorities and purpose.

Alexander and Responding to the Situation

With Alexander, a great deal of the coaching was about exploring how his habitual responses could be 'tailored' to deal with the troubling issues he was encountering at the time. Alexander was so identified with his organisation that he took it for granted that he was 'part of it' and had an impact. Nevertheless he was not immune from sometimes assuming he was powerless in a particular situation where perhaps he needed to be more assertive. His sense of agency could be compromised in a surprising manner – but these occasions were more 'blips' than major interruptions, and he was skilled in 're-balancing' – as he described it.

In terms of responding to the situation of the coaching, he seemed grateful for the 'opportunity to talk freely' and in complete confidence, and his partner had commented on its having made a difference to how he acted at home. Several major events in the organisation occurred while I was coaching Alexander, including a major downturn in the business. He did not allow this, however, to limit our sessions, despite his deep involvement in the crisis management and only once did he re-schedule a session on grounds of a work commitment. Overall, Alexander's approach to his work seemed to become more flexible as he began to recognise that he did not need to do so much of the critical work himself, but could rely on others to support him. This was something of a breakthrough, given his 'workhorse' sense of his role in maintaining the direction of the business.

Embodying

If there was an area in which Alexander had difficulty, it was in registering the effects of his workload on his physical wellbeing. Central to the Gestalt approach is the holistic orientation of its practitioners – giving weight to the non-verbal realm alongside the verbal. At least in Western cultures, the bias in favour of verbal rationality spreads into numerous human activities, including downplaying the significance of visceral, emotional, and sensual aspects of lived experience.

Gestalt coaches, therefore – even if they are deeply in touch with their body sensations and their emotion-based feelings – often have to operate in a climate that is inimical to the exploration of embodying. In some work contexts doing so is culturally, socially, or institutionally deemed unacceptable – to the point of such exploration being dismissed as 'irrelevant'. While many discover for themselves how much hinges on access to this mode of experiencing oneself – and the huge expansion of scope and possibility that it offers – these advantages are often recognised only by those who have 'taken the journey' already.

Being unable to recognise emotions and ways of regulating them, or being afraid or socially embarrassed to express strong feelings in context and when they serve a useful function, is to remain unembodied. This imposes serious limitations on people's capacity to function in the working world. To have no connection to what happens when we fail to breathe fully, or the inability to control our anger, or not noticing even acute bodily needs, are forms of incompetence or lack of development that can easily be overlooked. The consequences of such denial can be serious, not least for one's physical health.

So, arguably, there needs to be a coaching priority to encourage a more full-bodied, richly textured, deeply spirited engagement in life and work, all of which can stem from this exploration. The benefits for the client can be an immense expansion of range into areas that might hitherto have seemed 'dangerous' or shameful, or avoided altogether in the work place.

In terms of creating an experiential field in a coaching situation which will support and encourage being embodied – how can this be achieved? The notes below are some of the pointers.

(i) *Attention to the physical location of the coaching.* With attention to the body being important, the coach needs to attend to the location and space, its privacy, opportunities to move, and the objects, materials, props available for the client to feel comfortable, physically secure, and stimulated creatively. Questions of privacy, avoidance of being interrupted, and of being in a place that engenders a 'right frame of mind' have emotional and sensory relevance. The physical surroundings may dictate what is possible – for example, for 'enactments' or 'sculpts'; or in exploring relationships through modelling them in terms of physical proximity and distance between the parties.

(ii) *Setting a precedent early.* As part of establishing a context which enables embodying, the coach may need to engage with embodied reactions very near to the beginning of the coaching relationship, perhaps by including body references or a focus on bodily experience as an intrinsic part of what will form part of the coaching repertoire. Some reference may need to be made to establishing safety procedures, (including 'anytime pause buttons') and clear guidelines (including permissions and prohibitions) regarding touch, intimacy, freedom to move, make a noise, and so on. The relevance, importance, safety, and 'consumer satisfaction' of body- and feeling-based coaching activities, all need emphasis.

(iii) *Establishing that the life of the body has organisational relevance.* Especially in institutions where a predominantly male culture has been traditional, and where intellectuality, logic, and rational argument are the usual indicators of high performance, the life of the body may well be regarded as having no relevance to work or to organisational effectiveness, except as an interruption – for instance, through illness, emotional outbursts, or extreme fatigue. Coaching, itself sometimes considered counter-cultural, may be seen as even more unacceptable if embodying is featured as a central part of it – so special care is called for in introducing the exploration of embodiment. Often a more straightforward means of engaging clients with their bodies is to investigate clients' predominant attitudes around questions of health, energy levels, and stress; and their current patterns of physical and emotional self-maintenance in order to foster sustainable high performance: the analogy of being 'in form' in sport has relevance in the workplace too. Coaches need to be able to cite examples of what happens when the embodying realm is ignored, and be ready to give simple demonstrations, or exercises that show how even a small change (like a change in breathing) can sometimes have a profound effect on stress levels, and ability to perform.

(iv) *Recognising cultural or religious sensitivities.* The coach needs to be aware that certain cultures and religions may be strongly resistant to people exploring *any* body reactions, *in vivo* participation, or giving attention to sensations and feeling states. This bias needs addressing with care and sensitivity, with the coach making clear that everyone sets their own limits, for instance regarding touch, that will be respected. Even in the presence of cultural or religious attitudes that inhibit embodied exploration, the coach may still be able to shift the immediate 'culture' of the coaching relationship and the 'dance between' client and coach in an embodied direction, for instance, by providing enhanced sensory opportunities, perhaps through moving outside.

(v) *Selectively noticing and pointing out physical data.* The possibility that particular gestures, body positions, or movements may be relevant to the themes being investigated, can prove useful and assimilable to the client at certain points. Thus, even someone who is not practised in being embodied may grasp the possible significance of a clenched fist, or a sudden drop in the voice level, or an impatient tapping of a finger – when regarded in the context of becoming more aware of their 'unconscious' motives and reactivity. Developing a sensibility to the significance of one's posture in how one comes over at first meetings can be an important insight to acquire. Not all clients will learn to observe shifts in voice-tones as different topics are addressed; and registering changes in breathing, energy levels, but for some, it will give them a whole new and interesting domain that can, for instance, inform them about those who report to them. Using more observational data of these kinds may reveal more about a person's 'state of being' than anything they say.

(vi) *Exercising due care.* It is important to recognise that inviting attention to the body can sometimes rapidly trigger the release of long bottled-up emotions, so the coach needs to proceed with care and sensitivity. If coaches themselves feel out of their depth, they should be very wary of proceeding: if necessary they can suspend the session, or refer the person to a suitably qualified and experienced therapist or counsellor.

(vii) *Learning to access the 'felt sense'.* Coaches can bring focus to 'the felt sense' – as best described by Eugene Gendlin (1978), as the 'royal road' to discovering one's embodied state, readiness to engage, and emotional tone at any particular time. Coaches can demonstrate the felt sense by reporting their own, and giving information and encouragement to access it. Clients can learn to pay attention to the 'body's truth' – regarding, for instance, their enthusiasm for a proposal, their attitude to a 'difficult' colleague, or their response to a threat. They can learn the benefits of pursuing an inner dialectic between their felt sense – carefully 'listened to' or attuned to in the body – and the images or associations or verbal metaphors which best 'capture' the felt sense. Learning that they can continue to attend to both sides of the dialectic, they realise they have access to a powerful dimension of a self-monitoring and also a personal change process – given that the dialectic between feelings and thoughts is constantly changing and opening to new possibilities.

Alexander and Embodying

With Alexander, the issue of becoming more embodied was not straightforward, and it took some time gradually for him to expand his sense of his 'experience' – as being more than ideas and 'facts'. I had to find ways to talk about how my own performance was affected by how I was feeling and what I was sensing. Alexander became intrigued by the idea that attending to his felt reactions to events happening at Board level might give him relevant information in policy discussions with senior colleagues. He acknowledged that he might have a 'tin ear' for embodied data, when he learnt what these were. However, much shifted when he realised that by attending to his felt sense he could decide with more acuity when the time might 'feel right' as being the most advisable for a certain initiative and that it might be advisable to forego action if a contrary felt state was present.

Experimenting

Gestalt has always given emphasis to drawing upon the creative and exploratory potential of human beings. The central idea of 'creative adjustment' acknowledges how each person creates and innovates as part of surviving and flourishing in the world. Experimenting, in the same way as action research proceeds – investigating a situation by seeking to change it – is built into the very nature of coaching.

Experimenting is also about adopting an attitude of playfulness, open-mindedness, thinking 'outside the box', and going beyond the usual. To pursue this exploration is not to pursue novelty at any cost: newness is always in contrast to what is stable, familiar, settled, habitual, and known, and these qualities are clearly necessary alongside innovation and change. Experimenting is different in conditions of extreme instability, unpredictability, and uncertainty: here it takes the form of reaffirming and restoring elements of predictability, order, and reliability. Arguably, 'stability' at such times has become 'novel'.

In 'trying things out', one does not know the answer in advance; one is 'not operating on automatic' but exploring what may be possible, or likely, or 'could be the case'. Simulating, rehearsing, planning, modelling, are all ways in which organisational advances come about. Given that these were all familiar to the extremely accomplished Alexander, the exploration of experimenting was about his willingness and ability to step into the 'unknown' zone in some more personal areas with colleagues.

Creating an experiential field which is conducive to effective experimenting can proceed in a number of ways. Some of the design principles appear in the following notes.

(i) *Modelling an experimental, participatory stance from the start.* Coaches need to communicate from the beginning that: 'Trying things out is different from just describing them from a distance, or in theory'. Talking about an issue or dilemma can be a starting place, but if it continues in that vein, the dialogue can drift into being routine, detached, and unchallenging – no different from the kind of conversation that most people have with their friends in the pub or their families at home. Gestalt introduces difference from this pattern, offering possibilities for more direct inquiries into aspects of the client's organisational situation by 'bringing it into the room' – thus making the issue more 'alive', immediate, and often more cogent.

(ii) *Demonstrating versatility of approach.* The Gestalt coach aims to set a tone in which creativity, humour, improvisation; stepping out of ordinary conventions, changing frames, and shaking up fixed and automatic assumptions that have become routine and devalued in practice, all have a place. At the same time, Gestalt coaches need to be careful not to introduce new 'shoulds' – for instance, that a coaching session '*has* to be experimental' and that ordinary conversation 'isn't Gestalt'. Sometimes merely recognising that the 'here-and-now' is a place to begin any process of change is a sufficient experimental step for a client.

(iii) *Maintaining the balance between 'safety' and 'risk'.* The coach needs to recognise that for some people changing formats, discarding 'normal procedures', upsetting traditions, and departing from 'the known' can be very threatening, and 'newness' or 'change' need to be arrived at, if at all, at their own pace. Overall, the requirement is to establish a 'highly supportive' coaching field – whatever that means for the individual client or group. The idea that taking risks and making significant changes calls for a challenging coaching regime is illusory in most cases:

taking risks with new ideas and new behaviours is far more likely to happen if the client feels a fundamental safety. However, any 'rule' is suspect: the key is not to operate from a rule but from discovery of what clients need, and how they engage with the coach and the coaching situation.

(iv) *Working with resistance, not against it.* Some individuals or groups may seem 'resistant' to change: the Gestalt approach is always to honour such resistance, as it represents a strength, and it is worth investigating and allowing. 'Attempting to overcome the resistance' is usually abusive and self-defeating on the part of the coach. In honouring resistance to change, including reluctance even to 'trying things out', the coach creates conditions of trust and opportunity to introduce small gradations of 'newness' and 'difference' at a later point. Coaches need to be careful not to push for their client to do something which is 'standard practice' for the coach but may seem extreme or counter-cultural for a client – for instance, role-playing, or talking to an imaginary person in the room. Attention needs also to be given to what is familiar, supported, and reliable – after all, expeditions into the unknown require base-camps, safety procedures, and reminders of continuity to underpin confident adventuring.

(v) *Remembering the 'paradoxical' nature of supporting change.* Ideas of change in Gestalt therapy (see Wheeler and Axelsson, 2015) include the idea of the coach (or therapist) needing to affirm and underline 'what is already present' as the starting place for investigation, rather than actively seeking to bring about or support a change towards something new. The idea is that the more deeply a person or a team 'enters into' their current experience, frustration, or problematic situation, the more the potential for change may 'gather pace' and become a strong force for a naturally arising re-alignment, or perhaps for letting go of the need to change. In some cases a coach and client may discover that a change (say, of attitude) may not be the issue: there is a need to discriminate the kinds of experiments (or interferences with a familiar pattern) that are worth making from those which are not. Recognising that not all change is beneficial, necessary, or well-planned is an important element in sophisticated experimenting: a knee-jerk decision to alter a process in the case of difficulty may not be experimental at all, whereas doing nothing may be.

(vi) *Working with inevitable side-effects.* The experience of shame was discussed under Interrelating. The coach needs to be mindful that 'new' behaviour, role-plays, or steps into the unknown are likely to evoke embarrassment or shame issues – usually of a low order – simply through a measure of incompetence being demonstrated in doing anything for the first time. Any move away from the 'normal' range of responses needs corresponding supports – whether it's merely encouragement and the reassurance of the coach's presence and commitment, or something that meets the client's needs.

Alexander and experimenting

Alexander – having rarely confided in someone else apart from his spouse – was experimenting from the outset, simply by admitting to some of his difficulties and speaking to an outsider. At times, we experimented with Alexander preferring to write some statements down, rather than speak them out loud. I sensed my keeping silent (an experiment) was a sheer gift to him, given his history and experience as a senior executive among others who would interrupt and challenge him. Sometimes he needed a short period alone, or he asked me to close my eyes. All these I complied with willingly: I knew that he was 'breaking new ground' and trusted that he knew what he needed from the environment and from me. For me to have invited him to step into some more live approach – such as role-playing a meeting with a difficult colleague – I judged would have been 'disrespectful', given what he was already doing was risky and novel in his terms; and might have set the coaching back. Yet for another client, switching to role-playing might have been exactly what they needed to do, to open them to a whole new perspective, offering new vigour and interest. Experimenting is about championing 'business-as-unusual', and supporting the client in taking risks, but 'what is risky' needs fine calibration.

Self-Recognising

Central to Gestalt practice of all kinds is a focus on increasing awareness and noticing what one is doing, (or saying, feeling, or thinking) in the present moment, the 'here and now'. However, these varieties of becoming aware and of mindful attending, as important as they are, do not cover all that happens 'in present consciousness'. We also have important realisations about ourselves, our working lives, relationships, or tendencies to act and think in certain ways.

Self-recognising, in all its variants, is central to coaching work – as in other forms of Gestalt practice – and promoting it in clients is a primary objective for the practitioner. Those being coached will often describe their process and the changes they have gone through in terms of recognition – for example, registering for the first time that they have lost or foregone some aspect of their 'way of being' which was dominant in the past; or realising that how they see themselves is not how others see them.

The term 'self-recognising' is thus deliberately inclusive and expansive in scope. Knowing oneself takes many forms. In coaching, as in other modes of Gestalt inquiry, a whole sphere of possible discovery can open up for people. Often clients describe the process in terms of 'waking up' – an acknowledgement that they have been in something like a trance state hitherto, and the process of awakening can sometimes shock them, and much may ensue. The same process can occur with a group or team: some joint realisation or 'coming to terms with' a different outlook or set of assumptions, possibly arising with a change of leadership.

Of course, self-recognising is not just for clients: there is much to be explored or expanded in the continued professional development of the coach – after all, a practitioner's skillfulness in observing others, in spotting people's developmental stages, and in grasping how a person 'grows' or a team 'evolves over time', rests to a significant degree upon the sophistication of the practitioner, and his/her own 'level' of self-recognition and personal integration.

Creating an experiential field in coaching which is supportive of self-recognising can be variously achieved: the following notes may suggest how.

(i) *Explaining the central place of awareness work.* For those unfamiliar with Gestalt, some simple teaching may be in order: what it means to explore here-and-now experience; the importance of practising 'mindful' states of consciousness in a world that often seems to invite 'mindless' states induced by continuous distraction; and how new insights and experiences need assimilating into a coherent narrative of self-understanding. The coach can inquire into the way in which someone being coached already 'self-reviews', 'takes stock', or 'gains perspective', and affirm what they already do, as well as suggesting an expansion as a possible direction within coaching. The coach may point out that everyone has a considerable range of 'automatic' responses that we no longer pay attention to, and that part of self-recognising is to open these for exploration through their becoming 'strange' again. The subject matter is extensive, and the coach needs not to bypass or gloss over as inconsequential or irrelevant such issues as self-care, stress management, 'busyness', health maintenance, avoidance of burn-out; and the place of rest, vacations, 'down time', and the importance of time out in maintaining a good work-life balance, robust health, and sustainable high performance.

(ii) *Engaging with self-recognising as an intrinsic part of the coaching process itself.* Evoking a spirit of inquiry into self-recognising can be incorporated into every session. For instance, the coach can notice differences in interest-levels and personal energy levels – to which many people pay little or no attention – and invite the client (or group) to acknowledge (and confirm / disconfirm) such changes, and what they may be pointing to, or underlining. These can be indicators of genuine 'passions', which might need to be recognised rather than passed over or discounted immediately. The coach can also bring attention to the self-recognising function through noticing, alongside the client, longer-term developmental trends which become evident in the course of coaching. These may be highlighted in the context of inviting the client to review, say, the last six months taken as a whole. It is also important to invite attention to any 'unfinished business' which rankles, or is a focus for anxiety, or which interferes with present functioning or the client's benefitting from the coaching.

(iii) *Engaging with self, identity, and self-narrative.* Often themes of coaching have to do with the contradictions, complexities, and conflicts that arise as the client addresses variations on the themes of 'Who am I?' 'What am I doing here?' and 'What is next for me?' in a context of 'standing back' from the usual routines. The coach needs to attend to frames of discourse and to observe when a shift is called for. Thus, for instance, the question: 'What do you want (or need or desire)?' can sometimes be followed by: 'OK, and what do you *really* want (or need or desire)?' Such re-framing and playing with alternative question forms can sometimes evoke a forgotten or overlooked part of someone's sense of themselves. The coach may also need to reassure some clients that it is an entirely normal process to experience themselves as different selves emerging in different contexts (such as a person's different 'take' on work in Situation 1 and Situation 2), and exploring through dialogue how these divergences can lead to a productive partnership between selves, rather than being regarded as at odds with each other.

(iv) *The central place of story.* People make sense of themselves and achieve integration through telling their story and having it heard. Making a place for sharing narratives of working life is important for updating, extending, or replacing the formative, sometimes foundational, building blocks of thought about themselves and the organisation of which they are part. Reciting the history of the organisation is sometimes important, and doing so as a personalised story is often more so. Sometimes telling the story in different ways – including in archetypal / mythic language (perhaps as a fairy tale), and discouraging psychobabble clichés or management school jargon can also enrich the experience. An extension of story-telling and developing an integrative narrative is to open up and discuss values and ethics – of the client, of those involved in the client's world, and of the organisation as a whole, but also perhaps those of the coach as well. Reflecting on them and investigating disparities and confusions between them, allows space and encouragement to review current dilemmas in a more profound manner.

(v) *Reviewing and extending the coaching.* Self-recognising can include pursuing the 'work' facilitated by the coaching beyond the confines of the sessions, whether through 'homework', skill practice, or journalling. It is important that the coach ensures that links and resonances to themes of previous sessions are not lost – and that both parties have opportunities to reflect on the previous session and being ready to connect to the themes of it again, though this should not become an interfering ritual.

(vi) *'Gathering up' and summarising the effects of the coaching.* Looking back on the course of the coaching at the conclusion of it is also a time for self-recognising. As well as looking back, it can be a time to consider how the coaching may impact the future. By developing a sense of the journey already taken, and having a sense of 'the developmental next stage' or 'emerging growing edge', the coaching can be integrated into a larger and longer-term framework of inquiry as a phase in the client's personal and career development.

Alexander and Self-Recognising

Alexander derived a lot from reviewing themes that had emerged. He sought my input here, and I invited him to do more, and pointed out the benefits of his own self-monitoring and integrating. He had some blindspots regarding how he imagined others might see him, and even more so why colleagues might, for instance, find him awkward to work with. We looked at a video of a presentation he had given, and attended to how he came over, spoke, held the audience, and also occasionally lost them; this was a highpoint of the coaching. He often referred back to this, and again at the end, when he wanted to stop because his whole situation in the company shifted. Arguably it was not the right moment to stop, at least in terms of his own long-term development as a leader, but some of the work frustrations that had inspired him to have coaching in the first place were now much less apparent.

Conclusion

The five explorations offer a simple schema and model which a great many people can understand. To get a full picture of a coaching session or course of coaching, the checklist of different inquiries puts attention in places which can otherwise be overlooked or side-stepped. Acquaintance with the different dimensions and using them as interpretive and observational tools increases familiarity with them – and with progressively added familiarity, they can become a straightforward template or checklist that is useful.

In addition, the five explorations can themselves be identified, studied, and taught with a view to becoming a resource for clients.

Thus, for example, clients such as Alexander might appraise a critical meeting on the five dimensions:

- Did we *relate together* well, sharing information and handling differences effectively? Were we authentic rather than playing games? Was the meeting satisfying?
- Did we *respond to* the actual situation – get to the nub of what needed to happen? Were people taking responsibility, having a sense of ownership, behaving in ways that showed leadership?
- How *embodied* were we? Did we give credence to our 'gut sense' and were we in touch with ourselves at a feeling level? Or, alternatively, were we merely 'talking heads', as if that were sufficient?
- Did we take any new steps, or *experiment* with something fresh or different, or simply recycle the familiar without question, playing safe?
- And what did we learn – or *recognise* about ourselves, individually and as a group – and the ways we take part in

meetings of this kind? As a group, did we make intelligent choices? Were we 'on the ball'?

The above questions focus on the five dimensions one by one, but what is more important is *how they reinforce and enable each other's emergence.* The point is that whole intelligence depends on their *all* being present and in play. That is not to say that separate explorations, focusing on one dimension of whole intelligence at a time, are not useful: they are. But the principal interest is in their interaction and demonstration together. The combining of different dimensions is described elsewhere in detail (Parlett 2015), but the essential point is that all five dimensions have significance and all need to be present for a process or activity to be experienced as exceptional, whether in terms of effectiveness, practicality, performance, or human satisfaction. So if one of the dimensions is never explored, or leads nowhere in a particular organisational context, or is consistently undermined or devalued, then something important is likely to be missing that needs addressing urgently. Malfunctioning or poor performance arises through one or more of these dimensions going missing: their restoration leads to profound change and to increased whole intelligence. The model suggests that all the dimensions of the whole need to be represented.

Specifically here – in the context of coaching – readers might also wish to hold in mind two different ways that this thinking can be applied: 1. *Relating to the session itself*, the encounter, the live event between coach and client – also remembering that the session is also forming part of (and is an expression of) an ongoing relationship over time, with its developing patterns; and 2. *Relating to the client's context* and engagement with colleagues and stakeholders, which informs and is always present in the background of meaningful and effective coaching. The deep understanding and application of the explorations model may help to ensure that these two contexts remain closely interlinked in reviewing the coaching.

Finally, a reminder of the important Gestalt theme already underlined: that the five explorations model is not a standardised or fixed approach, but rather serves as an invitation for coaches to explore and test these ideas for themselves. As they helped with overseeing my experiences with Alexander, so perhaps they will support your own experiences with your clients.

References

Ancona, D., (2012). Sensemaking: Framing and acting in the unknown. Snook, S., Norhria, N., Khurana, R. (eds). *The Handbook for Teaching Leadership.* London: Sage.

Gendlin, E., (1978). *Focusing.* New York: Bantam Books.

Hawkins, P., (2012). *Creating a Coaching Culture.* New York: McGraw-Hill.

Kepner, J., (2003). The embodied field. *British Gestalt Journal,* 12, (1) 6-14.

Parlett, M., (1991). Reflections on field theory. *British Gestalt Journal,* 1, (2) 69-81.

Parlett, M., (2000). Creative adjustment in the global field. *British Gestalt Journal,* 9, (1) 15-27.

Parlett, M., (2003). Creative abilities and the art of living well. Spagnuolo Lobb, M. and Amendt-Lyon, N. (eds.) *Creative License: The Art of Gestalt Therapy.* Wien: Springer-Verlag.

Parlett, M., (2015). *Future Sense: Five Explorations of Whole Intelligence for a World That's Waking Up.* Leicester: Troubador.

Whittington, J., (2012). *Systemic Coaching and Constellations: An Introduction to the Principles, Practices and Application.* London: Kogan Page.

Wollants, G., (2008). *Gestalt Therapy: Therapy of the Situation.* London: Sage.

4

•••

The Aesthetics of Transformational Gestalt Coaching: A Heartfelt Research Project

Frances Johnston PhD

I have been repeatedly impressed by the strength of what I consider a Gestalt orientation to coaching. I appreciate the philosophy that as coaches we are strongest when we are able to access and appropriately utilize our whole selves. Our success working across cultures is supported by our approach that appreciates both individual coaches' diversity in styles and a shared practice framework which is unified by shared values and fundamental assumptions.

I hold the perspective that coaches are artists working with a palette of colors, with a dance troupe of humans. We can consider ourselves relational artists, able to work humbly and collaboratively with our clients on behalf of their aspirations for themselves. If we hold this as our intention, and work diligently through our careers to learn from our experiences, we experience the freedom to create and to be creative.

But I also want to explore how this notion of aesthetics in Gestalt coaching helps support health, healing and growth in our clients. What is the relationship between our approach and our results?

My opportunity to deeply explore this question came when my firm was hired to deliver a training program on personal impact and influence by a large, Fortune 50 multinational energy company. The program was ultimately delivered in more than 35 countries and was evaluated by an external party as their most successful program in helping people learn and retain the skills we 'taught'. To achieve this ambition, I intentionally found, trained and hired a group of Gestalt-influenced faculty coaches. These Gestalt-influenced coaches traveled the world and had significant success inspiring employees from multiple cultures to mindfully and intentionally grow in confidence, presence and their ability to use flexibly a variety of influencing styles to deepen their connection with their coworkers. The goal of the initiative was to help employees increase self and social awareness and enhance their ability to gain commitment from others. We wanted to help them focus on the elements of their jobs where they needed other people's support or behavioral change.

The program was very successful as evaluated by external evaluators, the participants themselves, their managers, and our own experiences as faculty coaches. You might say this was a very big experiment!

I was the leader of this troupe, and I *saw* beauty in action, I felt the artistry and self-expression of my fellow Gestalt coaches. I knew there was more to what we were doing than the techniques of coaching. There was an aesthetic quality to the way we approached the work. After the success of this training program, and other engagements our firm had achieved using a Gestalt-influenced coaching approach, I wanted to understand more deeply the essence of our success. To do this, I set out on a personal research project to explore the elements of our success in working across cultures, often with significant language barriers, and frequently in very different work cultures from our own. What follows are the results of a qualitative research project informed by our experience.

I particularly like the idea that beauty can be seen in our work with fellow humans. As one colleague remarked,

> *There is beauty in what is co-created with the client. When I am at my best, there is an elegance in my interventions. It could be in the succinctness of it, its brevity, or in the emotion of it, or in supporting the previously unseen connections.*

Often I am asked, what is 'Gestalt Coaching'? Much like the other authors in this book, I have settled, satisfied, into the place of identifying deeply with this approach. What stands out for me is the interchange between coach and client. I love that we notice and care about elements such as the structure of our respective worldviews, the vividness of attention, the contours of flow, the quality of connection and the balance and patterns of movement in the moment. That we notice, acknowledge and include our preferences, biases, attraction, creativity and affections, is an enormous advance in coaching practice. We use our emotional self-awareness and self-management to be present in an embodied way for the people with whom we work. I love that we challenge ourselves to get off our chairs and develop *experiences* to help our clients grow. We value our own experience, seek to deeply understand our clients, and above all are present and creative in our relationships.

My 'lenses' and interest in aesthetics

My parents, who were documentary filmmakers, often discussed how to describe and represent things that were hard to describe, such as emotions and connection. I also have this desire to express what is difficult to express. I want my research and writing to have the clear eye and awakened heart of a documentary. As an adult I use my eye to see systems and my heart to feel them. My work takes me across the world and enables me to work with leaders and their teams as they attempt to achieve the results they seek. The world of life in organizations is one full of relationship, potential, communication, and miscommunication whether with self or with others. As I have traveled and worked within this world, I have consistently relied on my early Gestalt training – a worldview and approach that has shaped me.

I am a scholar-practitioner in my approach and in my work as a leadership and organization development practitioner and coach. Having a grounded research-based approach when working with individual clients and large institutions is important to me. It affords a degree of integrity to what I do. When I make recommendations or design a training program, I want to be aware of the elements that will lead to success. And I want it to be beautiful. So, between my artistic self and my researcher self, I began this study and want to share my results. It is my hope that this chapter will stimulate you to consider your own experiences of coaching through the lens of *aesthetics*.

Aesthetics emerge from the relationship we hold with ourselves and from our interactions with others and the environment.

When we are coaching or leading a training program, we are performing in ways that invite us to dance, to interact in concert with others. There is a field of play that is created, and we have infinite choice about how we want to 'do ourselves' and how we want to 'show up'. Watching my diverse faculty of coach trainers, I saw such variety in how they approached their individuals and groups. This diversity stood out for me. As our clients are different, so our interactions with them will be.

As a trained field theorist for groups and organizations, I studied and assimilated the theories of Kurt Lewin and early perceptual social psychology, and I found the Gestalt orientation focused on whole systems, and diversity of perception and interactions, congruent with my worldview. While intellectually, I was at home with this approach that valued difference, as a young practitioner of coaching and group facilitation, I was challenged. How do I hold the idea that there isn't one true, best way, when I am such a novice and so thoroughly crave an answer to guide my practice? At pivotal points in my early career, I was fortunate to attend development programs that deepened my knowledge and appreciation of Gestalt systems theory.[1] These programs helped me be patient with myself and my emerging perceptions.

And then I learned that I could see aesthetics in our work! Studying with Sonia Nevis and Joseph Zinker on Cape Cod, Massachusetts, brought beauty to the forefront of my awareness. By watching and experiencing these true masters in our craft, I learned that our interactions with each other and our clients have an aesthetic quality. I saw smooth, elegant, easy and clean, yet creative approaches to supporting insight and shift. The idea that we can be artists as coaches and consultants became clear to me. This was such a revolutionary idea to apply to human relations, I barely knew what to do with it as a young person and practitioner.

Beyond 'technique' there was form, flow, metaphor, tone, feel, and intuition expressed in our interactions. Through observing a stylistically diverse group of faculty trainers, I noticed my interest in the choices they made and witnessed their individual artistry.

I marveled at the way the faculty trainers approached me and my fellow students, flexing their styles to match the situation. I saw the joy they expressed in their work. Nothing I experienced in graduate school matched what I found in this experience. Most profoundly, I appreciated the grounding approach of love and optimism embodied. This emotional quality enabled the students to take a deeper look at themselves with less defensiveness, and supported the faculty in taking more risk.[2] I saw the kindness and space each faculty brought to the others as they were 'being themselves,' different in style but common in values and approach. I noticed Joseph Zinker's attention to the exquisite beauty in each person and his assertion that all coaches and therapists are 'artists'. Up to this point in my professional life I had not been able to connect my intuitive sense of the importance of the quality and form of human interactions – of design – with personal emotional freedom. It would take me many more years of personal growth to liberate my artistic sense in my work in professional setting. This research study is a part of this journey to understand, validate and communicate the essential link between self-expression, professional interaction, and 'results'.

Research method

I conducted a review of aesthetics and neuropsychology literature. I reread Joseph Zinker's books (1977, 1994), because he had been my first exposure to the aesthetics of our work. I scanned but then put aside other Gestalt-oriented books because I wanted to build my own theory. After a few months, I found myself feeling ungrounded about the aesthetics of Gestalt coaching.

Aesthetics is highly subjective – what you like and dislike, what feels 'right' and what doesn't. Aesthetics also emerge from our commonality as humans with shared biology, shared norms of behavior and shared culture. I worried that because aesthetic appreciation is subjective, I would be imposing my own aesthetic as some sort of 'truth'. Therefore, I talked with Gestalt coaches who shared the experience of moments of transformation and transcendence in coaching.

Research approach and design

As a qualitative researcher, I knew that interviews and thematic analysis comprised a powerful approach to understanding social dynamics. To help illuminate the experience of Gestalt coaching from an aesthetic perspective, I talked with ten master Gestalt practitioners. I asked each person the same questions and transcribed their answers.[3] The questions were designed to help me explore what we shared in our collective self-concept as Gestalt coaches and where and when we were aware of aesthetics in our work. I also inquired about style and beauty, because these words are often associated with aesthetics. Interestingly, we didn't identify with 'style' as much as we were drawn to the idea of 'beauty'.

After the interviews, I conducted a thematic analysis that resulted in the identification of four themes, each with subthemes. The themes I identified as hallmarks of aesthetics in Gestalt coaching are:

1) *Paying Attention to our Experience of Self and Environment*
2) *What we Notice and Feel: Flow, movement, timing and rhythm*
3) *The Energy Coalesces: Transformational moments, connection and contact*
4) *Experimentation: Artistic, relational, and supporting shifts*

The interview data was independently read and studied by two Ph.D-qualified social scientists. Their perspective corroborated the initial themes, and sharpened the subthemes. The themes, are, of course, parts of a whole experience, and as such interrelate, cross over and influence one another.

Research results

My research revealed thematic similarities despite widely different approaches. Master Gestalt coaches described their experience of the aesthetics of their work as having elements of embodiment, movement, flow, timing and rhythm; attunement and present-centeredness. They each spoke of the use of experimentation and play in the process of supporting shifts in the other. These elements combine to create the 'colors' we work with in collaboration with our clients. The experience of us together is relational, artistic, broad and deep. Each coach was humbled, honored, in awe and enriched by their work with clients. For me this interplay between our self-expression, and our clients' exploration is sacred space.

In the next section, I will present the results of the thematic analysis of the interviews, supported by representative quotes. To illustrate each theme, I will provide a vignette from my experience as a Gestalt coach that provides a picture of the subjective descriptions from the interviews. Allowance for creative license will be necessary, as the vignettes are representational. For each theme, direct quotes are provided that illustrate the shared concept that constitutes the thematic cluster. Quotes are organized into subthemes and indented.

Theme One: Paying attention to our experience of self and environment – embodiment, worldview, attention, attunement

Humans constantly perceive stimuli in their environments and strive toward completeness, symmetry and 'good form.'

Aesthetics attract attention, attention leads to energy generation, and energy fuels change. We want to look at how we perceive the world to understand what is happening when successful coaching is occurring.

A Gestalt coach is aware of the emotional and physical conditions, both within themselves such as breath and other physiological data – and external to themselves. We are very keen to remain self-aware, which supports us to manage our inherent biases, broaden our awareness of novelty and hone our empathy. Here is an example I recall with help from my journal notes:

> *Our airport shuttle drove us past tall cranes and half-finished construction projects. The highway was new and smooth. Life in Baku, Azerbaijan was changing fast. We had flown over Iraq, Georgia and Europe. As I looked down on the arid, mountainous terrain, I thought of soldiers and tried to imagine what it would be like to live here. I dropped my bags in the Hilton Hotel, which was disconcertingly, and yet comfortingly, the same as so many I had stayed in before.*
>
> *I connected with my coaching colleagues to plan a venture into town. We walked past familiar luxury shops and unfamiliar alleys with restaurants, houses, stray dogs, and broken sidewalks and buildings. Our destination was the local market and a local restaurant. Walking in the market provided a rich sensory experience. We tasted, listened, saw, felt the character of the Azeri people, people we would meet, or at the least, people our participants knew. We noticed our differences and our sameness. Our goal was to sense the culture, to meet locals and inquire about their world.*

> *Although we were often tired and wanted to rest, we walked after arrival, because this attunement to the local culture – even if only enough to get that we didn't get it – and attention to the context we were working within, supported our ability to connect with the clients we met.*

The vignette above illustrates sensing and noticing functions. This first theme, 'what we notice and feel', speaks to the Gestalt coach's placement of value on perception and the process of tuning in. The theme constitutes the subthemes of embodiment, worldviews, attention and attunement.

Embodiment:
Gestalt coaches are attuned to themselves and their environments; they are interested in their own sensory experience as a means of orientation to the environment and to other person(s). In international work, we paid careful attention to the fact that 'within each culture certain possibilities of movement and structure are enhanced and more likely while others are not enhanced and less likely… a mis-attunement may be based on assumptions of a different embodied culture…' (Clemmens and Bursztyn 2003). For each theme, I will share sample quotes to illustrate the theme. Here I include:

- *'My Gestalt colleagues are more embodied, more present in the embodied from the start. More attention and resonance in the physical, emotional and inter-subjective, and an awareness of a broader contextual space. Being aware of the contextual field that the person and group is embedded in'.*

- *'It is not just a practice. It's a way of living. When I think about Gestalt and the practice of Gestalt, I think about*

> *what is the culmination of all my life experience and all the training I have'.*

Worldview:

Worldview is a construct created by the individual. It is the system of senses and meaning-making that determines how the individual physically, emotionally, and psychologically experiences reality. To make contact, one must approach and be in another's world. In Joseph Zinker's words, 'I always begin with what exists for the person (or the group) rather than with some arbitrary notions of what should be there. I try to understand and feel the other person's mode of being in the world' (Zinker 1977).

Working in Azerbaijan heightened our attention to the importance of slowing down to consider the importance of this essential meaning-making function, that of how humans construct meaning of what they perceive. This research reminds me of the importance of self-awareness of my own basic assumptions of how the world works.

> *'When you practice a Gestalt approach, it becomes a way of being in the world. This kind of being with each other is beauty'.*

> *'Beauty occurs when a client really feels we get their world. When they feel, 'Yeah, this is where I am''.*

> *'It's about the whole person, it's about the 'how' of their belief system – how they express this, it's about their physical nature, their voice tone, their carriage'.*

> *'The preference for the Gestalt person is to be curious about how the person is constructing their world or issue. How*

come, of everything you could talk about, you want to talk about this'?

'For me, in language, pacing, tone, reflecting, listen and feel into the other person's world. Let their responses to me shape me, let me be molded, modulated, so they can correct me. Especially early on before I try and correct their world. It's a gentleness... It's an energetic aesthetic'.

Attention:

Attention is consciously effortful. The use of the word 'attention' signals a purposive focus, made intentional by choosing the cognitive direction of perception toward a particular target. Attention is based on awareness (Korb *et al.* 1989). Paying attention is not always easy and is a muscle that must be developed. To pay attention to another when you don't easily share language, when you are jet-lagged and tired, or when you have heard a similar story many times takes intention, self-management and skill.

'I think attention is an aesthetic. Quality attention to another is one of the scarcest experiences people have. It seems to me, if something becomes rare, it becomes more precious'.

'When I think about the aesthetics of the work, I think about it in Zinker's (1994) description of good form. Paying attention to the energy, how energy can move or be constructed. Paying attention to the figure, how the figure gets formed, and how the figure gets interrupted. Pay attention to phenomena, you separate yourself from the phenomena, pay attention to it, look at it and start to question about it, wonder about how the person is experiencing it. Maybe ask a question about the experience'.

> *'It is easy to come up with a few clever questions; it is not easy to be present to the client, yourself, the physical, the spiritual all at once'.*

Attunement:
Attunement is a form of heightened in-the-moment awareness of others. This is beyond awareness. There are physical, emotional, and cognitive components of attunement, and a Gestalt coach may act on any one or a combination of these components in ways that impact the client. As a coach, we have the opportunity to co-create experiences grounded in a fundamental awareness of the current reality of the client.

> *'I think I am very emotionally and physically attuned to people. I move around a lot physically, I am energetically attuned, I move in response to the somatic reactions I get. I reflect back to people how I experience them'.*

> *'If you are smart and tuned in, you get a feel for what works, and all the other stuff falls away. What is the universal aesthetic? Number one, you really have a visceral sense of what is possible and what is not. Number two, it is guided by your engagement with the person or system'.*

> *'There are clients that I am more like that with – being present, emotionally attuned, co-creating, adapting. With those I am less like that with, I probably haven't found my place yet'.*

> *'A physical stillness, an absence of physical distraction. My own inner theatre is not being over-activated by the person I am with. I have this as an image as I sit down with someone. I mentally close my theatre. I am not trying to enact my*

> *play. Physical stillness, interior stillness and a kind of fuzzy focusing which just lets what gets talked about get talked about without needing to interrupt'.*

In Azerbaijan, we found a group of middle managers who spoke little or no English, and none of us spoke Azeri. As the research quotes remind us, what was central to our ability to deliver our training successfully, was our ability to attune to the participants, to be curious regarding their worldview, recognize that that worldview and our Western worldview would be both different and similar, and to pay careful, *careful* attention to our clients.

In summary, the first theme, *Experience of Self and Environment*, reveals embodiment, worldview, attention and attunement as essential elements of the Gestalt-influenced coach's perceptual field and initial orientation to others.

Theme Two: What we notice and feel – flow, movement, timing and rhythm

As we saw above, awareness of self and others is a central orientation for the Gestalt coach. We use our awareness of our own sensations and we try to be exquisitely attuned to our client. This is an interaction at a sensory, limbic and energetic level. For this reason, the self-development of the coach is essential – as distortions of perception can inhibit the interactions between coach and client. The next theme speaks to elements of this interaction. But first, an illustrative vignette:

> *I noticed that I was short of breath as my anxious client told his story. He wanted to succeed, to prove to his bosses that he was worthy of the new position. His words tumbled over each other as he spoke without pause for 15 minutes. I watched as he shifted in his chair, leaned in and out and used his hands*

> *for punctuation. When and how will I interrupt, I thought to myself? The faster he spoke, the shallower I breathed. Then I tried deep breathing. As my chest heaved up and down, he mirrored the movement and began to speak more slowly. After a few minutes of this rhythm, I spoke and inquired about his experience of the beginning and then the last part of our time together.*

Together, we moved as I made choices about how to work with the experience I was having in service of the dynamic I noticed and participated in. The theme of noticing and feeling was present in three ways:

Movement:
Gestalt has a dynamic orientation. We are interested in energy, we attend to shifts, and we explore environments – both literally and figuratively. A necessary precondition for movement is the existence of space. This idea is a great example of an aesthetic element. Space is what exists between the boundaries of two or more entities – be they ideas, people, or sensations. What does this tell us? Without space, there can be no movement. Without movement, there can be no contact. In movement, there is the potential for contact. When there is contact, there is bounded space. It is in these potentials where the work between a Gestalt coach and a client occurs. Many interviewees spoke of this development and use of space in interaction. In my client example above, without deep breath there was literally no space for my client to see himself, much less develop a perspective on change.

> *'There are these experiences that I have where we cross, we intersect. That cross moment is impactful. That space apart is the finding of the meaning for the client. Whatever it is that they are wanting to work on. When we are not touching,*

> *it gives them space to think, to want to move toward connection. I watch, I see their response, their face softens. You see it as you move toward or away'.*

> *'Witnessing someone accept a rejected, divorced part of themselves... whether it is a little kid part or a weakness part... Discovering that they can make that move. There is something beautiful about how people's stories develop'.*

> *'Sonia (Nevis) moves in and out... Out to observe to get the whole picture and then she moves in to deliver. When she is out, she is completely out of the picture... Gestalt has dramatic and fascinating strategies that can be very dramatic and deep. That is an aesthetic!'*

Flow:

Flow is more a way of becoming than a way of being, a constant state of emergence. Flow refers to an altered state of consciousness in which the individual is so immersed in an activity that performance is highly efficient and often involves a perception of time slowing down. Flow also describes a condition of non-resistance – effortless movement with the client(s). The metaphor is full of paradoxes – intersections, impact, changing structure, tensions. Perhaps a more apt metaphor is flux, a less attractive word but one that encompasses the concept of effortless mutability. So elemental, this idea came up organically in all of the interviews.

> *'Instead of thinking about the client in advance and planning what will happen, it's being ready and open intellectually, emotionally, and physically. It is about being fully present, able to go with the flow'.*

> *'The flow of verbal spoken language from the coach to the coachee. When it is done well, it's like moving water, sometimes calm, sometimes moving waves'.*

> *'There is something about flow. About that construct when everything makes sense. It could be insight, awareness, connection that has that feeling. Something becomes a little more stark, transparent, something happens. I don't see it visually...I feel expansiveness in my chest'.*

> *'When I feel in flow with a client, I feel like I am in a continuous figure of eight going through her and through me. There is a flow between me and her, a flow of thought because she becomes very engaged and focused. Everyone else has dropped away. I love this state, this feeling of connection with another person, a transcendental quality about it. A whole connection'.*

Timing and Rhythm:

Time is a measure of the interval between events. Timing is the calculated spacing of events, while rhythm is a description of a pattern in the timing. From a Gestalt perspective, one can think of timing and rhythm as the aesthetic arrangement of intervals of space. Timing and rhythm modulate experience, can undermine resistances, build tension in anticipation of contact, and bind the future to the past. As I waited to intervene with my client in the vignette above, I was considering the timing of when to speak even more than thinking about what I would say. I notice the rhythm of his speech and body language, and of our interaction pattern.

> *'For me, structure is something that develops or emerges from experience, form, what gets created between. The form*

is dynamic. It grows; it breathes life, like a heart. Aesthetics is rhythm that is not always so smooth but also is understood through its dissonance, the tension that gets created between'.

'The aesthetic has to do with the use of self. It becomes this experience with my clients that feels like a double helix... where there is a rhythm, a quality to that experience, and experience when time stops, things get really slow, intense, relational, connected, not always confluent, that is where the rhythm comes in'.

'The aesthetic is in the Gestalt, the totality of what we have created together. We get into a rhythm of dance together. We create something. It's a good feeling; I can feel it in myself. I can feel excited when we get into that rhythm, and relationship, connection, I can feel it in my balls (testicles)'.

'There is something about timing, and timing being based on my client's rhythm, not my own idea of how fast things should move. Based on clues I match and then push just the right amount'.

This theme – theme two – illuminates the experience of flow, movement, timing and co-created rhythm. Our perceptual sonar tells us what is out there in space and how we fit into that space. It notices resonance and dissonance, congruence and incongruence with the environment. A key element in this environment is the coach. We structure the relational environment, attend to flow and rhythm and direct attention. Our clients learn from the process of noticing themselves as they interact with us, their coaches.

Theme Three: the energy coalesces – transformational moments, connection, contact

Our interactions are intended to support growth. When the coach is at his or her best, connection is created, important moments emerge, and contact occurs. The themes above help create the conditions and inform the coach's insight. The themes below explore what else we may actually 'do' to support growth in our clients.

> *The waiter took our order and left. One by one, we shared observations from the afternoon's sessions on 'powerful presentations through use of self.' In this session, coaching happens in small groups of eight people. Each participant presents for 7 minutes, receives feedback, and then repeats their presentation, having integrated feedback on the spot. This is a challenging session for the coaches as they have to attune to the client who is presenting, attend to the other group members who are providing feedback, and manage a very tight time frame.*
>
> *One coach talked about a nervous, fast-speaking woman who needed to make a presentation to senior management the following week. The woman was hardly breathing as she stood almost behind a plastic potted plant. The coach became animated as she described the transformation that had occurred as the woman learned to take a breath, stand on her feet in the center of the room, and make the presentation slowly and with confidence:*
>
>> *'I invited her to stand and just look at us until she connected with the room. I checked in with her as the experience went along about what she needed from me, I could feel her energetically clinging to me at first,*

> *and then slowly, stand on her own two feet – actually and metaphorically'!*

Having experienced the shift, the client now knew she could make the presentation at work the following week with an entirely different personal presence.

Connection:
Connection shows up in the consideration of aesthetics in coaching as the linkages we make in relationships as we develop interdependencies. The client and coach form connections as they relate; they are structures that become part of the world we create for ourselves. Connections imply something more lasting than a contact moment, though by no means necessarily permanent or continuous. Connections change us, and with this realization, the Gestalt coach approaches them with mindful awareness and with an appreciation regarding the aesthetic nature of their lasting effect. The coaching that the woman in the above story received, enabled her to connect better with the human beings in the room.

'I don't think Gestalt is a strategy, I think it is a way of being in your life. Your way of being in connection with another person…you don't do this part of the way or in parts of your practice'.

'I love watching the connection get made. The emotional connections that get formed as new figures emerge for them. I don't intervene with physical touch very often. I use it occasionally. It feels most provocative when I use it with another man. It feels provocative to make observations about their physical mannerism, voice tone, eye movement, body shifts'.

'My connection with the client is primary. That is the vehicle I use mostly to support them in their work. I find...executives are isolated by their position or by virtue of their personality. So I use the form of our relationship to help them learn how to make contact'.

'One man was talking about how hard things were for his business, and the other man reached out and touched the other. It was so tender. It wasn't anything I did but be present and create a container. It was a moment of connection'.

Transformational moments:
Gestalt is famous for working in the 'here and now', preferring to work with experience in the present moment rather than in contemplation of the past and how we have come to this experience. We want to explore experience and emotions as they happen. We want to explore 'now.' This theme speaks to the aesthetic of this – a contact that exists at the crossroads of past and future. These moments of heightened lucidity and mindfulness are described thus because past is memory and future is imagination. Being in the moment involves all the senses processing what occurs here and now. It is described as transcendent, beautiful and incredibly transitory. We say, 'It is all here right now'. All the issues and opportunities our clients have can be found in the present.

'Beauty means for me, when people have these moments of awareness. When they suddenly see the light of day and realize they have only been in the dark, they describe it as colorful and brilliant, and they say, 'Where have I been?!'.

'There are moments of transcendence that feel like beauty. Something that happens that is out of the ordinary that

is experienced both within me and with me and the other person, and they are having an experience within themselves'.

'There was a moment when I realized my chest was tightened and my throat narrowed. I felt like I was going to cry. I looked at the couple I was working with. They just kept missing each other. I gave them that observation. I shared what I was experiencing inside myself as 'I am watching you miss each other, just in the smallest ways.' He started to cry and said, 'That is what happens all the time when we are together".

'To spot the moment when somebody is ready to entertain a departure from their well-worn story. It's a moment of huge risk to abandon your story. I think I have learned to be more respectful of this. When we are supported enough to leave our story behind and create something new'.

Contact:
Contact is a moment that results in the temporary absence of separation. Contact reaffirms identity because it allows those who make contact to understand – *and explore* – their own and others' boundaries. Contact is often highly provocative, especially if isolation has been the prevailing norm, which is so often the case in corporate work life. Contact can occur in physical, emotional, and psychological forms, or a combination of these. Contact is powerful because it carries with it the potential for change and growth and connection. To the Gestalt practitioner, contact is an aesthetic in practice and is beautiful for this reason. Contact is very dependent on awareness, attunement, and connection.

'How do you have a single point of contact with someone whose background is so different from you, that is so profound, so deep, and sustains itself? The Gestalt principle

> *is understanding the boundary of our own experience and being curious about the boundary of others'.*
>
> *'When I have named something that is really resonant with where that pain or discomfort is. Making the contact, you dispel the real pain because the person feels really listened to'.*
>
> *'The beauty piece is the contact. I make sure I point it out as generative and special, beautiful. I want them to understand it is powerful. That I saw it'.*

This theme helps us understand the relationship between the relational connection formed between coach and client and the emergence of energized moments where a special contact occurs. This contact can be within a client's holistic self, between coach and client, and simultaneously, within the coach's experience of themselves.

Part of the art of Gestalt coaching is in the variety of ways we can establish connection that supports the transformational moment of contact. Our creativity and freedom of expression serve us well here. As the next theme will reveal, we are not limited to verbal connection. The next theme explores the opportunity to take that moment and build powerful experiences within and around it.

Theme Four: Experimentation – artistic, relational, support shifts

Experimentation is the meat of Gestalt practice. Experiments are any conscious modification of behavior with the intended result of new ways of seeing and understanding that result from the participants' mindful awareness and sensory experience. These become data for reflection and may lead to change on small or grand scales. As one interviewee for the research said,

> *'There is an aesthetic about how to craft and create experiences between us, and the world that shapes the hope. We are really attuned to how it is that we are shaping toward what it is that you are longing for, wanting'.*

We are deeply interested in catching our clients right on their edge, often in playful and surprising ways. We want to get out of our seats and join our clients in reframing, re-experiencing what can be habitual patterns, repeated neural pathways of thought.

Experiments broaden, deepen and/or shift perspective on a sensory level. To improve and enhance the possibilities of growth through shifted sensory or perceptual experience, we have an idea, test it out and see if it is effective for a client. We are interested in seeing if it expands their range, changes the shape of how they may think, the way they see lines. Once experienced, we wonder what those things mean to them and what the impact of having had a new experience is. Experiments provide the opportunity for a new experience, for expanding the range of one's experience of existence.

In an experiment, you don't know what will happen, but you trust that whatever does, it will have some impact and meaning. To work this freely takes a willingness to risk, a developed relationship to support the work, and creativity. This is where science meets art, and it is a hallmark of seeing the aesthetic in Gestalt coaching.

> *The participant, 'Steven,' was in charge of a new process that added more work to his peers but could deliver results if they would focus their teams on the implementation. The new process and situation he described seemed complicated. His world was full of individuals that he cared for, yet who*

wouldn't follow his leadership. He tried to describe it so the rest of the group could understand. You could see in his face that he needed a break. He craved contact and hoped someone could unlock this puzzle. I recognized an emerging sensation of wanting to 'help' this guy.

I asked if he was interested in an experiment where we might explore his situation by utilizing some of his classmates. He said, yes, with a look of relief and fear. The group was willing to participate. Steven picked people from the group that reminded him of his peers. After a few minutes, we had 11 men and women assembled in a circle around Steven in roughly the geographic distribution of his national team. Each person had a sense of who they were 'playing' and the stance they held toward Steven and his new process. The set-up of this experiment was meaningful, as Steven had to carefully articulate each individual's point of view towards him and his initiative. As the players took on their roles, they began to move their bodies in relation to each other and Steven. I invited Steven to influence them in his typical style. He started to 'sell' them on the benefits of the process. You could tell they were not engaged. I asked Steven what he felt. He described what we had heard before, but this time with an emerging edge of desperation.

Wanting to upgrade the intensity, I asked the team to turn around and face their 'markets.' The remaining seminar participants then became demanding clients who tried to get the attention of their market leader. Immediately, the peers forgot about Steven and his needs as they engaged with their clients. Steven froze and then ran around trying to focus his peers' attention on his needs, to no avail.

> *The experiment was over. In the debrief, Steven articulated his experience of being ignored and forgotten, and the peers reported their relief at being able to go back to their markets and their unintentional but complete disregard for Steven and his agenda. Together, we discussed ways Steven might approach his influencing challenge differently now that he had heard about his peers' experience of his approach and felt the demands on their attention in very physical ways. Steven reported a week later that he was still 'feeling' that position, and once he felt it, he could consciously change his approach to his peers.*

This example demonstrates the construction of an experiment that involved artistry in the charging of the participants, and a reliance on the relationships between participants and Steven. They played because they cared about their fellow man. Steven took the risk because he trusted me, and was motivated to experience a shift. The entire experiment took nearly an hour to unfold and debrief. Everyone learned something meaningful from the experience, none of which could have been predicted. A Gestalt practitioner uses her intuitive sense to create a piece of social art, glued together with relationships that support shifts in perception. The 10 master practitioners I interviewed had much to say about experimentation.

Artistic:

There is a profound aesthetic in the crafting of experiments. It is essential that you have an intention and line of sight for each experiment, but it is equally important that you are unattached to any particular outcome. Gestalt practitioners have the ability to synthesize and see opportunity emerge from their 'data', both in the moment and based on prior interactions. We are able to recognize experience, to be in the moment, to think, support, articulate and act simultaneously. I process information in a holistic way; I feel my intuition and my analytic mind working together. I notice I want to move, to act, to jump out of my chair. As the research participants say:

> *'Joseph Zinker said 'give me a metaphor for what those feelings are like.' 'They are like a rotting, stinking swamp,' said I. He then asked the other woman, she said, 'it's like a beast that is hunting me.' 'Here is what you need to do,' said Zinker. 'You tell her what that swamp is like. You are sitting on the edge with a mountain on the other side where the beast is hunting. All you do is look at her and agree with her and tell her something you appreciate about her in this moment. Has to be true, but it can't be about an accomplishment. Then you will reverse it.' So we did it.... She told me what she liked about my eyebrows. Then she told me about her scary beast, and I told her something I liked about the sound of her voice. Then he asked us if the ledge we were sitting on was any wider. We did this for 45 minutes, telling stories and appreciating each other. The ledge just got wider and wider. His timing was superb. Contact makes it bearable. It got done completely by metaphor.'*

> *'There is a nexus of metaphor, storytelling and experiment. Storytelling and metaphor comes out of creativity, about making the familiar strange and the strange familiar. You take something you are working on, you put it in an alien language, and a new possibility emerges in the story. And the making the strange familiar by applying the learning to the dilemma...The aesthetic is to use the story at just the right moment'.*

Relational:
Experiments can be simple or complicated; and at their best, they are elegant social learning experiences. They are relational constructions, you and the client(s) working together in an unfolding story. By playing out his world, Steven, in the story above, heard and felt his story as he had to enact it with different players. He became aware of his habitual approach and was moved by the feedback he received from his fellow participants who 'played' his peers.

> *'Understanding that everything we say is an experiment... For instance, the difference between, "You say 'should' a lot" versus "Do you notice you say 'should' a lot?"... With Gestalt, the focus is on the intimacy of our relationship. The intimate part is using "I am noticing" and "I am wondering if it's helpful to you that I am noticing..." The "me" part of us adds more value than... just noticing and pointing out'.*

> *'The feedback I get is people describe that I get their world. It's collaborative, supportive of novelty, trying new things out. It's experimental'.*

> *'I was moved to try something, I didn't know if it would land well, but it worked. They all told me they had learned something about themselves through participating or watching the experiment'.*

Support shifts:
Clients trust us, and within that relationship of caring, they take risks and have experiences they would not have otherwise. This ability to take our attunement with clients and turn it into an action of some sort – a learning experience – often results in profound shifts in perspective, a new insight, empathy with

others and profound beginnings of change. Steven understood his relationships differently from the experience of doing the behaviors within a different set of relationships. This supported a profound shift in experience from being I-centered ('I need you to implement this process') to We-centered when he was able to empathize with the competing demands on his peers' attention.

> *'To enhance the possibilities of form, better form, we have an idea, test it out and see if it is effective for a client, if it expands their range. Changing the shape of how someone may think, the way they see lines, what those things mean to them, and having a new experience'.*
>
> *'There is something very beautiful when someone gets a fundamental shift, an a-ha moment. A deep contact, Yes, that really is what is getting to me, disturbing me, really connected with where I am at'.*
>
> *'There are moments of transcendence that feels like beauty. Something that happens that is out of the ordinary that is experienced both within me, and with me and the other person and they are having an experience within themselves'.*

The 'Steven' vignette demonstrates all the themes my interviewers reported. It was artistic in the sense that an emerging social field was created and held as it shifted. Steven and the participants trusted me, and each other, sufficiently to the point that they were willing to 'go for it' in service of Steven's learning. He was willing and able to tolerate a long time in the group spotlight – a live enactment of his back home challenge – because of the relational field we had all co-created; and finally, he was willing to bring his precious, complicated situation into the arena because he felt I had demonstrated capability to both 'get it' and support him in taking risk for his own good. The debrief of this elaborate experiment continued throughout the evening, long after the session was finished, as every person found things they related to within the different perspectives. Steven reported weeks later that he was still 'feeling' that position and once he felt it, could consciously change his approach to his peers.

Conclusion

During my twenty-year professional journey of working with clients and directing Gestalt-related development programs, I have found myself working to define what were specifically 'Gestalt' influences as they relate to our shared practice. For me, my seminal exposure to Sonia Nevis, Joseph Zinker, Joe Melnick and Penny Backman so long ago with their emphasis on the aesthetic and 'good form' as well as the power of optimism and compassion, sums up the essence of my Gestalt influence. There are other elements of course, but none that speak so centrally to my documentary filmmaker's eye and innate desire to believe that change is possible and can be approached with hope and optimism.

I decided to do this research project to deepen my awareness of my own coaching practice, as well as ground the approach my firm uses in our coach development program. I want coaches to see and feel the power of their use of self and connection with others as the vehicle of transformation, to value their own development as the essential core of their practice and ability to create connection with people very different from ourselves. I know from my own experience that transformational moments occur in a coaching relationship. When the relationship has that 'right' feel, that feeling of flow and connection, clients and I take risks.

I want us to be more explicit in our practice so that young practitioners like I once was, can more readily understand what Gestalt brings to coaching. I also want practicing Gestalt therapists to be able to see how Gestalt informs the professional practice of coaching.

A final thought

I would be remiss if I didn't directly address the fact that I am transformed by the relationships I have with my clients and fellow coaches. As I learn to more and more allow my heart, my creativity and mindful self-expression to guide my work, I expand my range as a person. This is the mutually transformational power of Gestalt-influenced coaching. We own that we are integral to our relationships, that we are connected through our limbic systems, and existentially. Our relationships are the container of creativity. I am a more whole person when I can bring this element of me to bear in my work. Too many of our workplaces and role-based relationships constrain and inhibit. Gestalt coaching explicitly is interested in broadening self-expression.

Attending to another person in the way this research reveals is a transformative experience for everyone involved. When we are mindful in attention, attunement, connection, and the flow between us; and when we use metaphor and experiments, we are in deep relationship. Such relationships are profound – a sacred space. In this space everyone grows from the experience.

I believe this is the power of Gestalt coaching, and that on some level all parties to it are aware of and present to this power. This fact equalizes the relationship between client and coach, and in doing so, is grounded in the formative values of equality and belief in democracy of the founders of Gestalt psychology. They might not have expressed so directly at the time the nature of the aesthetics of interaction, but I believe they would be pleased about how so many of us have taken their early work forward without losing sight of the essential value of self-directed, experientially-based personal growth, allied to the fact that neither coach nor client is the 'expert' but rather, that both are artists attempting to be the best they possibly can be in any given moment.

Notes

[1] In 1993, I came across the Gestalt Institute of Cleveland's Organizational and Systems' Development (OSD) program, and knew instantly that I had found a comprehensive theory of practice that felt like home. A second provocative experience happened a few years later when I studied with Sonia and Edwin Nevis, Joe Melnick, Penny Backman and Joseph Zinker at the Gestalt International Study Center on Cape Cod, Massachusetts, (USA).

[2] Recent neuroscience research on the power of positive emotions helps explain the science behind what I initially understood as a 'Gestalt-approach'. See Dan Goleman, Annie McKee, Richard Boyatzis and Barbara Fredrickson for seminal works on the power of positive emotions such as love and compassion.

[3] The questions I asked were:

1) Think of two colleagues you are fairly close to, one who has a gestalt orientation and one who does not. What is the difference in your opinion? What distinguishes a Gestalt Coach/therapist from other coaches/therapists?
2) Is it possible to practice with a gestalt orientation in part of your practice but not all of it? If so, what are the points of choice?
3) Are you aware of an aesthetical aspect to your work? If so, what does that mean to you?
4) When I ask you to describe Gestalt Aesthetics, what first comes to mind?

a. Why?
b. Describe a time when you were particularly aware of an aesthetic in your work. Where did you experience this aesthetic – in

yourself, in the interplay between you and the other, in the total arch of the intervention, etc.

5) How/where does beauty arise in your practice?

References

Clemmens, M.C. & Bursztyn, A. (2003). Culture and body: A phenomenological and dialogic inquiry. *British Gestalt Journal*, 2003, 12, (1) 15-21.

Korb, M.P. & Gorrell, J.J. and Van De Riet, V. (1989). *Gestalt Therapy: Practice and Theory* (2nd edition) New York: Pergamon.

Zinker, J. (1977). *Creative Process in Gestalt Therapy*. Oxford: Brunner/ Mazel.

Zinker, J. & Nevis, S. (1994). The aesthetics of Gestalt couples therapy. *On Intimate Ground: A Gestalt Approach to Working with Couples*. 356-399.

5

Breakdown and Possibility in Managerial Work: Reflections for Coaches

Rob Farrands PhD

For want of a nail the shoe was lost:
For want of the shoe, the horse was lost;
For want of the horse, the rider was lost;
For want of the rider, the battle was lost,
And all for want of a horseshoe nail.
Anon. Medieval Rhyme

Introduction

This chapter is based on the idea that coaching managers requires an understanding of managerial work and how it relates to the organisation they are managing. For this reason the chapter provides a parallel exploration of coaching and managing.

The first stage of parallel development is based around an understanding of the significance of commitment-making for both management and coaching. This gives rise to the idea of the manager as a conservator of the organisation, which inducts manager and coach into the essential vulnerabilities of the organisation. From conservation comes a shared understanding of the essence of the organisation and its possibilities for fulfilment in its current context – a stage referred to as completion. The structure of Commitment – Conservation – Completion grounds management and coaching in a progressively enriched understanding of what sustains the organisation in the world. The approach presumes that complex systems such as hospitals, banks and other organisations are only ever partly articulated and acts as an antidote to premature or narrowly-based change.

My own beliefs about the work of managing are based largely on my experience as the Industrial Relations Manager in a large UK car plant. The first part of the chapter will show how this experience led to conclusions about the nature of managerial work, which predisposed me towards a view of management as a system of commitments aimed at conserving the organisation by anticipating breakdowns. Viewing management as a system of commitments is the initial connection that ties management and coaching together. This connection is so strong that, potentially, coaching provides the best developmental process available to managers. The parallel exploration of management work and coaching is intended to support such a strong claim.

My view of coaching and managerial work did not leap directly out of my experience. I have relied upon friends and the work of others to help me make sense of that experience. As a result many of the core ideas, including the one concerning commitment, have been drawn from the work of others. Ideas that have left their mark have been those that made sense of some aspect of my experience, or which set up memorable inquiries for me as coach and consultant. Increasingly, the ideas that made sense or inspired fresh inquiry have been shaped by an interest in the philosophy of Martin Heidegger and Maurice Merleau-Ponty, their interpreters and my friends with whom I have shared my interest[1]. Remembering this community of correspondents, I feel myself to be a part of a larger movement to reclaim a world that, paraphrasing Heidegger, we are always already thrown into. Working out what we do and how we think, when we are always already a part of what we think and do is a problem that haunts this chapter.

Managerial work

The experience of being a manager in a large car plant was a personally intense one that left me with strong, definite impressions that have affected the course of my coaching and consulting. The roots of these definite impressions lie in the practical *doing* of the managerial work. Subsequent study has not supplanted the power of the original experiences in shaping my basic beliefs about what it is to be a manager. Writing the chapter has reminded me that 'beliefs' don't only exist as concepts but may also be rooted in feeling. I have been surprised, for example, to discover a fierce loyalty to the managers I worked with even where there was no particular friendship at the time. I take this loyalty to be a residue of the commitments that once bound us together. From this 'residue' has sprung a determination to make my time with them count for something: to take my experience seriously as a kind of honouring of them and the world we shared for a while.

As an industrial relations manager I found myself in the middle of a strongly differentiated polarity that had been defined for me as the essence of my job. On the one hand, scientific management – urging forward new 'rational' arrangements that would sweep away the reified practices from the past – and, on the other hand, a defensive shop steward movement, determined to cling to all past practices as a form of currency for pay negotiations. The sense of polarisation was strongly reinforced by a history of poor relations and mistrust between trade unions and management. There was little sympathy for each other and very little dialogue that was not part of the public posturing of high profile negotiations.

I rapidly learned that I could not work with a completely estranged management and trade union movement. I had to forge links in order to be able to do my job even if I had to resort to subterfuge in order to make the connections. In doing so I learned that I was only doing what many others were already doing. The public face of difference was underpinned by networks of connections. Making practical connections to get things done changed my ideas around what I was doing. I deconstructed the polarity which I had been given as the basis of my job, first in practice and then conceptually.

Re-thinking occurred in the cut-and-thrust of meetings over trying to solve problems and disputes. I was in almost constant interaction with other managers and trade union representatives. There were some formal meetings and many other informal ones, either standing by a stationary production track, meeting secretly in pubs, or grabbing food with colleagues at lunchtime, or at shift handover. At the more formal meetings the problems came in the shape of reports of critical numbers, which showed variances of one kind or another and predicted gathering storms. We clustered around these reports, interpreting them like runes and trying to foresee and forestall incipient problems. We would review plans, make fresh ones and commit to actions and mutual support. Reason and history were in active consideration in all of these exchanges: what we did last time was in play alongside what it was reasonable to do this time. We threaded our way together back and forth between past and present in service of the future – what we would do next.

From out of such exchanges – often aggressive and stressful – I came to understand what I would later name as 'engaged agency'. Managers and trade unionists tended to act in service of what they did last time, as they referenced their experience and acted out of that experience. Managers and trade unionists were equally motivated by their past, but not determined by it. Conversely, they were amenable to reason, but it was never detached. Reason was hard won in battles over the past and the possibilities for the future. Agency was possible but it arose from somewhere – it was never, in my experience and increasingly in the way I conceptualised, detached.

The circumstances of my work impressed upon me the social nature of the experience that my co-respondents were explicitly and implicitly accessing as a basis for acting. Both trade unionists and managers referenced a conception of social history in the form of precedents and past practice. In fact, at this particular plant, there was a Byzantine structure of embedded practices that had resulted from years of piecework practice. Mostly these were un-recorded (part of my job was to write them down) and disputed, but still exercised a powerful spell over the way work was done. Not surprisingly, then, I found that, along with re-thinking reason, I was also having to re-think experience as a collective practice. At the time I was being exposed to 'mental models' in management training courses. I took the point about our thinking being conditioned – it helped me understand engaged agency, but I was inclined to be sceptical about the mental part: in my world the 'models' were out there in the plant in the form of historic collective practices.

Surviving as an industrial relations manager forced me to let go of the simple framing of my job and get my hands dirty in a host of interactions in which reason and history were in play. In the struggle I began to act as an existential manager long before I could conceptualise it as such. I had to live out in the world of the plant; I was forced to dispute history and challenge it for the future; and I had to apply reason in respect of social practices that visibly and invisibly were shaping affairs and determining outcomes.

If this was a consequence of my work it was not my preoccupation at the time. Reason and history occurred in the context of problems actual or anticipated. This was a volatile industrial relations environment in which management were trying to force through new technologies that disrupted established practice. All the old ways of handling things were in the air. All the existing procedures were being challenged. There were many disputes, some of them major national affairs. In these circumstances, building trust was essential to getting things done. I rapidly learned whom I could rely on to do what they promised and also say what they really thought. Simultaneously, I learned to be careful with my own promises and to honour them when I made them. In such an unstructured environment trust was essential and became a major determinant for me of managerial credibility and competence.

In those frantic days the plant was effectively held together by a network of promises – 'commitments' as I would later learn to call them. I quickly learned to carry a notebook and to write down every commitment I made and every one I received. At the end of each day I would go through 'the book' (as it was known to myself and my colleagues) and check the commitments register. As the Industrial Relations Manager I sat at the centre of a complex of commitments and if the complex didn't function as it should, things would simply stop. Realising this affected how I saw the organisation and how I have seen organisations ever since.

The plant seemed to me, from what I knew from informal and formal sources, to be constantly on the verge of breaking down. It was held in place by all the work that managers did to prevent a gross failure. Problems and reports of potential problems were early warning signals that things were failing somewhere, somehow. Our job as managers was to get in place the promises that would prevent the plant breaking. Later I would learn to say that my awareness was heightened by privation – the pain and the problem. Focusing on the potential for failure motivated shared creativity around anticipatory action, which resulted in a fresh network of promises. The outcome I learned to most treasure was an absence: a strike that did not occur, an engineering change that did not over-run, not being called out in the middle of the night, walking down the tracks and not feeling a mood of discontent.

My experience in industrial relations pre-disposed me to a view of management as a kind of conservation of organisation. The ways that the organisation was likely to break down soon became familiar enough to enable the planning of anticipatory action, but not predictable with enough exactness that formal procedures and policies would quite do the job. Managers needed to have active processes of detecting anomalies and reaching agreements to act together. The agreements were often reached in back-rooms or through attending a dispute in which time was of the essence, so it *was essential that agreements would function as commitments.* Trust was essential or the organisation would not be held open in the face of a tough environment – it would break and close down. Later I saw the limits of this view but I never rejected it. My experience as a coach and as a consultant has tended to confirm important aspects of my earlier view while also pointing out inadequacies.

The inadequacies of my inherited perspective have manifested in my under-emphasising the role of formal structures and processes and their effect in shaping managerial work, in favour of reliance on networks and on trust. I have had to accommodate these missing aspects into my worldview. Nevertheless, the felt experience of the car plant has been retained as a memory of institutional chaos where nothing seemed to work. The pace of change was so desperate and the resistance so violent that all understanding about what to do and how to do it seemed temporary. This seemed to strip management back to a basic process of coping. I became intensely interested in how managers coped because it was of vital personal interest. *What I learned for myself, and more generally in respect of management as a whole, was that the ability to make binding commitments and to attract them from others was absolutely essential to managerial work*[2].

Starting with an understanding of the significance of the process of giving and attracting commitment has proved to be a fruitful way to understand management. Not the only way of course but significantly for this chapter it has had the advantage of providing a creative connection to coaching, which in regard to commitment bears many similarities to management. Pursuing the latent parallelism of coaching and managing around commitment has enabled me to develop coaching as a simulacrum of managing, which has added extra creativity and drama to the coaching.

Commitment and coaching

Commitment is universally significant for managers, although it often goes under other names with which it is strongly associated, especially trust and loyalty. The word is especially appropriate for a description of management because its meaning covers and draws together three vital aspects of managerial work:

1. It means dedication, specifically, dedication to an organisation. Dedication is a highly respected part of being a manager. It shows up in hours of work, consuming interest and a strong priority in the manager's life: a concern with work-life balance indicates the extent of dedication. Dedication is connected to loyalty.
2. Commitment indicates a pledge, an undertaking, or a promise. When used in this sense, commitment describes a primary field of competence for managers: an ability to make commitments and to attract them from others. The measure of commitment in this second sense is reliability – was the commitment honoured? Reliability in this sense connects to trust.
3. Commitment means an engagement or an obligation. The word is used in this sense to indicate a constraint on freedom of action as when we say, 'I'm already committed'. Managers are given authority over a certain domain, which also works as a limit. As a result to get things done they often have to engage with other managers.

Taken together, these three aspects give commitment special significance in relation to the social aspect of managerial work. Each manager's authority to commit is constrained and the commitments made are usually dependent upon commitments made by others. The network of commitments that result, ties managers together in a web of mutual obligation. Commitment, then, is systemic. The efficacy of the network depends crucially on whether individual commitments are honoured. Seen in this light reliability in relation to commitment is a systemic virtue: promises have to be kept or the whole network is threatened.

Reliability, defined as managers doing what they say they will do, is a fundamental behavioural requirement for commitment to work. Above all other behaviours and personal characteristics, reliability is therefore the one most useful to managers *qua* managers – arguably it is the one most admired and sought after, and the one that most quickly builds or confounds reputations. Reliability is about delivering on what is committed but, before that, there is the giving of the commitment. If the original act of commitment is not believed then it will weaken the network of other commitments, because other managers will be less likely to rely on it. This lack of reliance will be likely to introduce a systemic weakness long before it is discovered whether the original commitment was in fact honoured. In other words, the network of commitments is a promissory system in which lack of credibility in any one part is likely to weaken the whole. The initial believability of the manager making the commitment is therefore highly significant. In regard to believability, the reputation of the manager for authenticity is highly relevant. Whether managers have a reputation for saying what they truly think or believe is vital to their ability to be able to credibly give a commitment. If they cannot credibly provide a commitment (or attract one from another) their status as managers is damaged and the network of commitment is weakened.

The ability to make and honour commitments is not just a matter of good intentions. Organisations are complex places in which managers face competing demands for time and resources. To reliably and authentically make a commitment depends on foresight and inquiry. Foresight manifests, in management, as planning: quite simply, it is risky for a manager to make a commitment without knowing whether she has the spare capacity or available resources, which she can only know if she has invested in planning her time and her resources. It is also risky for a manager to make a commitment without first conducting the inquiries to understand fully what is required or expected. Managers who commit too easily are worrisome ('can do' is all very well as long as it results in 'have done'); those who demand or force commitments without acquiring an understanding of the other's situation are equally worrying, because they may threaten other parts of the whole promissory system by disrupting other commitments.

For the manager, a commitment aims at being an act accomplished with words. When the commitment is properly made it transcends description, which is normally assumed to be the province of language. To be 'properly' given the words of commitment need to be supported by personal reputation and credibility, but it is just as important that the words are uttered under the right circumstances and in the right place. An analogy will help to emphasise the point being made here. When a couple exchange vows in a church the words are solemnised and act to change the couple's social status as perceived by themselves, their families and the broader world. The setting, the ceremony and the witnesses are all designed to make the act of commitment just that – an act, rather than a mere description of a state of affairs[3] (a similar kind of solemnisation occurs in a court room). The places where this occurs for managers are not as recognisable as a church or a courtroom and the ceremonies are more culturally specific: the coach needs a degree of immersion in the client's organisational world to detect such places.

Despite variation, the places of managerial solemnisation are normally to be found in certain kinds of meeting, officiated by a manager of authority. The relevant meetings are regularised so that trust may be measured through the completion, or not, of commitments previously made, and are formalised briefly in minutes. The style of such meetings is sparse. Much is taken for granted, worked through in advance and reduced to a report, which may just be a table of numbers and which will usually go unchallenged in its essentials. Preparation and tradition (for example, taken for granted assumptions) clear the way for the meeting to focus on commitments: those already given and being reviewed for completion, or those being promised afresh.

Coaching as a simulation of managing

Focusing on committing illuminates the basics of management. It grounds managerial work in dedication to an organisation, social interaction and core personal capabilities around reliability and credibility. We may also understand coaching as being grounded in commitment. To do this, coaching has to be approached as an opportunity to simulate and perfect the crafting of commitments and the building of commitment-ability. Linking coaching to management through commitment makes it more relevant to managers and also strengthens the coaching process by founding it on trust.

To some extent this argument builds on what coaches already understand and what is reported in the literature[4]. It is well understood that coaching relies on building trust between coach and client. Trust in coaching as in managing depends on reliability and authenticity. Ultimately coaching cannot succeed as such unless coach and manager can find each other believable, can rely on each other and learn how to enter into binding commitments. In this sense there is a parallelism between managing and coaching: they both participate in an emphasis on commitment.

Without commitment the manager will not be able to deliver sufficient continuity and quality of contact for the coaching to be effective. Commitment can be demonstrated and fostered in various ways. For example, by the manager's readiness to integrate the coaching with her work. This can be accomplished in several ways: situating coaching sessions in the manager's place of work; inviting the coach to accompany them to meetings; taking experiments back into the work place. This kind of activity opens up pathways between the work-place and coaching-place, increases understanding and builds trust. The manager takes some risk in bringing the coach to work, showing his work-place and introducing the coach into this world. He puts himself in an exposed position and also shows himself differently to colleagues and staff – perhaps as someone who is seeking support. He may also demonstrate through his day-to-day behaviour that he is someone who is not taking the coaching lightly – someone who is committed to it and thereby honours it as something worthy.

Parallelism between coaching and managing may develop into simulation. The opportunity for the coaching to be a simulation of managing arises because commitment, or lack of it, is readily demonstrable through the course of the coaching. As such, it is directly observable and open for discussion, based on the first-hand experience of the coach and manager. In a practical way, the coaching becomes an opportunity for the real-time development of 'commitment-ability'. For example, whether the manager turns up on time, or cancels at the last minute (these things might seem trivial but they go directly to reliability and are a major every-day shaper of reputation in managerial settings). Also, does the client complete any experiments co-created in the coaching? How does the client make commitments to the coach in the first place – what does it take for a promise to become a commitment for this manager and coach? How well does the client equip herself with the basic preconditions for commitment – for instance, in planning or inquiry?

If it is possible to undertake the coaching in the manager's place of work this supports simulation in the form of empathic resonance between coach and client. The coach, for example, can use her own felt responses to person and place as a pretty reliable representation of what the manager's colleagues are experiencing – or at least as a starting place for inquiry. Similarly the manager may notice how the coach responds to the place and to the people she meets there. In the past I have extended the opportunities for resonance by arranging for the manager being coached to receive feedback from colleagues in my presence. The actual content of the feedback was of course affected by my presence, but I also learned from simply seeing manager and colleague in contact with each other[5].

An eye for the possibilities of live simulation may also go to enliven the coaching session with fresh drama. For example, working once for a petrochemical company in a head office in The Hague, the client and I found ourselves assigned to meet in a large office almost completely filled with a large conference table. We rather playfully decided to hold a mock meeting that rapidly became very serious. We 'invited' the seven people who were the main ones engaged with her issue. Each person was given a name-board and the client sat in each place in turn to address her virtual self, sitting at the head of the table. She adopted the persona of each person in turn, provided the advice, stood up, shook her body and moved into the next place. Round the table she went while I took notes and managed each transition. We came together face to face at the end when I presented my notes and we discussed the experience and the offerings that had been made. We persisted with the playfulness as we also considered the effectiveness of the meeting, such as the quality of the listening. In this 'serious play' an attempt had been made to incorporate a social format – meeting around a conference table (recognisable in the manager's world) – into the coaching world, in order to develop the parallel between managing and coaching.

By focusing on commitment-ability and its related aspects of managerial work the manager has simultaneously developed an understanding of his work and coaching's contribution. If the coaching has gone well the manager has developed his ability to credibly commit himself and to attract credible commitments from others. This may have also developed into understanding that management has to be respected as providing essential care and conservation of the organisation. The manager and the coach also have an improved understanding of their own ways of trusting and have discovered something about how they can foster trust in others. They both have a fuller appreciation of managerial work and the particular organisation in which it is taking place.

With the coach's help the manager may also have acquired a growing appreciation of the total network of anticipatory action and has an expanded perspective of those parts of the network most important to her. This approaches a more strategic understanding of why exactly the organisation is built the way it is, which equips her to engage with making deliberate changes to the distribution of accountabilities within her own sphere.

The coach, too, has learned from the journey by gaining access to the world of the client's organisation. This learning provides a developing context for the coaching work. The coach's sensibility is being shaped by her access to the organisation; she notices things in her client that would not have arisen before; her intuitions connect more frequently and her respect for the whole set up of client and organisation has increased.

The emphasis so far has been on commitment as a personal capability that can be developed through simulation in coaching. I have shown how this creates an understanding of the organisation as being conserved through a network of commitment into which the coach is drawn. The next section will examine in more detail how managers create the context within which commitments and commitment-making has meaning, and how the coach accompanies the manager on this journey.

The context for conservation

Commitments are social bonds: forms of promise that are created in meetings with other managers. As we saw in the previous section, these meetings provide an important context for making commitments. In this section we will take up the story of managerial work and its relationship to coaching by seeing how managers sustain the contexts within which commitment exchanges take place.

Managers create the meetings necessary for the whole process of commitment. Meetings are places where managers gather around anomaly reports that indicate the need for anticipatory action. They are also places where words can turn into actions that create processes as well as commit and allocate resources. The most significant meetings of this kind are instituted so they acquire more permanent presence around which support activity is organised, such as a secretariat or a more or less fixed place such as a conference room or manager's office. Institution brings with it traditions, processes and a particular style of doing things. These meetings form the operational core of the organisation. They are the place where the recurrence of breakdowns is addressed and where anticipatory action is put in place. We can say that these operational meetings are key places in which the network of commitments surfaces and becomes visible.

For the manager, these instituted places are sites of managerial performance. They are where he demonstrates or not his trustworthiness and where his reputation for reliability and authenticity is consolidated. Performance in these meetings is likely to be a crucial aspect of the coaching. As a general rule, the primary preoccupation of managers in relation to these meetings is with the ability to make themselves heard. It is important for them to be able to gain the necessary commitment of others, and in order to do this they need to speak skilfully. This preoccupation with advocacy and presence is something of an illusion though. Of equal or even greater significance are the abilities to listen and inquire, which are frequently under-regarded and most in need of support from the coach. The reason for suggesting a rebalancing is to do with the dynamic nature of commitment-making and also with the elusiveness of purpose in organisations.

The point relating to purpose will be explored further in the next section. For now, suffice it to say that the manager's concern with conservation of the organisation tends to focus her on the work that is being done to accomplish this aim and that the purpose of the organisation tends to fade from view in the face of everyday operational activity. Purpose needs to be listened for and this will be seen to be an important part of the manager's maturation.

Of more immediate importance to this section is the semi-structured nature of the network of commitments in which the manager participates. As we will see, the network does translate into structure to a greater or lesser extent, depending on the nature of the organisation, but this is never complete. It is crucial for the manager to listen for changes in the shape and alignment of the network. This listening provides early warning of subtle shifts in challenge and emphasis that may be highly significant for managers' own priorities. 'Listening' is something of a misnomer in this situation in so far as it indicates an auditory function only. What needs achieving is more like tuning in to how the network is manifesting through the meeting. To say we need to listen with our eyes and the rest of our body as well sounds rather strange, but that is effectively what is meant by 'tuning in'. Once the manager and the coach 'tune in' it quickly becomes apparent that many of the stories that emerge from these meetings are concerned with making sense of subtle shifts in the complex network of commitment.

Taking the focus on listening one stage further we can almost say that the network is constituted by the listening! What is meant by this, is that as the network is only ever partly visible, listening for *how it is manifesting itself at any one* time brings it to life for the manager. In this sense listening then calls forth the speaking, because it frames what might be articulated. Articulation brings the network to language, which makes it available for interpretation and modification, starting with the very way in which it is expressed as people begin to speak out of their listening.

Through these dynamic processes of listening and articulating, within the recognised setting of certain kinds of meeting, managers sustain the operational logic of their organisation, based on recurrent breakdowns, anticipatory action and networks of commitment. The meetings in which this occurs are central to the manager's role in conserving the organisation. They are therefore also central to coaching. Continuing the theme of parallelism and simulation, we can notice that the coaching also takes place in a meeting and that the capabilities around listening, tuning in and articulation could be as much in play in coaching as they are in an operations meeting. Manager and coach can agree that they are in play and can take the coaching forward by noticing and working directly with meeting skills relevant to the manager's world.

The broader context for coaching

Meetings take place within broader organisational settings. The work needed to conserve and keep the organisation in place is not infinitely variable. Organisations have their own vulnerability – their own way of breaking down. In consequence, anticipatory action tends to concentrate around historic vulnerabilities and create a tradition of attitudes, beliefs and practices that manifest as structures and processes. The structures and processes that 'flesh out' the organisation provide a wider setting for the meetings, which themselves provide contexts for the core process of commitment-making that results in networks. This layered system works dynamically so that change works in both directions: the organisation is shaped ultimately by the network of commitment, but that network is also shaped by the way in which it becomes expressed as organisation. Examples from actual cases can illustrate the way in which commitment gives rise to organisation and the effect this has on the manager's work, including her understanding of her commitment.

> ***Example 1.*** An organisation created to extract oil from the North Sea through exposed oil rigs, creates what, to a casual observer, looks like a bloated Health and Safety function and manifests, every day, in an obsession with accident prevention (a specific kind of anticipatory action). Every meeting in this organisation starts with a safety story; walking up the stairs with hands in pocket in a Head Office thousands of miles away from the oil field leads to a chorus of firm admonitions to 'hold the hand-rail'; and the entrance hall to the Head Office displays safety statistics alongside ones showing production and profit. Every manager in this organisation is sensible to the historic ways in which reality threatens it with breakdowns in the form of the death and injury of people working offshore

and the consequences for reputation and production. Such sensibility guides the way in which managers prepare and read reports, listen to colleagues, exercise commitment-ability – as well as go up and down staircases.

Example 2. A currency function in a country's Central Bank had experienced a distressing series of counterfeiting crises in the 1980s that had embarrassed the Bank by highlighting its lack of control. Over the next four years the currency function of the bank built up the largest and best-organised anti-counterfeiting and currency education department in the world – bigger and better than that in any other central bank. Twenty years later, this nation-wide operation was still functioning via regional centres and a large central function in the capital city. Now that counterfeiting had fallen to negligible figures and a new highly secure currency had been introduced, the Bank decided that the time was ripe to re-visit the extensive costly operation. The attempt to deconstruct it provoked intense resistance among managers who argued that the latent threat was still present.

Example 3. The Francis Report (2012) reports on the failure and collapse of the Mid Staffordshire National Health Service hospital in Britain, where patients died in terrible circumstances of neglect. The report shows that the failure occurred because focusing on 'reaching national access targets, achieving financial balance and seeking foundation trust status' had been 'at the cost of delivering acceptable standards of care'[6]. The strength and energy with which the hospital focused on a few perfectly rational targets had the effect of distorting a largely unarticulated, embodied care practice. The findings of the report illustrate how a focus

> on care in a hospital is designed to protect patients from a latency in modern medicine: its tendency to objectify persons into biomechanical machines to be drugged and manipulated back into health. The institutionalisation of care through nursing anticipates the recurrence of such a breakdown. Over-riding care (and not listening to nurses), especially with efficiency measures that tended themselves to objectify patients and staff, created a mood of objectification within which cruel and undignified treatment emerged.

In all these organisations, visible structure and process is the result of managers working to standardise commitment-making processes around vulnerabilities to breakdown. An analogy would be to compare this visible organisation to scar tissue. Structure and process arise on the sites of previous breakdowns. The breakdowns may actually have been forgotten but the scar remains. In other words, where there is little risk managers pay little attention, and the absence of attention and risk appears as the absence of visible organisation.

In each of the three cases, actual or anticipated breakdown led to internal conflicts within the management system. The way in which these conflicts were handled was highly significant to the outcome for the organisation. In each case the subject matter of the conflict was the likely recurrence of breakdowns, the need for anticipatory action, and the nature of the managerial commitments being made. In the Bank the conflict was essentially about the alignment of resources around the likelihood of the recurrence of a particular dramatic breakdown. The strength of resistance to the idea that the time was ripe for change illuminated the strength of the commitment built up around this previous breakdown.

In the case of the oil company and the hospital, the death of people in the care of the organisation led to a major review of the organisation and its breakdown avoidance strategies (in the case of the hospital *via* a Public Inquiry). In the oil company case, five men died as four rushed to save a friend who collapsed while welding the inside of a giant pipe. The managerial conversation afterwards focused on breach of the procedures put in place to prevent this kind of breakdown (it was explicitly prohibited for men to try to save someone in these circumstances without the rescue team). Only a question concerning the *courage* of the men who went to help their *friends* shocked the discussion to a different level. Then there was remembrance of the organisation's history of exploration and mutual care in dangerous places. A shift occurred: what possibilities were there for safely encouraging men to help each other? Could we have made it safe for the 'friends' to have gone to the rescue? The new inquiry deepened the conversation and led to a project to investigate returning to this organisation's first principles around health and safety.

Coaching can help the manager to include the organisational context within his understanding of his conservation work. Considering the history of commitment and breakdown can be a useful way for the coach to enter this territory and encourage a tuning-in to the organisation. In the Central Bank the coach helped the manager to understand the events of the previous counterfeiting crisis in the Central Bank; rediscover the humiliation that was felt when the currency function was caught completely off-guard and re-visit the commitments that were made as a consequence. In so doing, coach and manager explored and recalled why counterfeiting was such a continuing threat to the people's economic welfare. Basic questions arose about the real value of the Bank's currency production and protection service and its relation to economic health. Similarly, in the oil and gas company, the coach led the manager back to the roots of the business in discovery, adventure and danger. What was disclosed was a remembrance of comradeship and care for each other that had long ago been covered over with rational health and safety procedures and rules.

The coach deepens understanding of the organisation in order to extend it by guiding the manager back through the layers of covered-over richness that constitute the organisation's heritage. In so doing, the coach raises with the manager the possibility of transmuting the conservation work by addressing the possibility of the organisation.

Completion: essence and articulation

As the manager engages in conservation work he also comes to understand what is essential to the organisation. This aspect of his understanding does not arise as a set of ideas through which he grips hold of the organisation, as when the manager, for example, develops a theory about the organisation, perhaps under the encouragement of a deliberate attempt to develop a vision, or a strategy. Instead his understanding of essence arises directly from his practical engagement and is experienced first as a sensible feel for what is right for the organisation, as when he says, 'We don't do that here!' This feeling for what is right is nothing more than the expression of what he has already learned to conserve and care for, although he did not start with a full understanding of what that precisely was (even if others had been telling him he did not properly 'get it'): it only came to him as he found his place through conservation of the organisation. In effect, the hard work of conserving the organisation has immersed the manager into the organisational world, from where it is deeply affecting his sensibility and, ultimately, the very process of meaning-making.

The essence of the organisation emerges spontaneously and simultaneously with its care and conservation. It is as if a bargain has been struck with the manager: the organisation rewards his commitment to conservation with insight into its essence. Given that the essence is disclosed as an affect and shows up as an ethical understanding – what is right for this organisation in this situation – there is a question of how it might be articulated. Before this, though, it is helpful to consider how the manager only gradually came to understand what was essential to the organisation. We have shown that the manager is first practically engaged with the organisation through the whole process of committing to conservation in order to keep the organisation in place. Through practical engagement she[7] comes to take for granted what is important as she picks it up through what she does and how she does it. Her understanding becomes sublimated into her bodily response.

An analogy for the manager's understanding of organisational essence is a human being's understanding of their feelings. People do not create their feelings, they arrive unannounced and regardless of whether they are wanted. Something in the world reaches out to touch the person. He may try to close down receptivity and yet do the opposite, too – strive to be more open but he cannot completely control his feeling. However, although complete control may be impossible it is also true that feelings are not given entirely and completely. Through language a person can articulate what he feels and through increased refinement of language, open to greater differentiation and sensitivity.

By analogy, a manager's apprenticeship in conservation opens her to the organisation, enables her to respond to it with greater refinement and to see the world through an organisational lens. Language then, does more than simply describe something already there. It expresses feelings and in so doing brings the organisation freshly to life in the current context. In this sense, the manager can be said to 'complete' the organisation.

Spinosa, Flores and Dreyfus refer to the process we have described as one of articulation[8]. The quote below misses the embodied aspect of being 'implicit' but its active tense reinforces the sense of the manager's agency in completing the organisation:

> *There are two forms of articulation. All articulating makes what is implicit explicit. If what is implicit is vague or confused, then we speak of gathering from dispersion. If it was once important and has been lost, then we have the special kind of articulation that we call retrieval.*
> (p25. Emphases in the original)

Both involve some kind of restoration. I am adding the idea that articulation also involves the transfer of something from one realm – an ethical, felt one – to one of language and thought. This helps us understand the manager's progression towards insight into his organisation as one that necessarily begins with practical, skilful engagement – for this is how he acquires his felt sense in the first place.

For example, a multiplicity of practices such as care practices in a hospital may be taken for granted. The original reasons for the practices may have ceased to be well articulated, perhaps because the original reasons for them are lost in time: re-articulating them restores them even as it both refreshes some important part of the hospital's history and brings them up to date with current challenges. The practice of holding the hand-rail in the head office of an oil and gas company may decay because it is deemed trivial or because it is obstructive of office workers making the most of the exercise potential of bounding up the stairs. To be reminded that the original practice injunction was an act of solidarity with colleagues working in a dangerous gas field, or off-shore on an exposed oil rig, restores the practice by retrieving the original logic in a way that resonates back into the riskier environments. Caring for patients and ameliorating the risks to staff are aspects of something essential for these organisations and expressing this rejuvenates practice and purpose.

Acts of articulation may be strategic and have significant effects on the structure, vision and strategy of the organisation. For example, since the banking crisis of 2008/9, banks in Europe and America have been struggling to re-articulate their purpose in respect of their retail and small business customers. In some cases this is leading to a division of the bank, and the strengthening of boundaries between investment and retail sectors; also to momentous changes to remuneration structures. We can see the public mood also shifting in a claimed remembrance of basic purpose: for example, a newspaper seeks to remind a bank of its Quaker past and of the values articulated by its founders – a kind of retrieval. More generally, there have been several books of late that have sought to remind us that business organisation was once about freedom and dignity, or that ownership was once a form of commitment rather than detached investment[9]. The books 'retrieve' for us aspects of how the creation of modern organisations was once part of a revolution in the human condition.

By now, coaching has moved from creating basic commitment-ability to do its work in the dense territory where experience and language collide to complete each other. The coach teaches the manager to take her articulation seriously, and to use the coaching process to sort out the words that mean something and to see where they have become mundane and shorn of essential meaning. To speak words, as it were, for the first time, fattens them out, fills them up again. 'Care or 'safety' or 'value' are savoured once more – given space to move and breathe, first in the coaching and then at work. *Via* the coaching, the critical words come to express something worthwhile and by so doing are gathered up from dispersion, forgetfulness and embodied practice to do real work again. The real work is to rejuvenate experience and feeling; to enable fresh definition and differentiation and bring things and people to life again. By such rejuvenation possibility emerges from careful conservation.

Unless possibility is linked in practice to conservation as described in this chapter then there is always the risk that organisations become subject to the detached reasoning that, many years ago, I was erroneously told they should be: then our organisations were at risk of perfectly rational forms of cleverness, based on the disingenuous idea that everything was possible. There is then no completion but only ungrounded change. The risk arises because good intentions and an idealistic spirit are not enough. The tragic story of the Mid Staffordshire hospital and other emerging cases from the NHS, demonstrates that actually everything is not possible, nor desirable. The belief that it is may result in showing only that everything may be destroyed[10] for it turns out to be a lot easier to destroy and exploit an organisation than to conserve and cherish it. The experienced manager understands how the organisation is vulnerable to breakdown. Through this he may gain access to the organisation's essence. This is the route towards completing our organisations by bringing back to life the rich complex of concerns and dreams on which the organisation was founded.

For the loss of a nail…

It is obvious that there can be no coaching unless the manager and the coach turn up. In this chapter 'turning up' stands metaphorically for a broader commitment of the coach and manager to each other and also to the organisation that is so often the silent third party. Teasing into the light of day the complex of tripartite commitment on which the coaching rests is fundamental work. In this work the coach's commitment to the manager and to the organisation is as much in question as is the manager's commitment to the coach and to the organisation (and, we might add, the organisation's commitment to the coach and the manager). What is more, in this chapter commitment is presented rather strangely to a modern sensibility, supported by the medieval rhyme quoted at the beginning.

The chapter presents commitment as being related to an absence – the absence of the particular breakdown that, it is suggested, constantly threatens attempts to conserve organisation (in the way that the risk of objectifying and killing patients attracts a counterbalancing commitment to personal care in a hospital). Commitment in coaching, then, refers to the steps that coach, manager and organisation take to protect the organisation from entropy. The chapter accentuates the significance of this as a kind of holding open of the organisation towards its world. The rhyme supports this understanding with an odd (on examination, even uncanny) description of a systemic process of nail/shoe/horse/rider/battle. The nail in the ancient rhyme is not present and this is consequential. We have become used to thinking in terms of positive present figures. The idea of an absent figure is likely to seem, at best, contradictory.

What is not present in Gestalt form is the ground and in this chapter it is the ground that solicits further inquiry: the role of the figure is subordinated to being a means of opening up the ground – enabling, allowing entry. What is discovered in the ground are the remnants of a forgotten, or taken-for-granted, organisation that calls to be re-articulated and re-expressed as a form of current-day completion. Coaching explores the rich ground, just as managers are forced by circumstances to deepen their understanding of the web of commitment that conserves their organisation and makes completion some kind of possibility in the first place.

Organisations tend towards hierarchy, almost by definition. Power has its needs. A primary one is to mark its presence with change. Coaches are often co-opted into this project. Focusing on change often leads to the premature identification of needs that are vested with more specificity than is justified or possible. Hospitals that kill and banks that go bankrupt constitute the resulting debris. Coaching needs to catch hold of something already present in the manager's DNA – the need to commit and conserve, and to embody this in grounded coaching that aims at renewing our organisations as places of deep purpose.

Notes

1. The conversation has been going on for many years, but has come to something of a head just lately, due to the re-creation of our consulting and coaching practice as a company called 'Figure Ground Consulting'. Around this new entity, I have had many stimulating conversations that have been incorporated into this chapter. Most immediately these have engaged Heidegger scholars Dominik Heil and Matthew Hancocks and the coaching specialist and co-founder of FGC, Bridget Farrands. I have also been challenged and provoked by our associates Lars and Margareta Marmgren and driven to clearer articulation by the challenge and interest of our associate Roger Martin. As to Merleau-Ponty and Heidegger, the secondary texts of most immediate relevance to this chapter are Mauro Carbonne,

'Variations of the Sensible', in *Merleau-Ponty and the Possibilities of Philosophy: Transforming the Tradition*, 2009; Mark Wrathall, 'Motives, Reasons, and Causes', in *The Cambridge Companion to Merleau-Ponty*, 2005; and Charles Taylor, 'Engaged agency and background in Heidegger', in *The Cambridge Companion to Heidegger*, 1993.

2. Exploring commitment was inspired by reading the 1986 work of Terry Winograd and Fernando Flores, *Understanding Computers and Cognition: A New Foundation for Design*. The connection may seem improbable but in trying to understand managers as users of technology they critique the traditional decision-making model and introduce the idea of organisations as networks of commitments. You may see how the work helped me to make sense of my experience from this quotation:

   > *'Careful observers of what successful managers do (such as Mintzberg, in The Nature of Managerial Work, 1973) have remarked that their activities are not well represented by the stereotype of a reflecting solitary mind studying complex alternatives. Instead, managers appear to be absorbed in many short interactions, most of them lasting between two and twenty minutes... We may say that managers engage in conversations in which they create, take care of, and initiate new commitments within an organisation' (page 151, ibid)*

3. The immediate source for these claims is the work of J.L. Austin, see *How to Do Things With Words*, 1962. See also Charles Taylor, 'Heidegger, Language and Ecology', in *Heidegger: A Critical Reader*, 1992.

4. The book on coaching that has most impressed me is James Flaherty's work, *Coaching*, 2011 (3rd Edition), which grounds coaching in basic principles of respect, trust and freedom of expression. It also contains an excellent reading list. In the Gestalt literature, see articles by Stuart N. Simon, Ann Attayek Carr, Mary Anne Walk and Marion Gillie in *Gestalt Review*, 2009, 13(3) and also, 'Field-relational coaching: PAIR model', by

Sally Denham-Vaughan and Mark Gawlinski. See chapter 2 of this book.

5. For examples from my own practice see Opening to the World through the Lived Body in *International Journal of Action Research*, 2009, 5 (1).

6. Report of the Mid Staffordshire NHS Foundation Trust Public Inquiry, Executive Summary, page 3. See also my article in the *Royal Society of Arts and Science Journal,* July 2013, on this subject, 'Hospitals: Human Bodies' (http://www.thersa.org/fellowship/journal).

7. When speaking generally of 'managers' I intend no distinction between male and female. The chapter does not address gender differences around commitment, conservation or completion, which is not to say that they do not exist.

8. See Spinosa, C., Flores, F., and Dreyfus, H. L. (1997) Disclosing New Worlds: Entrepreneurship, Democratic Action and the Cultivation of Solidarity. The MIT Press, Cambridge M.A., and London, England.

9. For references to the idealistic sources of capitalism and its current structural problems see D. N. McCloskey, *Bourgeois Dignity*, 2010; C. Mayer, *Firm Commitment*, 2013; R.S. Sisodia and D.B. Wolfe, *Firms of Endearment*, 2011.

10. This is influenced by Hannah Arendt's analysis of totalitarianism as based on the belief that it was possible to start again and wipe the slate clean. See D.R. Villa's article, 'Arendt's theory of totalitarianism: a reassessment', in *The Cambridge Companion to Hannah Arendt*, 2000. For a consistent analysis of the dangers of ungrounded change, see the introduction to Connor Cruise O'Brian's biography of Edmund Burke, *The Great Melody*, 1992.

6

Resources for Relational Leadership

Mark Fairfield and Maggie Shelton

This paper is a collaborative work produced by the two authors, who are also the subjects of a story presented in this paper. We thought it fitting to write this chapter together since our topic is shared leadership.

We work as part of a team at The Relational Center – a Los Angeles based nonprofit community organization that operates several projects with the objective of catalyzing a culture of mutual support. Our staff and volunteers provide training, capacity building and services to individuals, families and organizations, coordinating their work with a fleet of grassroots community organizers to build a social movement for radical engagement and social justice.

Mark founded The Relational Center in 2007 after 15 years of social work practice that focused on community health, organizational management and higher education. He was also very involved in teaching and training Gestalt practitioners and contributing to the Gestalt literature with his focus on group development, harm reduction, and community building practices.

Mark invited Maggie to join his staff in 2010 because he needed help in designing and overseeing a training track for organizational practitioners. Maggie came to the organization with a strong reputation in her field and extensive experience in family therapy, social work education, nonprofit management, and leadership coaching. Also, her familiarity with social constructionist philosophies enriched the organizational culture by expanding the Center's knowledge base, refining skills and extending its community of practice.

Prior to working together, both of us had been engaged in leading other nonprofit organizations, in some cases managing very difficult change projects. Since starting at The Relational Center, we have had the opportunity to experiment with some key leadership practices that were either not entirely welcomed or not able to be realized in our previous work settings. Over the last several years, we have been fortunate to have the support to explore these leadership practices in depth. We have endeavored to develop strategies that harness momentum and leverage available resources to produce the widest possible beneficial change. The main outcome of our work has been the articulation of a curriculum for social health and sustainable development.

As we implement this curriculum, we find ourselves relying heavily on 'coaching' as an obvious modality for helping communities and organizations build their capacity to achieve and sustain their objectives, especially where there is positive social impact. Rather than aiming to eliminate problems, resolve conflicts, or reduce symptoms – objectives commonly associated with advisors, mediators, and psychotherapists – we coach *to support people to develop in ways that can be sustained.* From our perspective, coaching elucidates what can support people to grow and adapt in ways that secure commitments from the communities and systems that sustain them.

In developing and testing our model, we have been significantly influenced by important contributions from organizers and consultants who identify their work as 'relational'. Some of these include Gordon Wheeler (2000), Kenneth Gergen (2009), Robert Kolodny and Cathe Carlson (2009), Malcolm Parlett (2003), Dian Marie Hosking and Sheila McNamee (2006), Sally Denham-Vaughan and Marie-Anne Chidiac (2009) and Mark Fairfield (2013).

We ground our coaching work in the principles of dialogue, pragmatism and evolutionary theory. But we have come to see that the validity of a model is put to no greater test than when its advocates themselves struggle to follow it. For it has been especially in those moments of our own hopelessness and frustration that we have come to see the importance and usefulness of this framework. In this paper we discuss what, through our struggles, we learned about the impact our commitments have had on the way we engage in leadership coaching.

Our Story

The story is set in the early days of The Relational Center's development. Mark, its founder and Executive Director, set out on a journey in the hope of leaving behind the familiar isolation and sacrifice of the heroic leader and in search of a world of support and transformation. And the first challenge he encountered was the discovery that no one person is capable of changing the outcome.

Mark hired Sam to manage the daily operations of the organization's mental health program. Sam was overwhelmed and underprepared, struggling in what would quickly become an unmanageable role. And not surprisingly, both Sam and his role fell apart. Feeling he was entirely to blame for creating this dilemma, Mark also came close to falling apart. Even the thought that he should have known how to prevent this 'failure' paralyzed him.

But Mark looked for help and got it from a consultant who had been assessing the organization's staffing structure. On the consultant's advice, Mark decided to eliminate Sam's position to free up enough money to create two part-time high-level leadership roles that would bring more expertise and professional credibility to the organization. This restructuring would also break up the work functions that had been previously combined in Sam's role; which was a fusion of responsibilities that had contributed substantially to the impossibility of that job.

Mark was truly convinced he must scrap the position and reallocate the attached resources. But Sam believed his contribution was being undervalued. Moreover, Mark had been focusing on Sam's job performance without much consideration for the job's viability. So not surprisingly, Sam saw Mark's decision to eliminate his position as punitive. In his frustration and paralysis, Mark had pinned too much of the problem on Sam. Mark had valued some of what Sam offered to the organization, so Sam's perspective was painful to acknowledge. But most painful was Mark's realization that in his decision to lay Sam off, he had not kept the culture to which he was so committed, one that privileged collaborative decision-making.

Eventually, Sam found the courage to confront Mark and ask whether there might be some way to replay the events differently. Mark agreed to try this because he knew *he needed more support* in order to consider factors he could not easily see himself, and which played a part in Sam's struggle with his role. Other conversations happened that involved Sam more actively. A different process was followed, but Mark continued to frame the problem as something to do with Sam's competency. He could not yet see the systemic factors at play. Haunted by his own myopia, Mark felt he had stumbled too far from his dearly held values. He became weighed down by guilt, but simultaneously overcome with the impulse to blame someone.

Meanwhile, publicly Mark and Sam presented a unified front. They maintained that the outcome was the best possible one for all involved. But in actuality their relationship became strained. Later they toyed with the idea of creating a volunteer position that would better match Sam's skills and interests. But these conversations fizzled out, as Sam felt increasingly *less supported* to grieve this abrupt loss in his life and to process his complex reactions. And Mark became less available for conversation as the challenges of carrying on eclipsed any attention to the damage needing repair.

Work with the Board of Directors simultaneously challenged Mark, as he found himself again in a pattern of needing support, this time from his superiors, to help him address a pressing financial crisis. But Mark did not trust that he could ask for the support he needed. And, at the time, the Board was comprised mostly of members who were themselves overwhelmed by the financial demands on the organization and needing mentoring and training if they were to *grow* their capacity for stronger leadership.

The organization needed more cash flow. Mark felt pressure to raise money quickly. What the Board had to offer addressed long-term sustainability needs, a kind of support that cut across short-term exigencies. Their help was valuable, but it did not address what was most distressing to Mark. This was a familiar and painful impasse – where those around Mark did not mirror back the same urgency he felt. Yet ironically he felt responsible to *protect* his Board from having to see his distress.

Our response

We now include two conversations that highlight ways we revisited our commitment to relational leadership practices during this crisis, with a fresh appreciation for how constrained we all are by discourses of individualism in organizational work.

Coaching Conversation #1

Mark admits openly that he feels shame about having failed to handle this organizational transition in a way that was faithful to his ideals. Maggie can see that ideas about personal responsibility and blame have pushed aside Mark's awareness that he might have needed support. So she steps into a coaching role with him, hoping she can inspire him to find resources that expand his capacity.

Through our conversation, it becomes clear to us that Mark's sense of lacking support is buried under his persistent story that the layoff was necessary and that Sam did not appear to have the necessary competencies. But the story conceals the complexities. In Mark's thinking, Sam could not offer him what he needed. And Mark's efforts to compensate for that had only made the problem worse by keeping Sam in a position for which he was under-qualified. Furthermore, Mark inferred from others' comments that he too was appearing incompetent because he was not confronting Sam's incompetence!

Drawing on her own past leadership experiences, Maggie recognizes this trap, reminding herself that other more complex understandings are being overlooked. With this in mind, Maggie asks whether she and Mark can find other ways to think about the problem. Swayed by familiar leadership discourses, Mark needs reminding of their danger: how they make the impulse to blame others inevitable. But now he can also appreciate how blaming serves as a bookmark for curiosity. They realize that they would eventually have to return to these questions about Sam's performance and the viability of the role if Mark was going to understand the sources of the problem. The question 'Who's to blame?' *interferes* with curiosity but also *signals the need for it*. In the light of this recognition, we ask the more complex question: 'What systemic factors contributed to what happened?'

When considering a systemic explanation, we can think of the current 'problematic' structure as itself a creative adjustment of the past. We can appreciate how, when resources were more limited, it would have been wise to hire someone who may not have had all the needed skills but was willing to accept a lower-paying job. It would also be obvious that Mark could not have foreseen how quickly the demands of that position might have grown, potentially more quickly than Sam's capacity to meet them. Without that knowledge, it would not have been feasible for the two of them to plan for such an event.

We can also appreciate how in those days the need for money led Mark to focus his time and energies more externally (for example, fundraising, development, community relations and marketing), leaving Sam more alone and therefore insufficiently supervised.

Later, when Sam was not handling what *Mark needed* him to handle, Mark – addressing the demands of his *own* position – concluded that he lacked the support he required.

This expanded perspective elicits compassion for everyone involved. We notice that as Mark considers alternative perspectives, he can entertain the possibility that nobody has failed; the organization is right where it should be, given the context. But without this expanded picture, he can easily get stuck in a blame/shame holding pattern: first, maintaining that Sam had failed *him*; and later wondering whether *he* had failed the organization.

Once we assume the influences are complex and systemic, we consider the power of capitalism and individualism in our own histories. We have both been compelled to take responsibility for inadequate finances as a *personal failure* or the result of *poor leadership*. This is all the more poignant in the nonprofit world where financial security is assumed to be the direct result of an Executive Director's fundraising prowess.

Coaching conversation #2

The second conversation between us comes a few months later, after a new organizational structure is now in place and Sam has been invited to contemplate taking up a 'volunteer' role.

As we speak, it becomes clearer to us how hard Mark is working to conceal his distress about money. Loyalty to the *competent leader story* seems to have become central to his very dignity: isolation is almost a reasonable price to pay in exchange for being seen as dutiful. When Maggie suggests that he might consider sharing this experience more openly, Mark protests that nobody wants to hear it. His voice strains in a build-up of frustration that

Maggie can hear. As she mirrors it back, Mark cannot deny how angry he feels at being left alone with such an overwhelming job (a predicament eerily similar to Sam's).

Fortunately, Mark has now configured the situation in such a way that he can deconstruct his feeling of powerlessness as a signal of influential conditions that no one person could overcome. Now that he feels his own powerlessness more vividly – supported by Maggie's resonance – he starts scanning for the discourses into which he has been drawn. Joining him, Maggie also gets a closer glimpse of the oppressive impact the desperate pursuit of money is having once again. Success in fundraising has not only threatened to supplant 'belonging' as the primary source of Mark's well-being, but it has distracted him from actively valuing the social capital we have always prized the most – the people who believe and invest their passion in The Relational Center's mission.

We, Maggie and Mark, leave this conversation knowing that if Mark cannot resist the seduction of a *hero leader* narrative, The Relational Center will be co-opted by its tyranny. So we commit to helping Mark experiment with inviting others to share in leadership, an invitation that stimulates celebration and confidence rather than doubt and suspicion. *Sharing responsibility is a wise and honorable leadership practice.* This realization inspires Mark to interrupt his performances of solitary sacrifice to make room for a culture of mutual support.

Not long thereafter, Mark reaches out to his Board of Directors to let them know he cannot be left to worry about money on his own. He begins frequently describing the kind of culture he needs in order to inhabit an inspiring, visionary role. Maggie collaborates with Mark to pilot a relational leadership development program at The Relational Center that lays the foundation for a wider leadership core. He also begins to speak more openly about critical organizational needs in his donor appeals.

Soon a major donor responds with a gift that encourages other major gifts. Giving grows enough to address The Relational Center's short-term crisis while also creating space for the Board to engage in larger conversations about how to create an organizational *culture of asking.* Fundraising becomes an opportunity to invite more investment in a shared vision and a culture of shared ownership. And membership on the Board expands while those members who have been working diligently to keep the ship afloat now have access to more support and therefore have more to offer.

Leadership resources

The story we have presented is an example of the struggle to respond to urgent, difficult organizational challenges with an assumption of resourcefulness and resilience and an appreciation of the complex, systemic influences that prefigure change. And what catalyzes these conditions is the intentional valuing of our humanity.

As illustrated by the encouragement Maggie offered, we advocate a form of coaching that favors a relational/developmental paradigm. Rather than adhering to a 'skills-acquisition' model, we assume competency comes from the assimilation of accessible resources paired with the coordination of effective action with one's environment. We assume that growth is a synthesis of support (which can be anything from an expression of confidence to a new strategy to a whole technological system). Support is not merely an enhancement to skills building; it *enables* skills to emerge and persist. So growth comes with support that endures.

Given our assumptions about growth, we take the position that coaching should *raise awareness of the conditions needed* for personal/professional 'success' and highlight what conditions cultivate or undermine them. In organizations, context is often omitted in discussions about competency. For those who are thought of as successful, the factors responsible for fostering confidence and ease of performance are mostly invisible. People are not likely to notice how their environment has been constructed unless it impinges on their interests or ignores their needs. For example, they are not likely to notice that a work environment led by attractive, Western European men in their early 30s will probably tend to consider good-looking, white, young men to be its most competent workers instead of being more conscious of the need for diversity.

For those who receive hundreds of subtle cues each day that they belong and can essentially do no wrong, work is forever an opportunity to demonstrate talents and abilities. Challenges are seen as adventures. But for those who receive hundreds of subtle cues each day that they do *not* belong and are always on the verge of some blunder, work is a continual process of enduring scrutiny. Challenges feel more like trickery than adventure. For everyone, competency is constructed contextually.

In our story, Mark's context inclined him to anticipate that his requests for help would be seen as leadership failures. Mark needed explicit signals from those around him that they actually *expected him to feel overwhelmed* when he tried to go it alone. He needed to hear from others that they wanted him to distribute responsibilities and that not doing so would be unwise. Mark needed evidence that his experiences were to be expected and his choices were therefore understandable. It was only when he received the confidence of others that he could feel confidence in himself. His impulse to turn to others for help was transformed from incompetency to wisdom when the culture shifted toward a relational leadership paradigm with its emphasis on context and support.

Outside a relational perspective, maturation has to be conceptualized as linear and stage-bound, overemphasizing personal mastery while minimizing the important role that social and environmental factors play in constructing growth. A skills-acquisition perspective collapses the complexities of human development. It also fails to credit the supporters who function as stewards of collective competence, and whose mutual co-operation and networks of access often determine success far more than any one person's actions. But a skills acquisition perspective also promotes an idea of success that comes from an individual's hard work and talents: some individuals cut it, while others simply do not. It leaves out any mention of the benefits of being 'simply human.'

The human species has evolved innate capacities that persist regardless of individual abilities or talents (Fairfield, 2013). The authors' own experience as organizational leaders magnifies the importance of maintaining access to these human capacities, a challenging thing to do in work contexts that treat human beings like machines. In fact, we believe that our own vulnerabilities are also our greatest strengths for survival because they prompt us to rely on and care for each other.

We have four capacities in mind that we considered leadership resources for Mark in the story we presented, as well as focus points for relational leadership coaching. These four capacities are *sensitivity*, *diversity*, *dependency*, *and resiliency.*

Sensitivity

Following the advent in the 1990s of *emotional intelligence* as introduced by Salovey & Mayer(1990), a slew of books hit the business market with titles promoting a different brand of leadership that recognized and appreciated the role of feelings in navigating the workplace (Caruso & Salovey, 2004; Goleman, 1995). Simultaneously, readers were introduced to a resurgence of mindfulness practices, a tradition that for the past 20 years has been highlighting a synergy between contemporary neurobiology and ancient Eastern meditative practices (especially socially engaged forms of Buddhism). Neurobiologists now endorse the use of embodied awareness in cultivating brain integration and regulating hyperarousal, promoting peaceful social engagement, moderation of consumption and creative synthesis of physical, emotional and communal phenomena (Siegel, 1999). The general consensus from science and industry is that *appreciating* emotional experience helps people make good decisions in life and in business.

And let's remember that feelings are called feelings because they are felt – that is, they are sensed in the body. Yet the paradigm of individualism dismisses the very validity of the body, encouraging a tradition of disembodied rationalism that stands at odds with the claims made by the field of emotional intelligence. And we enact that paradigm every day through our mechanistic metaphors in the world of work, advocating practices that reward stoics by promoting them to higher levels of leadership, which assumes that the best leader is the most emotionally unaffected. Despite the advent of emotional intelligence, in business it is radical even *to notice* that one has a body, let alone to value embodied experience.

Of course, experience is always and necessarily *shared*. John Heron and Peter Reason, qualitative researchers who have written extensively on the subject of epistemology, propose a form of 'experiential knowing' rooted in sensory encounters. They argue that knowledge that circumvents communal experience runs the risk of merely reasserting a dominant agenda:

> *The threat to quality knowing here is that co-researchers create a defensive inquiry which guards against the discovery of the novel and different, and which reproduces in encounter the habitual social and personal taken-for-granted. Quality inquiry will courageously challenge habits, seek new encounters and deepen contact with experience.* (2008, p. 378)

So in our coaching framework we give emphasis to the exploration of the continuum of experience – including embodied sensing – assuming that what people feel in their bodies provides unique information for *locating* important resources that would otherwise be *hard to find*. Our habit of tracking each other's felt experience at work has proven beneficial by increasing our ability to track specific experience and how it points to conditions of the larger context that contribute to or constrain change. We want to re-sensitize others and ourselves to what is happening within and all around us. If the context does not support the possibility of this kind of sensitivity, we coach in ways that call attention to this lack and catalyze more awareness of the conditions that may interfere with our ability to notice what is happening around us.

Discussion

Maggie was closely tracking her own body sensations as she worked with Mark. She noticed her shoulders tighten when Mark described the 'burden' of leading a poorly resourced organization. She noticed her foot tapping nervously as he mapped out a territory of nothing more than perpetual, solitary responsibility. At each point, she noticed her own felt experience and described it vividly to Mark. Hearing her descriptions invited Mark to attend more closely to his own experience. In his body, Mark felt a familiar heaviness on his chest, a knot in his stomach, tension around his eyes. Sitting in these sensations, Mark could reconnect with his fatigue and grief. He could feel the sadness of going it alone. The power of his experience broke through his repetitive mantras so that he could truly hear the story he was telling — the narrative of certain isolation and sacrifice. Now he was able to notice how his previous experience had been so profoundly influenced by discourses of individualistic leadership: the narrative of *the lonely hero*. And those discourses *desensitized* Mark to his own sadness. To be a leader is to be alone, or so the story goes. And to survive on that lonely journey, a leader has little choice but to lose sensitivity to the pain of isolation. Having the support to reengage with his feeling of loneliness armed Mark to challenge that powerful (dehumanizing) narrative.

Living through these moments together offered us the opportunity to notice how deeply important our sensitivity is to our ability to look for what we need in challenging situations. It was only from within this space that Mark could integrate his sense of isolation into a more complex expression of needing support. Then he and Maggie could move toward identifying a different set of questions that reached beyond what Mark had already concluded was 'inevitable.' Of course, with new questions came new possibilities for getting his needs met.

Diversity

The structuring of experience into what Gestaltists describe as figures and grounds links to an evolutionary imperative to access multiple perspectives as a matter of survival. Noticing potential danger and changing course would be next to impossible if people could not at least imagine the intelligence of a different path. Simultaneously this ability to look at the world from different points of view has carried our species forward in evolutionary terms into increasingly complex brain developments.

Increasing mobility and technological advancements have also increased our contact with multiple cultures, ushering in even more opportunities to appreciate different perspectives. Understanding who the different players are in a multicultural world requires an increased capacity to listen with a different ear. Kenneth Gergen refers to this capacity as 'polyphony', meaning 'multi-voiced.'

> *Mary Ann Hazen proposes that an organization becomes polyphonic when people celebrate their differences. She uses the carnival tradition of Mardi Gras to illustrate the point. In the festival, people from many different walks of life come together to dance, play, sing, and laugh. On the level of day-to-day decision-making, the practical implications are clear: establish dialogues that include as many participants as practicable. Any manager who finds him- or herself alone at the desk, formulating an autonomous decision, poses a threat to organizational life... Unfortunately our individualist tradition often stands in the way of collaborative decision-making.* (Gergen, 2009, p. 324)

Twenty-first century humans must not only anticipate multiple realities in the present, they must also be equipped to project an almost unlimited range of future scenarios based on that present experience. This will make good use of the distinctly human capacity for scenario planning. As our species has evolved, so has our view of the future. Humans are moving toward increasingly more complex understandings of causation and future outcomes. While it is true that simplistic explanations (for example, '*a* causes *b*') help people attend to their short-term survival needs, we need more complex explanations (for instance, 'sometimes *a* and *b* seem to happen along with *c* and *d*') for long-term sustainability planning. People can usually find *safety* with less negotiation; for *thriving*, they need others' input and assistance to organize a multipart plan.

We can coach people in ways that stimulate the consideration of multiple perspectives. In the workplace, tradition or expediency often blocks the expression of diversity. A coach is often most helpful when provoking attention to choice points. Sometimes the road forks at points of differing opinions, sometimes at possibilities for new solutions. Often what needs highlighting is the contrast between short- and long-term benefits, a distinction that can be difficult to hold in mind in the midst of crisis or pressure. Coaching can elicit more effective leadership when it cultivates an interest in diverse points of view.

Discussion

In our story, Mark despaired when his board recommended fundraising strategies that led him to believe they did not appreciate the urgency of the organization's short-term cash needs. Maggie highlighted the mismatch in a way that reminded Mark of the value of the Board's ideas *from the long view*, while validating the strain it put on Mark to get less support in looking at things *from the short view*. This showed us more clearly the resourcefulness that comes with holding diverse perspectives together in a more complex picture. It helped us to appreciate how effective coaching can be when it inquires into an experience such that figures and grounds can be reversed.

Furthermore, Maggie could draw on her experience of being pulled by multiple perspectives so that she could remember to encourage Mark's curiosity about the stories that might be shaping what was possible in this situation. Specifically, Maggie named some potentially contradictory discourses of leadership influencing Mark's expectations of himself and others. This supported Maggie and Mark to bring attention to the shame and dread imposed by stories of failure and poverty. These stories tend to polarize success *vs* failure or prosperity *vs* poverty by inviting leaders to take too much responsibility for one or the other. Mark was caught in this kind of polarization.

Mark was pulled into shame about ways *he alone* had failed to act according to his own explicit commitments. This led to a story he had begun to tell about himself, one that characterized him as a fraud that should not be leading other people in a system committed to collaboration. Mark was spinning a tale of individual responsibility. Maggie noticed the story and what it evoked for her. She had many similar experiences and could reflect on their effects in her life. She could also contrast those experiences with her current preferred values and commitments. Maggie noticed that Mark was at that moment accepting the invitation into 'failure' because he lost touch with the possibility of alternative perspectives. Again, our experience of enduring these events and reflecting on them together heightened our appreciation of the support we were deriving from our ability to look at things from many different angles.

Dependency

Humans cannot escape being 'under the influence' of something. Each year, social neuroscience adds to its already impressive canon of research to paint a vivid picture of the remarkable 'plasticity' of the human nervous system (Gallese, Fadiga, Fogassi, & Rizzolatti,

1996; Gallese, 2001; Siegel, 1999; Lewis, Amini, & Lannon, 2001). In one sense, this points to something humans often dread, that they are at risk of being hurt and *dependent* on the environment. But hiding in the background of these potentially troubling aspects is a host of advantages.

Humans benefit from this 'ability' to be moved and shaped by their social and physical environments because their survival has for ages hinged on a sophisticated skill for mutual understanding and a reliance on collective coordination (Hrdy, 2009). While it is habitual, particularly in the West, to use this skill for intricate coordination as a way to co-construct an elaborate *illusion of independence* – a cultural narrative of personal responsibility and individual mastery – still everything that happens does so as the result of these wonderfully coordinated actions. Nothing can be accomplished without some form of cooperation – *including* competition, segregation, isolation and war. 'As we participate, so do we create the value of various activities and outcomes – or not. Depending on the relationships, we would joyously work 12 hours a day or blow ourselves apart with a bomb' (Gergen, 2009). Ignoring or *hiding* our inevitably interdependent condition makes it no less real.

Assuming people are always influencing each other and coordinating outcomes has important implications for understanding and planning change, especially change in organizational systems. From this viewpoint, change can only happen when interrelated forces cooperate to allow for new behaviors, new experiences, and fresh perspectives. People simply cannot overcome the conditions of their context alone. So it is pointless to coach anyone to attempt this. When people want specific results, they need to consider how to invite the coordinated actions of those who can contribute to supporting or blocking the desired outcome.

In organizations, it is common to overlook some of the coordinating players by *underestimating* the impact of their compliance or resistance. Organizational leaders often need help keeping track of the taken-for-granted workers, functions, and areas on which business depends. If coaching is about helping people work more effectively, the coach has to consider conditions beyond just an individual's habits and capabilities. Change will require the support of others who are part of the individual's context, support that comes most readily when others are invested in the change. Everyone is dependent.

Conversely, attempts to make a change *without* considering supporting conditions will result in failure, either because the change will be blocked at the outset or because it cannot be sustained without others' commitments and intentions. A striving for self-reliance will almost inevitably contribute to a sense of failure. The bottom line is that everyone needs help to make a change that sticks.

Anyone practicing leadership hopefully inspires others to take initiative for embodying a larger vision. Often the most inspiring leadership demonstrates how to carry some share of the workload while ensuring the load does not crush anyone. Trying to *control* what happens and how others respond is an unmanageable task and usually leads to failure. Arguably, effective leadership eschews this habit, pointing the way to possibilities for distributing responsibility equitably and sharing ownership of outcomes.

While the myth of independence can easily catapult people into self blame, they can just as easily resort to blaming others.

Blaming oneself or others signals a rupture in the fabric that ties people together. Human beings are wired to recognize implicitly that they are embedded among a web of others whose cooperation they need to make anything happen, good or bad. So they naturally feel compelled to point out when the spotlight does not capture the invisible-but-powerful actions of the *others who are also responsible.*

Discussion

In our story, Mark fell prey to pursuing independence because he could not access input and support. He was seduced by the notion that a good leader does not need help, but knows what to do and does it without regret. When Mark flirted with blame, Maggie wondered about the wider arrangements that coordinated his solitary leadership. She listened to Mark's story for themes of loneliness and burden, imagining them as *invitations to distribute responsibility* among a wider group of players.

But Mark had literally *forgotten the context* that gave rise to his choices. The forgetting led to misunderstanding the ways the larger context shaped what was possible. In stressful situations that require rapid decisions, it may be too difficult to attend to all the factors shaping what is happening. Under stress, people are especially prone to collapsing complexity and missing systemic influences. Once Mark could tolerate remembering there were forces beyond his control, he could take up Maggie's invitation to consider a wider picture, one that included the whole organizational system and the social landscape in which it was situated. And if we understood his impulse to *blame* someone (even himself) as an invitation to explore the contextual influences, we could take more of the picture into account. This was an important discovery for us. Prior to this realization, we understood how a collapsed view of things would easily lead to blame. What we see more clearly now is the useful information that comes in the form of blaming.

Maggie also reminded Mark that collaborative practices are 'practices' after all: we learn from them by noticing *in retrospect* what was possible and then remembering this the next time we have an opportunity to experiment. Thus Maggie grounded Mark in one of the core values organizing his work – that is, supporting developmental strivings. Now Mark could see how his 'poor decisions' were actually *collective strivings* that offered opportunities to reflect with others on his actions and use those reflections to learn how to coordinate systemic changes.

So now Mark could notice his impulse to blame, and see how it could be read as a signal that he needed more information. He could then point this out to those around him so they could see it with him and also *notice him seeing it*. In collective reflection, Mark could engage others in the system to notice missed opportunities and current possibilities. Ironically, the situation that had previously seemed necessarily lonely to Mark now emerged as a highly creative opportunity for shared action. *We see this transformation of isolation into collaboration as a function of leadership that recognizes and values dependency. And we regard the encouragement of this kind of leadership as a key practice of relational coaching.*

Resiliency

Resiliency has been shown to be more than just the ability to cope well under adversity; it includes both the capacity of individuals to navigate their way to the psychological, social, cultural, and physical resources that sustain their well-being, and their capacity, individually and collectively, to negotiate for these resources to be provided and experienced in culturally meaningful ways

(Zautra, Hall, & Murray, 2010). Resiliency research has shown that adaptive behaviors do not actually *cause* resiliency but rather 'are the positive developmental *outcomes* demonstrating that this innate capacity is engaged' (Benard, 2004, p. 23). These outcomes, in turn, contribute to improved social, health and occupational behaviors and reduced health-risk.

The research has identified protective factors including respectful relationships, high expectations, and opportunities for participation and contribution. These factors predict when human beings are likely to engage their capacities to adapt creatively to adversity (Benard, 2004).

We consider a healthy organization to provide the same protective factors for its workers, offering a culture of respect and care, reasonable but stimulating challenges, and ample opportunities to participate in decision-making and to provide leadership wherever possible. When some or all of these factors are absent, the few workers who have them elsewhere in their lives will likely be able to compensate, but over time the whole organization will suffer with increasing rates of turnover and decreasing rates of effectiveness.

As relational coaches, we are always in some way coaching *whole systems* (that include ourselves as parts). Therefore, our intention is to encourage workers to make use of the strengths, assets, resources and supports within reach. Those who are part of the system co-create the environment that shapes their experience. So we explore the *qualities of the environment that can be adjusted* in ways that improve functioning for the whole system. If workers are unhappy with a past outcome, what can be learned from the context that gave rise to the unfavorable result? Instead of asking 'What more could I have done?', we inquire, 'What kind of situation would have shaped things in the way we hoped they would go?'

Relational coaching *assumes* clients are resilient when exposed to a culture that activates their capacities to adapt creatively. So we actively search for ways to inspire such a culture or to notice when some of those conditions are already emerging in a client's context and encourage their further development.

Discussion

In our story, the proverbial buck was bound to stop with Mark – the *leader*. Mark felt shame about needing more support than was available, and anxiety about asking for it. So exploring his needs for support would surely activate his shame and anxiety. Fortunately, the organizational culture fostered appreciation of these core human emotions that kept Mark from shutting down in the face of them. This culture served as a protective factor that activated his emotional courage.

Maggie understood that Mark could never have arrived at where he now was if he did not have a vision for change. In the early days of founding and growing The Relational Center, Mark encountered significant adversity and scarcity of resources. He responded to that challenge mostly by *looking for* support in unusual forms. He used the passion and investment of social capital and voluntary labor to compensate for a lack of money. Now the economic challenges had grown to the point where money was the only support that would suffice. Still, Maggie trusted that he could be resilient to this struggle as long as he maintained access also to his broader support base.

Recall that it was the very idea that he had exhausted what he saw as all *available* support, that led Mark to resort to isolation

– which made him brittle and more likely to make unilateral decisions on his own. When Mark saw this mismatch between his preferred practices and what he ultimately did, he felt ashamed: he was a *failure.* So Maggie pointed out that in naming the 'failure' Mark was already demonstrating resiliency by reaching out and exposing his distress.

In the early days of the organization, Mark showed resiliency in the form of strength of vision and unflinching persistence. The downside was that he often vacillated between concealing his struggles or showing them with bitterness or contempt, encouraging an organizational culture in which people assumed Mark could either handle things just fine on his own or that he was unhappy with what they were doing. So people did not realize Mark needed them to be available to him for support. In fact, without hearing his clear and sincere plea for support, they most likely felt inadequate to contribute anything to him.

Now Mark was showing a new kind of resiliency that emerged at the very moment when heroic sacrifice could no longer sustain the organization. He was *shamelessly* reaching for support, considering his embodied experience as useful information, imagining alternative ways of thinking and organizing, and looking for collaboration to coordinate sustainable change.

Update

At the time of writing this chapter, two important developments have taken place. First, after a considerable period of estrangement, Mark and Sam have met a handful of times and shared their feelings about what took place. Actually, it turns out they both have a similar understanding of the complex factors shaping the past events. This shared picture interrupts the impulse they both feel to blame each other. They are now in the process of exploring whether there is any ground for a new collegial relationship.

Second, the Board of Directors is now in a dramatically different position, with much more capacity to share responsibility and work together to ensure the organization's sustainability. Mark continues to access the Board's support by keeping them more actively engaged and involved in the mission and work of the organization. While efforts to engage donors and volunteers continuously demand Mark's attention, he now has a clearer understanding of the role dependency plays in deepening the commitment of his supporters.

Conclusion

In our story, we describe a shift in Mark's experience from shame and inadequacy to hope and resiliency. We first acknowledged sensory detail that challenged repetitive, binary stories (developing sensitivity as a capacity); and then wondered about alternative discourses that could offer us more support (through increased diversity). Next, we agreed to think about leadership as shared responsibility rather than as invulnerability and competency (a different view of dependency). Finally, we assumed there was wisdom and strength available by virtue of the very problems and pains Mark was encountering (a different sense of resiliency). All of this learning transformed the notion of failure into an opportunity for inquiry, in which the impulse to blame could be understood as a signal of the need to distribute responsibility more thoughtfully.

A caveat: making use of these capacities does require a quality of engagement with others that takes some effort and some willingness to appear 'hungry' for support. No degree of theoretical discussion can eliminate the sting of recrimination that comes from the usual and customary practices of eschewing dependency and rewarding stoic endurance, practices pervasive in many organizational cultures. So while we have indeed measured success around challenges pertaining to The Relational Center's sustainability and leadership, we have also encountered 'push-back' from within and without. The discourses of individualism still clamor and we are still under their spell much of the time.

Our hope lies in our vision of what is possible when a critical mass of our organizational community cooperate in lifting up the standards of distributed leadership and collaborative decision-making. Now that we have seen that this is possible and have experienced its momentum, we can aim for this vision and remind one another of the benefits that come when we do. In fact, our access to imagining such a scenario is itself an embodiment of the human capacities on which this chapter has focused.

References

Bakhtin, M. M. (1986). *Speech Genres and Other Late Essays.* (V. McGee, trans.) Austin: University of Texas Press.

Benard, B. (2004). *Resiliency: What We Have Learned.* San Francisco: WestEd.

Carlson, C., & Kolodny, R. (2009). Embodying field theory in how we work with groups and large systems. Ullman, D. & Wheeler, G. *Cocreating the field: Intention and Practice in the Age of Complexity.* (pp.135-175). New York: GestaltPress.

Caruso, D., & Salovey, P. (2004). *The Emotionally Intelligent Manager: How to Develop and Use the Four Key Emotional Skills of Leadership.* San Francisco: Jossey-Bass.

Denham-Vaughan, S., & Chidiac, M. A. (2009). Dialogue goes to work: Relational Organisational Gestalt. Jacobs, L. & Hycner, R.

Relational Approaches in Gestalt Therapy (pp. 249-298). Orleans, MA: GestaltPress.

Fairfield, M. (2013). The relational movement. *British Gestalt Journal, 22,* (1) 22-35.

Fairfield, M., & O'Shea, L. (2008). Getting 'Beyond Individualism'. *British Gestalt Journal,* 17, (2) 24-38.

Gallese, V. (2001). The 'Shared Manifold' hypothesis: from mirror neurons to empathy. *Journal of Consciousness Studies, 8*, 33-50.

Gallese, V., Fadiga, L., Fogassi, L., & Rizzolatti. (1996). Action reecognition in the premotor cortex. *Brain, 119,* (2) 593-609.

Gergen, K. (2009). *Relational Being: Beyond Self and Community.* Oxford: Oxford University Press.

Goleman, D. (1995). *Emotional Intelligence.* New York: Bantam Books.

Heron, J., & Reason, P. (2008). Extending epistemology within a co-operative inquiry. In Reason, P. & Bradbury,H. *The SAGE Handbook of Action Research: Participative inquiry and practice* (pp. 366-380). Thousand Oaks, CA: SAGE.

Hosking, D. M., & McNamee, S. (2006). *The Social Construction of Organization: Advances in Organization Studies.* Copenhagen: Copenhagen Business School Press.

Hrdy, S. B. (2009). *Mothers and Others: The Evolutionary Origins of Mutual Understanding.* Cambridge MA: The Bellknap Press of Harvard University Press.

Lewis, T., Amini, F., & Lannon, R. (2001). *A General Theory of Love.* New York: Vintage Books.

Parlett, M. (2003). Creative abilities and the art of living well. Spagnuolo Lobb, M. & Amendt-Lyon, N. *Creative License: The Art of*

Gestalt Therapy (pp. 51-62). New York: Springer Wien.

Salovey, P., & Mayer, J. (1990). Emotional intelligence. *Imagination, Cognition, and Personality., 9,* (3) 185-211.

Siegel, D. (1999). *The Developing Mind: How Relationships and the Brain Interact to Shape Who We Are.* New York: Guilford Press.

Wheeler, G. (2000). *Beyond Individualism: Toward a New Understanding of Self, Relationship and Experience.* Cambridge: GIC Press.

Zautra, A. J., Hall, J. S., & Murray, K. E. (2010). Resilience: A new definition of health for people and communities. Reich, J.W., Zautra, A. J., & Hall, J.S. *Handbook of Adult Resilience* (pp. 3-34). New York: Guilford Press.

7

Working with the Imaginal Field

Sue Congram PhD

If someone asked me, 'What do you value most about the way that you coach?' it would be using imagery and imagination – through metaphor, story, myth, poetry – to access the deeper psychological layers of the client's experience. For example, I work with *reflective images* that arise out of the dynamic field of coaching and offer them for the client to consider. In other words I pay attention to imagery that has arisen for the client, or offer images arising from my own present experience, that I believe will mirror the client's experience.

I trust this process because I do not see emerging imagery as *mine,* or *the client's,* but as arising from the relational space between us. As a fundamental aspect of 'the field' it is *ours* to be worked with. Francis (2005) describes this process as 'reading the field' to determine 'what might be emergent, or even striving for expression' (p. 30). Coaching from a perspective of the 'imaginal field' (Congram 2011), takes learning to a greater depth, where deeply-held processes that influence and affect the way people act, are brought into awareness. I refer to this as *in-depth* coaching.

With leaders, it looks beyond the individual in the role of leader, taking into account the relational processes of a wide range of people who collectively contribute to the direction-finding and direction-giving functions of leadership.

One of the most foundational practices of leadership is relating. Successful coaching calls for an understanding of the deeper layers of relational dynamics, and an exploration of how coaching can result in a more systemically-expanded leadership capacity; by individuals in leader roles, by leadership teams and by people exercising influence at all levels of the wider organisational system. I suggest that exploring images that arise in the coaching encounter is one way of working in-depth on these relational dynamics. This chapter describes three case studies where in-depth coaching of this kind, brought about transformational change. First, I explain how taking a field theory perspective is at the heart of both coaching and leadership.

Taking a Field Theory perspective for in-depth leadership coaching

Lewinian and post-Lewinian thinking on field theory has made an impression on me, in my coaching and in understanding leadership. Field theory has helped me appreciate that coaching is more than a conversational exchange between coach and client; it is located in a social and cultural environment that influences and is influenced by the exchange. In addition, adopting a field perspective invites phenomenological practice, where the moment-by-moment flow of interaction between myself and the client is where insights are gained.

Field theory has also given me a perspective of leadership as an emergent property of a system (team, group, organisation), which arises out of relationships and connections (O'Connor & Quinn

2004), and is shaped by deeper social and cultural layers (Congram 2013). As such, the role of leader is one aspect of the dynamic field, but not the whole of it. Developing leadership capacity is about the leader *and* all the people who contribute to the leadership of the organisation in different ways. This perspective remains consistent in my coaching, whether an organisation operates a conventional leader-follower structure, or a more progressive distributed leadership model (Spillane 2006).

To guide me in my coaching, I differentiate between psychological layers that are at play in the dynamic field. I use the analogy of a tree to explain what I mean by layers, where all layers are relevant, interconnected and dynamic (not fixed and static). The first layer is *above the surface;* the second layer refers to *roots just beneath the surface;* the third layer comprises *the deepest roots of the tree.* I explain that coaching in-depth means working at the third layer, calling for a different set of skills than those used to coach within the first two layers.

(1) The first layer, above the surface, is the tree itself, open to the environment, visible and easy to describe as it changes over time in relation to the weather and the seasons. Here are the observable phenomena – behaviours, expression, voice, what is said and how it is said; how people present themselves in relationship; and how others respond. Much coaching is interested in cognition, behaviour and performance, often drawing on rationality and logic. However, without deeper insights and awareness, both coaching and leadership can feel dry and lifeless.

(2) The second layer, just beneath the surface, is a critical point where the roots meet the tree, acting as a life-source. Life here is not separate from that above the surface, but in a world where the value of rational thinking is greater than emotional well-being,

this layer can appear less important. Here exist many aspects of life that are not generally in awareness on a daily basis unless stimulated. Emotions, knowledge, personal values and attitudes, life history, family patterns, longings, thoughts, intuitions and questions of personal identity may all belong at this level.

Coaching beneath the surface is concerned with emotional awareness, self-reflection, perceptions, assumptions and interpretations being made and acted on; intentions not yet articulated; and other hidden processes that are fairly accessible. All these can contribute to the richness of social interaction. Take emotions, for instance. We cannot 'see' an emotion, we can only see how an emotion manifests through the body.

This second layer is fairly accessible in coaching and much of the time is expressed through speech and body language; and part of the client's learning may be through developing a language to express emotional, reflective and intuitive experiences. Mindfulness and reflective practice can lead to much greater self-awareness and emotional self-understanding; and to a capacity to respond well to situations that life presents.

(3) The third layer, in which lie the deepest roots of the tree, is far less accessible. These roots have two specific functions: to nourish the tree and to keep it stable and in balance. Just as the tree cannot survive without these roots, so too, people draw on their roots in their daily interactions – their cultural values and beliefs, deep assumptions, and aspects of life which are taken-for-granted and help to keep it in balance. Significant change calls for accessing these deeper roots of a person's life, and is characteristic of what I mean by 'in-depth coaching' and 'in-depth leadership': both draw on the deep roots of life. Through my own research I have

discovered how many forces that influence and shape leadership capacity have their roots in this deeper layer.

I wish to emphasise that in-depth coaching is not to be mistaken for therapy, which is usually personal and remedial. It is not my intention to address this distinction here. Rogers (2004) provides useful information on managing the boundary between coaching and therapy, which is a critical issue in professional practice.

Developing in-depth leadership capacity calls for a different language in coaching than applies with reflective practice that is confined to the first two layers. Deep roots carry the language of the metaphoric and symbolic, requiring coaching capabilities that work at this level: coaches could find themselves engaged with and listening deeply into the stories that the client brings, picking up projective expressions through the client's use of symbolism, and may involve poetic or artistic expression. This layer is pertinent to coaching leadership capacity because ideologies, attitudes and beliefs concerning leadership are culturally embedded, underpinning as well as limiting leadership capacity.

In-depth coaching practice for developing in-depth leadership

In this section I describe three case studies in which coaching included investigations at the third level. All three studies are with individual leaders rather than leadership teams; each demonstrates how deeply-embedded attitudes and beliefs have a limiting effect on their own leadership capacity as well as on their teams and the wider systems they lead.

Case study 1: Abbie – re-integrating 'other'

This case study demonstrates how discounted parts of one's self, which are considered '*other*' (such as vulnerability, talents, qualities, attitudes, prejudices, biases, beliefs) can limit leadership capacity. What I mean by *other*, is that which is neither integrated as an aspect of the self, nor an aspect of the system, and yet is experienced as something that is 'out there' and not 'within'. Because of this phenomenon, leadership can fail to achieve full capacity because part of the whole is not recognised and valued. The coaching question is to help uncover what is disowned, and then to encourage its integration.

I used story and metaphor for working in-depth with my client in this case study. Story is a particularly valuable approach to coaching clients for two reasons: there are those who disown aspects of themselves; and because stories play a part in social exchange. In everyday conversation stories act as 'glue' for communities, enabling social interaction and bonding. They carry all three layers described above. Clients will always have a story to tell: this is what they naturally do when they come for coaching. Whilst stories of past experiences are constructions of the actual experience and can be different at different times, embellishments are generally not intended to deceive but to accentuate points, and to bring past experiences to life in the present moment. As human beings we tell stories and amplify them based on our beliefs, perceptions and perspectives. Stories of people's experiences offer an extremely rich source of material to work with in coaching, where fabrications are rich in metaphor and symbolism, and reveal deeply held beliefs and values that are largely out of awareness.

Abbie held a senior management position in a large commercial organisation, a post she had taken as a career move from middle management in another organisation. She had been in the position for almost a year when she came for coaching, believing that she was capable of carrying out her leadership role, but constantly finding herself on what she described as 'her back foot', which pushed her 'off balance' and behind in her work. The metaphor 'off balance' caught my attention, Rather than making my own assumptions about it, I asked her what needed to be brought into balance? She continued her story, telling me how much under pressure she felt and how she could never complete projects on time, and asked me to coach her on a time management plan. I responded that I was not willing to do that, explaining that I believed that both her sense of being 'off balance' and her time management issues, were a symptom of a deeper imbalance. I explained that I did not believe coaching her on time management would change things in a sustainable way.

Whilst staying with her language and encouraging Abbie to be aware of her embodied experience of being 'pushed off balance', I noticed how she was increasingly determined that managing her time would make things better. We were confronted with a choice point: either to pursue her stuckness, the metaphor of being pushed off-balance (a layer 2-type issue); or the question of time management (an issue at layer 1). There were several possibilities here with which I could have worked. I sensed that Abbie knew this place of stuckness well: she portrayed herself as a victim of the system (layer 2), which seemed to serve her in some unknown way: this would have been another coaching thread to follow, a field dynamic that could be explored. Instead, my interest was to consider what might be missing from her story that was rooted in-depth (in layer 3).

Any combination of these layers offered potential for learning through coaching. The question was (and always is in coaching), 'what is the overall purpose of the coaching in this particular situation; what is the coaching contract?' My coaching contract with Abbie had been to help her become a better leader, and that hadn't changed.

I remembered an image that had caught my attention during the previous coaching session, of a talented, imaginative, vibrant woman who had become pale and washed out. I saw the same paleness in her face now and decided to share my observations as well as the image. This observation resonated with Abbie, although she argued that the working environment was not the place for imagination and vibrancy, and that a leader's role was to 'get results', which meant keeping on schedule and working tightly to deadlines. For Abbie, there was no place at work for the kind of imagination that coloured her home life. Whilst Abbie held strong beliefs concerning how to get results and was very good at getting them, she had disregarded her imaginative and vibrant self in her leadership. Furthermore, she did not realise that her imagination could help bring her work life back into balance, as well as get results.

Abbie's belief system discounted a part of her self, and gave preference to what she believed was expected of her, supported by a convincing self-rationalisation. Here was a situation where a range of leadership qualities were not recognised or valued, neither within Abbie, nor within the organisation in which she worked. The qualities that were being discounted in Abbie's case were imagination and vibrancy, which Abbie had 'toned down' in order to fit in, convincing herself of the rightness of this.

In my work I notice that people frequently edit out what they don't feel comfortable with. When challenged, they rationalise why they shouldn't do something that might otherwise be beneficial, convincing themselves through applying material from their own belief system. A well-established rationalisation can sound convincing because it once served a purpose and has not been modified over time in the context of seeing the world differently. A coach who is coaching for greater leadership capacity has to be prepared for this and to spot it, whilst at the same time appreciating why the client would think in this conventional way. Coaching can help self-limiting belief systems to become visible, so they can be challenged. At the same time there is a need to ensure that internal support systems are strong enough to sustain the discomforts of change as new ways of thinking become established.

Coaching Abbie included the use of imagery, working with colour and embodiment practices such as I describe below. From my perspective, I saw the opportunity to encourage Abbie to use her imagination to expand her sense of her leadership possibilities. This was a moderate step-by-step process where I would pick up on words and images that Abbie came up with and reflect them back to her. For example, when she described her 'vibrant' self at work as 'toned down', I brought into question what she was toning down and what colour might emerge if she 'toned up'. This colour work was inspired by Abbie as we started to explore the meaning of 'imagination and vibrancy' in leadership. She drew on colours from the furnishings and objects in the room to explore what was vibrant and what was not. I asked her to identify which colours brought her alive and where she felt them in her body, compared with colours that softened, dulled or muted her mood; and how she experienced these. Later she used coloured pens and crayons for her own reflective journal. She found this helpful as it provided a powerful reference point, a daily reminder that did not take too long to do. She also started wearing small and simple items of clothing and jewellery with the symbolic colours that she had chosen (a scarf, a necklace with a coloured stone, a T-shirt), and placed coloured objects on her desk at work, bringing a symbolism of new life into her daily work as a constant reminder of her ongoing development and intentions. Each colour reminded her of an aspect of herself that was valuable to her leadership. Developing imaginative ways of working in her role followed a similar path, a step-by-step process of testing out, and to her surprise, speaking out.

Body-work was an integrated aspect of the coaching process, particularly in helping Abbie to 'feel' the colours that she was exploring and to 'feel' a balanced posture. It included how she held her body when she was standing, walking and sitting, when she felt 'balanced', 'out of balance', 'toned down', 'toned up' and 'vibrant'. She also imagined how others may have been responding or reacting to her body and facial expressions, an exercise that proved particularly insightful when considering relationships that Abbie described as 'more difficult'. She began to appreciate her own contribution to the difficulties. With new awareness, Abbie was able to question and inquire of herself and of her leadership practice. She could now move away from a situation where a great deal of energy had been absorbed in *surviving*, towards *living* leadership with greater capacity, and also encouraging the same in people around her. By demonstrating a more vibrant version of herself to her team, they also became liberated, engaging their collective leadership in a way that Abbie had not previously appreciated.

Many circumstances surrounding Abbie are typical of the workplace. Rational, authoritative and directive leadership qualities are held in high regard, they are the basis on which success is traditionally measured. Whilst these qualities are greatly valued, *other* qualities that contribute to leadership are often not recognised. Inevitably therefore, Abbie disregarded them within herself, believing them neither to be useful to her own success, nor to others. This is an example of how belief systems concerning leadership often run deep and go unquestioned.

Case study 2: Tim – the eclipse

This case study illustrates how deeply-embedded beliefs and attitudes can eclipse practices that are important to leadership, but are undervalued. In my research (Congram 2013), I found that leadership capacity is limited by attitudes and beliefs about what leadership is – largely based on the heroic, leader-follower paradigm. Despite the emergence of more progressive thinking (Fitzsimons *et al* 2011; Western 2008), traditional mindsets continue to dominate organisational discourse (Koenig *et al* 2011). People think and talk in terms of leadership as being about the role of 'the leader', and coaching practices largely match this view. This ideology is deeply embedded in our culture, eclipsing practices that could otherwise serve leadership well.

For Tim, in a 360° feedback process the message was blatantly clear: 'Be more assertive in your leadership'. I asked him what this meant and he explained that he understood it to mean that he should be more directive and authoritative. He had said that what he would like to achieve through coaching was to develop a more successful team and he believed that this was the direction in which to go. In the past twelve months, the morale in his team had dropped, and was made worse by bad end-of-year results. He believed that his team could have done better, were not good at self-monitoring, and that by his setting goals for them and monitoring their progress on a regular basis, they could achieve success. From a 3-layers coaching perspective, Tim's attitude towards his own leadership and the performance of his team were presented as if from layer (1), whilst his belief system was deeply rooted in layer (3).

According to the information that Tim had provided, the leadership capacity of this team was well below what they could achieve. Yet, to my eyes, it appeared that he was moving further away from growing the team's capabilities. He was thinking only at a rational level and describing what his leadership could be over the coming months in a purely logical way. I was puzzled by this, as Tim had earlier described an experience in which he had worked sensitively and successfully on a difficult issue with a team member. When I asked him about it he brushed it off, explaining that 'that wasn't leadership, I just had to deal with it on that day'. I noted also how he had involved others to support the person in question in the future – again he brushed it aside as a 'management issue that anyone would have dealt with'.

This differentiation between management and leadership may hold some validity, yet my interest was in how to draw out Tim's relational strengths, which he appeared to discount. A strength had become eclipsed by his own ideology of what leadership 'should be'. I found this same phenomenon in my research, where relational practices exist but are obscured by traditional ways of thinking, and therefore not strongly associated with leadership (Congram 2013). Tim subscribed to the commonly-held ideology of leader-follower that is embedded in our culture generally. It was a model strongly practised in the organisation in which he worked and was accentuated by the company's competency framework.

I was faced with a coaching dilemma: whether to keep a focus within the traditional leader-follower parameters demonstrated by Tim and operated by his organisation; or discuss with him a more progressive way of thinking. My own knowledge, experience and view on developing leadership capacity moves me towards a relational, inclusive and systemic approach. Yet I had contracted to help Tim achieve team success, which in his mind was goal-oriented and leader-driven. It was a position that he wanted to get better at and one that I considered could act against his long-term aspirations for team success.

My resolution was to share this dilemma with Tim, to be clear about our differences. It was important to 'hold' our differences – not to try to resolve them, but to work with them creatively. As a coach I believe this demonstrates healthy role-modelling of difference in relationships, a point that I came back to a few sessions later in the coaching. As we discussed this difference, what emerged from the discussion were two images of *stones* and *feathers,* which metaphorically defined our two positions. This was an emergent process in which a number of descriptions had infused the conversation, such as 'hard to get hold of', 'lightness', 'solid', 'grounded', 'sharp edges', ' soft skills', and so on. These I had reflected back as part of our coaching process. We later used *real* stones and feathers to symbolise these two positions.

Although we were exploring a polarity (rather than a plurality, involving many positions, which would be more representative of modern leadership thinking), this provided a starting point for generating metaphors and images of interest to *me*, while not losing sight of *Tim's* preference for rational thinking. Through this approach, Tim found a way (a third position), which was a combination of our differences, where he worked with coloured stones and a range of different feathers. Coaching involved supporting him to bring ignored practices into view, and to own them as valuable qualities, and then to draw on these in a way that would best serve a different leadership approach. Working with the stones and feathers provided a profound platform from which Tim was able to make new meaning of leadership for himself – one which involved people and relational activities, without standing too far outside the generally-accepted practices of the organisation. Instead of learning how to be more assertive, Tim learned how to make a difference through building relationships; to influence through giving voice to his ideas; and to stay present when confronted with difficult situations. He developed this, not through input of new skills, but by drawing out and shining a light on his natural strengths.

In my work, I have become aware of the extent to which professional people, including coaches and consultants, can also be caught in deeply-established cultural practices, where dominant, accepted forms of working, eclipse important practices which then go unrecognised. These practices, often referred to as 'soft skills' or 'feminised practices', are critical to leadership because they 'create the conditions out of which leadership can emerge and success can be achieved' (Congram 2013, p. 195).

Case study 3: Ian – a question of self-belief or self-confidence?
The following case study illustrates how apparent high confidence masked low self-belief; led to diminished leadership capacity; and how exploring a non-work-related issue held the key to developing greater leadership capacity. Of particular relevance here is that working at the deeper layer (3) painted a different picture from one that attended to personal work alone. The issue that arrived in the coaching room was stress (layers 1 & 2), but the stress was a symptom of a deeper problem.

Ian was in a senior role in a large public sector organisation. He knew the practical side of his role well, but he had recently experienced a highly stressful situation in which he had felt publicly exposed for something that he hadn't been directly responsible for. The situation had affected him deeply and was the reason for the coaching. As I sat with him listening to his story I felt as though he had a tough veneer around him. He seemed overly keen for me to know how good he was at his job, and the difficulties of operating in a blame culture. Ian also mentioned having a wife and two young children, but moved on quickly from that topic to focus on work issues. He seemed particularly anxious, showing physical symptoms such as mild perspiration and intermittent shakiness in his hands.

Having noticed a high number of incidences of a similar pattern with clients in the past, my interest led me to differentiate between *self-belief* and *self-confidence*. Both of these I believe are necessary in leadership, but become conflated – so that only the term 'self-confidence' is emphasised. While self-confidence is talked about widely in my client work, self-belief is rarely mentioned. Studies suggest that both are closely connected to self-identity. For myself, in my own life journey, developing self-belief has been enormously important, more so than building confidence in what I do. To believe in myself has compelled me to step forward with the passion and conviction of my beliefs. To build self-confidence has meant learning the skills and art of my work. The combination of these is a dynamic and powerful force. The years that I lived with low self-belief were only half-lived, and the moments that still catch me out lead to contractions of my capacity to lead and of my professional expertise.

However, low self-belief is not only personal: it is also a dynamic of the field in social interaction and leadership. Organisational cultures have strongly privileged *doing* (giving attention to self-confidence) over *being* (giving attention to self-belief). Professional work is measured and rewarded on performance and skills. I believe that this strong 'doing' attitude exacerbates problems associated with low self-belief, added to by living in a culture where many of us, myself included, grew up to diminish the value of positive feedback – 'not to boast' and not to get 'too big for your boots'. Yet absorbing positive feedback is like nourishing food – we need it to boost our self-belief and to be ready to give honest feedback, which might boost the self-belief of others.

Clients who have shown symptoms of low self-belief, often do this through stories designed to show how excellent they are in their work. It's a process that I have come to understand as concealing the vulnerable self. I believe that people learn how to protect themselves well from their vulnerabilities, often through telling a story. It's how they navigate through life despite a diminished sense of self. Although coaching cannot provide what is needed for dealing with deep psychological wounds, it can provide development for self-belief and stronger identity for people who have good enough internal support to make the changes needed. How this happens is different for everyone, guided by a sense of what is emerging in the coaching field.

During the third coaching session with Ian, I sensed a need to establish better contact and wondered if sharing as parents, something that we had in common, might achieve this. I asked him about his wife and two young children, and what it was like being a father, explaining that mothering for me had been both joyful and challenging. His response came as a surprise: 'Their mother is a better parent than I am'. I asked him what he meant by this and he told me about feeling he was not a good father. A gentle exploration revealed how he carried a belief about himself that he never could be a good father, whilst at the same time holding a deep longing to be the father he dreamed of for his two children. As he finished his story I showed my appreciation for what he had shared and then asked 'Do you believe in yourself enough to be the father you want to be?' We sat in a very long silence, until he looked at me and said with deep emotion 'I can, can't I?'

It occurred to me that there might be a strong correlation between fathering and leadership, for Ian. If he were to become the father he wanted to be, and to find the courage to step out of his old belief system, it might enable him to grow in his greater leadership capacity in the workplace, by helping him grow his self-belief and self-worth. Six months later, Ian took several bold steps in his role as a senior manager, which proved to be life-changing for him.

Self-belief can be a powerful dynamic in the relational field of leadership. In the context of a team, where the leader holds strong self-belief, this can be a powerful infusion in the team dynamics which can nourish the relationships within the team and encourage strong 'team belief'. People become inspired, and at times liberated in their own self-belief, although they may not be able to put words to their experience. An increase in self-belief on the part of the leader, can strengthen the leadership capacity of a whole team. Likewise, when self-belief is low in a leader, then the leadership capacity of the team can also be negatively impacted.

Coaching in-depth means raising awareness of unhelpful attitudes at level 3 concerning what is valued and what is not in the culture at large. It is also about seeing the current world through fresh eyes, and creating the conditions that will support a revised perception of self.

Thoughts, reflections and inspirations for this work

My reflections return to what I value most in the way that I coach: using imagery and imagination; accessing the deeper psychological layers; and creating an 'imaginal field'. The three case studies here demonstrate a small range of coaching processes for developing in-depth leadership, selected from a mass of creative possibilities that emerge in coaching. What enhances coaching in-depth is going beyond the rational mind, to unfolding metaphor and imagery, holding this up as a mirror for self-reflection, and connecting it with body experience (as described in the case of Abbie). In this work I am informed by, and draw inspiration from, Gestalt Field Theory, studies on culture and leadership, and depth psychology – particularly the work of Carl Jung and Active Imagination (Schaverien 2005; Chodorow 1997; Von Franz 1997; Woodman 1992, 1990,1982).

Active Imagination, as Jung developed it, follows a similar path to Field Theory in which imagery arises through an emergent rather than structured process. There is an important distinction to be made between two forms of imaginative practice: *active imagination* and *imaginative activities.* Carl Jung distinguished between *imaginative activities,* which he argued relate to conscious processes and 'the surface of personal things and conscious expectations' (Jung 1976 [1935]: para. 397), which is equivalent to layers 1 & 2 in the tree analogy used here. He related *active imagination* to the deeper unconscious where 'images have a life of their own and... symbolic events develop according to their own logic' (*ibid.* para. 397), equivalent to layer 3 of the tree – its deep roots. Imaginative activities have structure, whereas active imagination is emergent and flowing. Both have their place in coaching, each with a different purpose and different result.

There is also synchronicity, or in Field Theory terms 'the principle of possible relevance' (Parlett 1991), where unplanned and unexpected events that spontaneously occur, or exist within the dynamic field of the work, can become meaningful. An example here is where Abbie used the colours in the room to explore 'vibrancy'. This was not a preconceived idea (or exercise), but spontaneously emerged through her work. The colours happened to be there. Jung believed synchronicity to be 'an acausal connecting principle' (Jung 1955), whilst Jaworski (1996)

– in a study of synchronicity and leadership – describes it as 'an unfolding creative order' (p. ix). To stay open to synchronicity offers up unexpected meaning-making sources both in coaching, and to leadership.

The coach-client dynamic field is one of courage, adventure, facing an unknown terrain and new endeavours. If leaders and coaches alike conform to conventional thinking rather than challenging it, then leadership capacity will not grow. Coaching in this sense is demanding of both the coach and the client, requiring both parties to challenge their own strongly held cultural norms at a deep level and then to discover what it takes to work together at a deep level.

Leadership coaching does not necessarily attract clients who want or expect to be working with image, metaphor and the body. Most of my clients expect to engage in more conventional coaching that has greater rationality and logic to it. I find this a welcoming challenge, through which we navigate our way. A good starting point is to accept that everyday conversation carries levels of metaphor (Lakoff & Johnson 1980) all the time. Limitations to in-depth coaching do not arise through the lack of material to work on, but through a lack of capability, understanding or imagination by the coach and/or client, to bring the material alive. Working in-depth can be liberating not just for the client but for the coach as well.

References

Chodorow, J. (1997). *Jung on Active Imagination*. London: Routledge.

Congram, S. (2011). Narrative supervision: the experiential field and the 'imaginal'. J. Passmore (ed), *Supervision in Coaching*. 81-98. London: Kogan Page.

Congram, S. (2013). *Dynamic Fields of Leadership: A Study of Underlying Social, Cultural and Collective Influences.* Ph.D Thesis. University of Cardiff.

Fitzsimons, D., Turnbull James, K. & Denyer, D. (2011). Alternative approaches for studying shared and distributed leadership. *International Journal of Management Reviews, 13*, 313-328.

Francis, T. (2005). Working with the field. *British Gestalt Journal, 14,* (1) 26-33.

Jaworski, J. (1996). *Synchronicity: The Inner Path of Leadership*. San Francisco: Berrett-Koehler.

Jung, C.G. (1955). *Synchronicity: An Acausal Connecting Principle.* London: Routledge.

Jung, C.G. (1976). The Tavistock lectures: On the theory and practice of analytical psychology. *The Collected Works of C.G. Jung* (vol.18). Princeton: Princeton University Press. (Original work published in 1935).

Koenig, A.M., Eagly, A.H., Mitchell, A.A. & Ristikari, T. (2011). Are leader stereotypes masculine? A meta-analysis of three research paradigms. *Psychological Bulletin, 137,* (4) 616-642.

Lakoff, G., & Johnson, M. (1980). *Metaphors We Live By*. Chicago: University of Chicago Press.

O'Connor, P.M.G. & Quinn, L. (2004). Organizational capacity for leadership. McCauley, C.D. & Van Velsor, E. (eds.), *The Center for Creative Leadership Handbook of Leadership Development* (2nd ed.) 417– 437. San Francisco, CA: Jossey-Bass.

Parlett, M. (1991). Reflections on field theory. *British Gestalt Journal, 1,* (2) 63-81.

Rogers, J. (2004). *Coaching skills: A Handbook*. Maidenhead: Open University Press.

Schaverien, J. (2005). Art, dreams and active imagination: A post-Jungian approach to transference and the image. *Journal of Analytical Psychology*, *50*, 127-153.

Spillane, J.P. (2006). *Distributed Leadership*. San Francisco: Jossey-Bass.

von Franz, M-L. (1997). *Alchemical Active Imagination*. London: Shambhala. (Original work published in 1979).

Western, S. (2008). *Leadership: A Critical Text*. London: Sage.

Woodman, M. (1982). *Addiction to Perfection: The Still Unravished Bride*. Toronto: Inner City Books.

Woodman, M. (1990). *The Ravaged Bridegroom: Masculinity in Women*. Toronto: Inner City Books.

Woodman, M. (1992). *Leaving My Father's House: A Journey to Conscious Femininity* (1st ed.). Boston: Shambhala.

8

Making the Relational Turn: Some New Perspectives on Coaching Groups

Catherine Carlson MEd and Robert Kolodny PhD

Introduction

We have come to challenge all of our most settled notions about groups, about how groups develop, and about how to coach them. Our long-established coaching practices have dramatically shifted in response to the 'Relational Turn' – an emerging paradigm that represents new ways of thinking about our human nature and that emphasizes our relatedness rather than emphasizing our self-differentiation.

Here are a few examples of how our own practice as coaches has shifted[1]. To begin with, when we are coaching a group, we no longer see ourselves as the people who are supposed to make something happen, but rather as participants in an emergent process with a focus on discovering how we might support the next step in a group's development. Also, while our emphasis is still on development, we no longer think of it as assessing and filling gaps or deficits in skill, or as seeing ourselves as the ones who identify strengths and weaknesses and offer experiments to improve what is underdeveloped. Rather, we see development as fostering conditions to enable the richest possible relational environment for experimentation and learning, so that development occurs naturally.

In addition, we no longer find it useful to see groups as progressing through pre-determined stages (such as forming, storming, norming and performing…), but rather see them and their current state as emerging from a complex set of conditions that defy predictive mapping. Rather than holding ourselves apart and expecting group members to focus on one other, we understand that we are also part of the mix and must be available to explore our own experience and our impact along with everyone else; and that when we do this, something fundamental shifts for all of us. Finally, we no longer accept the mythology that has cast a spell on much of our coaching field, namely, that if you skill yourself up enough (by getting accredited, developing your 'use of self' and achieving 'personal mastery'), you will be able to whip any group into shape, regardless of all the other contextual factors at play.

This revolution in our practice has been driven by a shift in our understanding of how human systems develop – a shift from an individualistic view to a relational emphasis. We used to believe people and groups would develop by becoming newly aware of something we could see that they had not. Fundamentally, we treated development as if it was enhanced by adding positive behaviors and subtracting negative ones. We have come to see that people and groups develop naturally, by contacting and relating, and incorporating what is available to them in their overall situation – they take shape in relation to the supports their context (or as we think of it, the relational field) has to offer.

Another way of saying this is that development is *emergent* (not predictable or pre-determined: groups cannot be 'aimed', though we used to coach as if they could); and *non-linear* (much more moment-to-moment, involving trial-and-error, trying on and testing out, than our earlier expectations allowed).

This has caused us to think of our coaching work with groups as contributing to the co-creation of an emergent developmental field that is inclusive, supportive and creative. That is, we see our challenge not as getting a client group from point A to point B (or teaching the skills they need to get themselves there), but learning what will enhance the emerging relational field that we and our clients co-create moment-to-moment[2].

A working summary of what's different in our coaching

As a way to capture our emerging understanding of the basic guidelines, orientating concepts, and key skills and sensibilities that inform us in co-creating an emergent developmental field, we have contrasted these with our previous ways of understanding and working from a Gestalt perspective. We think contrasts can help to sharpen distinctions that can be subtle and elusive. Drawing contrasts can also suggest an either-or positioning and imply that one approach is better or more correct than the other. While we certainly have a bias in favor of the relational orientation, our intention is not to devalue our earlier training or more familiar approaches. We are looking to incorporate what has gone before in a new synthesis that includes both.

1. Implications for our practice as coaches

Here are some key shifts that have reorganized our coaching practice:

- We understand development as a function of the conditions of the field, as different from addressing some deficiency or dysfunction that can be identified independently and then 'fixed.'

- We do not automatically favor 'positive' outcomes or affective states (cohesion, understanding, enthusiasm) over those that don't feel so good (struggle, confusion, doubt, shame).
- We no longer think of support as offering what *we* think a group needs, but rather as a process of mutually discovering what a group can assimilate and make productive use of.
- We have come to more fully appreciate how the experience of shame and shame-avoidance are inevitable in group settings, and are key challenges to development. Supporting ourselves and our clients in the face of shame is key for our work, as contrasted with overlooking it, avoiding it, or blaming it on our client rather than seeing it as a phenomenon of the relational field that is co-created.
- We have found that groups grow and flourish through members recognizing their interdependence rather than by our coaching each member individually to become more autonomous and self-sufficient.
- We are now more likely to make what we are privately thinking and feeling as coaches explicitly available (rather than allowing our interior process to remain a powerful but unacknowledged variable) and to see this as critical to the emergent developmental field. Making ourselves vulnerable in this way represents our number-one challenge in working from this orientation.

While we use contrast to highlight changes in our practice, we want to be clear that a relational orientation includes the previous (individualistic) paradigm – we are not simply replacing one with the other.

2. Implications for the understanding we bring to groups

These changes in how we show up as coaches are influenced by a number of shifts in how we see groups and how we understand their development:

- A group is a constantly emerging reflection of multiple, changing influences and conditions that forms in relation to some need in the environment, rather than being some kind of fixed, identifiable entity with its own more or less unchanging character (meanwhile recognizing that there are aspects of groups that become habitual and may appear to be repetitive, and non-changing).
- Individual and group needs are intertwined in complex ways and are best served by balanced attention, rather than seeing them as potentially pitted against each other, or in an either/or contest.
- Change and development grow out of group members contacting and relating together. This stands in contrast to seeing change as prompted by some kind of isolated internal awareness arrived at individually, with the coach being the 'better knower' and primary source of this kind of awareness.
- The larger fields that lie outside a group have an influence on the group and what development is possible. For example, the corporate culture in the case of a work group; the multiple affiliations and allegiances for the members of a social group, and the rich mix of ethnic and cultural backgrounds that increasingly characterizes all kinds of groups. These larger fields, often nested one within another, need to be attended to rather than treating an individual or group as if they are not embedded reflections of such fields.

3. Implications for the skills we need as coaches

The above guidelines and key orientating concepts grew out of several coaching experiences over the last several years. These experiences have led us to a set of 'relational practices' which guide us as coaches to engage in, and contribute to, an emergent developmental field. While there is no all-purpose list of ingredients for coaching from this perspective, these practices are ways of working that we find enormously supportive.

- *Sensing into the field* is the capacity to connect to the field using the full range of our sensory capacity. We are not simply trying to understand what is going on in the larger context or field, as if studying it from a distance. We accept the reality that we are *of* the field that we are attempting to understand. Attending to our embodied experience more fully is what gives us access to the field. Using our full array of senses helps us be receptive to, and continuously listen for, the subtext (the affect, mood and relational music behind the text) that is being created by a group, including the influential echoes of relationships that exist in the larger context 'outside' the current group that are impacting what is occurring 'within.' This practice includes, first and foremost, listening for the unarticulated wants and the developmental longings that lie behind what is actually being said (which can often be heard as strivings we are being invited to support). It involves sensing that which is organizing our field but has been out of awareness – considering such influences as structure, power, expectations, and demands; attending to the quality of the field and how what's going on between people (including the coach's interactions with others) impacts the field and vice versa; as well as the impact of social and cultural influences. The interplay between contextual influences (and our experience of these influences) is not merely background, and they are not separate 'things' that we try to understand through reasoning. Field or contextual influences get integrated into our appreciation of what is developing. This practice can be thought of as developing a particular kind of 'field sensitivity' or 'context sensitivity' and calls for the use of phenomenological tracking – a method that supports us to be aware of our awareness process – sensing what is present based on staying as close as possible to our phenomenal or subjective experience and calibrating and recalibrating to what is occurring. This involves the capacity to organize and reorganize our response to others and to situations and is a key support for self-regulation for individuals and for groups.

- *Empathic attunement.* In the same way that *sensing into the field* allows us to connect to the field using our senses, empathic attunement allows us to connect to others using our emotional resonance. However, this practice goes beyond awareness – it involves empathy (sensing with a particular focus on listening from within another's perspective so that you can grasp the other's experience). It includes attending to what is happening here and now between you and another. One of the paths to attunement is sharing the impact others are having on you and hearing the impact you are having on others. Only in this way can one 'hear' what is not being spoken, and 'see' what is not visible, which helps support our capacity to 'incorporate' the experience of others. It is how we 'get' others – temporarily experiencing a situation as they experience it – seeing the world the way it looks to them, in a way that they sense that you grasp what it is like for them. This requires suspending our own reactions and ways of making meaning in favor of trying on another's. It also involves finding ways of communicating and testing this attunement. At a group level, it involves being emotionally connected to each person and to the larger field so that you can support what is emerging with the collective, as contrasted with just staying with one person's want. This, too, involves phenomenological method and is a critical support for self-regulation.

- *Cultivating dialogic sensibility* refers to listening to ourselves and to others in a fresh way that enables emergence of new possibilities, and fostering field conditions that support others to do the same. This practice embraces the notion that meaning is made between us in our engagement with each other, rather than by each of us taking counsel primarily with ourselves. It involves presenting our take on things without assuming that our take is the right one – that we are the 'better knower' of what is a shared reality. It holds what is 'true' about a situation to be an emergent property of that situation, only knowable through the sharing of different perspectives, replacing answers with questions, inequality with equality, power with respect. Once again this relies on phenomenological method and supports self-regulation.
- *Being strategic while simultaneously supporting emergence.* Being strategic in terms of planning, structuring and having a clear intention informing one's actions, has traditionally been seen as a key factor in working with groups. Strategic forethought and intention brought to a situation provides a way of channeling energy and possibility. If everything is open and all choices are possible, then the field can be too under-bounded for energy to gather and focus. Structure and forethought, when applied in a measured way, can reduce anxiety and allow groups to be more creative. At the same time it is important to attend to our embodied

experience and tune-in to what is emerging, particularly the developmental striving that is seeking expression. By tapping into the collective wisdom of the field, shifts will occur naturally. This practice challenges our capacity to be *both* strategic *and* support emergence at the same time – not a matter of landing on one or the other but simultaneously enacting both. It refers to a way of coaching that reflects a synthesis and integration of both ways of orienting. We contrast this practice with the more popular understanding of knowing which way to be at different points in time – when to be strategic and when to be emergent. From a relational understanding the value of being strategic while *simultaneously* supporting emergence is that it enables conditions that facilitate mutual co-regulation.

- *Expanding experiential range* is both a relational practice and one of the ways we define development. Development includes expanding into more creative ways of responding and more resourceful ways of handling complexity. In this process we often expand the range of contact that is permissible and the kinds of support that are acceptable[3]. Where we habitually avoid experiencing certain kinds of situations and relationships, we limit our possibilities and the developmental opportunities for the groups we coach. When we shy away from challenging experiences – shame, vulnerability, or complexity – we are going to be less able to support others to stay with them. And we risk reinforcing the belief that they are too difficult to handle.

We want to emphasize that these relational practices are more attitudinal stances, or ways of being, than they are recipes for 'being a relational coach.' Moreover, they are connected and typically manifest jointly. For example, sensing into the field relies on accessing bodily experience and empathic attunement;

and expanding our experiential range might follow from putting our faith in dialogue. While we pulled them apart in order to highlight features of each, they are an integrated constellation of orienting and guiding sensibilities.

Some illustrations from our work

Co-creating an emergent developmental field as coaches is not without its risks and difficulties. Much of what we report here about our new sense of ourselves as coaches and our revised picture of groups crystallized for us with two recent coaching engagements.

In the first, we were working with group practitioners (facilitators, coaches, leaders) in an advanced development program which we had the primary role in designing. The program was intended to introduce participants to a relational perspective on groups and the implications for coaching.

In the second assignment, we each coached a sub-group of senior executives enrolled in an ambitious leadership development program in a Fortune 500 company that had already been designed by others. The teams were expected to produce outcomes – concrete recommendations for addressing key strategic issues identified by the organization. Both assignments involved multiple group meetings and work sessions over a ten-month period.

The practitioner's program

In this assignment, our challenge was to introduce a fundamentally different model of working with groups to people expecting a more familiar approach, based on a practice model they already found valuable. We knew from our own experience that the relational emphasis we were bringing and the way we would show up as coaches would be new and different. Still, because the relational approach gives so much attention to support and collaboration, we imagined it would feel inherently appealing.

Looking back, we now can appreciate that the way we began relating did not fit participants' view of what a coach should do. The usual supports were not emphasized – particularly a clear boundary placing us as 'outside' the group – and a clear differentiation based on us being the 'better knowers', having more knowledge and expertise as well as positional authority, so that we could help participants 'improve'.

The familiar model has the coach fundamentally separate from the group. Both parties mutually reinforce the coach knowing what the client needs and taking more of a leadership or facilitation role in relation to the group. These kinds of supports are familiar in the larger world of coaching (and consulting). So while our wish was for people to feel supported, our efforts took such an unfamiliar (counter-cultural) form that they did not feel supportive to people in the group – at least initially (and even longer, for a few people) – and so could not be readily assimilated.

Despite this initial potential for missing each other, we believe the relational orientation itself – not being separate and apart but *being in relationship, being fully in it with them* – made it possible for us to create a rich developmental experience together and to recognize deeply our mutual co-influence and co-regulation of the field. We focused our attention on what was going on between us and how we were impacting and being impacted by the relational context we were shaping together. Encouraging them to tell us when they didn't feel supported meant we could do things they judged as 'wrong' and still work these through in a way that preserved or restored our connection.

So, the difference in orientation that was a big source of our difficulties provided, in another sense, the very resources we needed in order to work through the real discomfort (experienced by us all) of trying something new and therefore awkward. In the more familiar model, the coaches would have been expected to take responsibility, independently of the group, for figuring out what was 'going wrong,' and then for deciding what was required to put things 'right.' In this relational orientation we were positioned to live through the dilemma together – to work it out jointly rather than 'figure it out' separately.

Early on, an issue arose around confidentiality. Some participants (who had felt seriously harmed by disclosures in a previous program they had jointly attended) felt that events in sub-groups should not be shared in any form with participants or coaches who had not been part of that group. One of us was coach to a subgroup that took this issue up and happened to include the program participants who were most invested in it. Our experience was that members of this subgroup were so locked into their views on either side that the situation seemed intractable. We could see how difficult it would be to run an effective process under such a restriction, yet could also see that these concerns could not be ignored or overridden without enormous damage to us as a collective.

It seemed to us that the very future of our work together was at stake, and it is difficult to convey how risky it felt not to intervene from a position of authority or 'superior knowledge,' and instead, to allow the dispute to unfold. At the same time, privately we were struggling to figure out how to bridge the gap. So it was paradoxically a comfort to decide to trust our evolving theory of coaching and participate in the dialogue as a part of the group without trying to pull rank. In the face of our worst fears, the process of people's views being heard and acknowledged seemed to resolve the concerns on both sides (it is impossible to replay – or even fully know – the intricacy of new awareness, contact, movement and change, that occurred). No formal 'agreement' or 'policy' seemed to be needed, and the issue simply faded.

This was a vivid example of a principle at the heart of our different way of coaching groups – *we don't have 'to get them somewhere'*. Similarly we encouraged group members consciously to envision themselves as *of* the group when they were practicing as group coaches – not as standing apart and alone as the person supposed to make things happen. At first, people practicing found it hard to shake the expectation that it was up to them to figure out what would be good for the group and its members, and then get everyone to go in that direction[4]. As time went on, they started reporting feeling less anxious and less on-the-spot as they worked. Rather than trying individually to figure out on behalf of everyone, they relied on the wisdom of the group (which included their wisdom) to find its way.

A key discovery participants made was that the more someone tried to control the group, the less influence she or he had. People taking turns practicing coaching sometimes began armed with a plan – a proposed activity for the group that the coach believed would teach them something or point them in some 'better' direction. This approach seemed to derive from some felt need to be 'in control' of the process – to know what to do. It almost always triggered strong reactions among group members, usually feelings of being patronized or manipulated, which then rebounded on the coach, leaving them feeling 'inadequate' and 'not doing it right.'

One of us was with a subgroup during a practice session that turned out to be a pivotal moment in our experience as a learning community. A participant taking a turn in the coach role was operating from an 'aiming' orientation, prescribing for the group a task they thought would be helpful. The group pushed back, triggering traumatic personal memories from a previous experience for this 'coach.' She then chose to reveal an extremely shaming life episode, one that might take years in a private therapeutic relationship before coming up. This revelation was followed, over the course of the afternoon, by reports of other profoundly shameful experiences by three others in the group.

The context of our engagement was clearly not therapy, nor was working with shame the intentional focus of our work. So this turn of events was a surprise and presented a significant challenge to everyone, particularly to us as coaches for the session. One of our impulses was to move away from this deeply interpersonal and emotionally charged work, to get back to something more comfortable and part of our 'learning agenda' together. We think it was fortunate that another set of impulses prevailed. These included helping to slow things down, responding to each person who spoke by telling them the impact their reports were having on us, doing what we could to ensure that the words of others didn't reinjure the speaker, and generally working to muster enough support in the room so that people could say as much as they needed to say. None of these were prepared responses based on some coaching formula, nor were they clinical interventions. Rather they emerged from doing our best to sense into the field to see what was needed, and from our efforts to stay present with our own anxiety and doubt and not be disabled by them.

We think that a number of the things we had been doing as coaches helped to foster conditions that made possible a deep exploration of shame, one of the most difficult of human emotions and one that participants clearly longed to address. Foremost among these was something we didn't do. We didn't try to get the group somewhere different than where we already were – some 'better' place where we thought they 'should' be – which has the inherent potential to be shaming in itself. We also think that what we had been doing regularly – attending to and working with interactions where people missed one another, doing our best to park our own judgments, acknowledging our own need for support and vulnerability to shame and uncertainty – all helped to create the context that made this extraordinary session possible.

We have a lot of evidence that this shift in approach changed the nature of our relationship, particularly as contrasted with the 'better knower' orientation participants were accustomed to. Paradoxically, it made shame more available to be explored, even as it normalized and de-stigmatized it. With hindsight, we can see the threat of shame was alive among us from the beginning. However, early in our work, we were only able to approach it more conceptually. We had not yet discovered, as a group, what would support a fuller, more personal exploration. In time, our collective ability to foster conditions that reduced its disabling impact, made shame more available to be explored and worked with. Sometimes shame was an in-the-moment experience of not feeling included or 'gotten' by other group members (or by us). Other times it was exploring past life events that had been held as so shameful that they had never been discussed publicly before.

We think our commitment to dialogue – *really being in relationship with them* and accepting the vulnerability this inevitably demands – played a key role in helping us *meet* one another and join together in a way that would not have been possible if we tried to stay outside or apart. The practice of dialogue was our primary method for unpacking the diversity of our different experiences. What we have just described is fundamentally different from simply *having a relationship* with a client, which is possible without *being truly in dialogue with them.*

Dealing with shame throughout this engagement as it emerged was key to what else became possible for us as a learning community. Because of the group's ability to hold it and deal with it, we think people felt less like it belonged to them alone and were more ready to acknowledge shame and override the instinct to try to suppress and hide it. We took this as a sign that our experiential range as a group was expanding, thus enlarging the range of permissible contact.

Participants reported themselves as feeling more 'freed up' and 'less preoccupied with performance,' as well as feeling more creative, more open to try new things, and 'more interested in others' as the program evolved. As the narrowing, preoccupying experience of chronic worry about how we are being received faded, we became more available and present – a fundamental support for development.

The leadership development program

Our second illustration as coaches unfolded in a leadership program for senior executives in a global business organization.

At the outset there were signs that we, and our relational orientation to coaching groups, would be welcomed. The person managing the leadership development effort sought us out because of perceived shortcomings among the coaches who had worked in previous programs and was eager for our advice and assistance. The senior leaders who were in charge of the strategic issues each of the teams would work on were similarly willing to take our guidance. We were encouraged by what appeared to be real eagerness for professional development in our early contact with some participants.

We were also fresh from the experience we have just described of introducing a very unfamiliar approach to coaching and the extraordinary learning that emerged from it. It was tempting to think we could embark on this new assignment in similar fashion and expect to reproduce the same rich outcomes as if we were taking the recipe for a successful dish and cooking it again. We were soon reminded that this was a very different setting, with very different constraints and challenges. In most respects it was not possible to do what we did in the practitioner's program.

One of the key values of a relational orientation is that it emphasizes that *behavior can only be understood within the context in which it occurs.* Thus much of our focus was on how the context was influencing and being influenced by what was going on among all of us who were party to the events. The dominant culture of this organization was highly individualistic and competitive – not dissimilar to other North American business corporations of its size and complexity.

The company said it was seeking more collaboration between functions, geographies and levels (building collaborative skills and behaviors was a primary program objective), yet it simultaneously held leaders (and us) individually responsible for success or failure and had a pretty low tolerance when expected results weren't delivered. There seemed to be limited awareness of the multiple contextual factors that were influencing outcomes that were being attributed to individuals. The program was structured to foster individual development (mostly in the form of knowledge acquisition), as contrasted with one having more potential for systemic impact. In fact, the development aspect of the program for which we were responsible, was situated within an executive education program run by university faculty lecturing on specific content areas (strategy, globalization, innovation)[5].

It gradually became apparent that participants were not necessarily there by choice, and only some fully wanted to be. Task accomplishment was routinely more valued and rewarded than learning or experimenting with something new, even in a setting that was explicitly developmental. People regularly organized around power and hierarchy and the avoidance of being shamed, with blaming others being one preferred tactic for evading shame.

Both of us recognized the shaming/blaming pattern because we were subject to it ourselves: we heard it in the summing up observations participants made at the end of our first week together, and we saw it in their written evaluations of this session. Tuning into this allowed us to acknowledge their doubts about us as coaches and to seek each out individually before the next gathering to ask how we could better support them. We could have taken another approach and contributed to the prevailing pattern by putting the blame on them – minimizing their discomfort as just resistance to trying anything new, or concluding they just didn't understand the difficulty and complexity of our role, or even attributing it to their individual limitations – the very deficiencies the program was supposed to remedy.

With one group that we coached, following up individually made a big difference. The group became more interested in what their coach had to say. Over time, and with our help, this team created a kind of collaborative counter-culture within the program. They showed a more balanced interest in task and learning, and were willing to devote major time outside the program parameters to support each other in getting feedback and pursuing their own development. They experienced themselves as very cohesive and innovative (and were seen in this way by others in the program and by the senior leadership of the company). They regularly remarked on how different this was from prior teamwork experiences. From our point of view as coaches, they were a rich and rewarding team to work with – appreciative and supportive of us in our role and rewarding in the creativity they brought to their work together. At the same time, we wondered how much of what they had learned about leadership and collaboration could successfully be brought back to their roles in the company without the unique supports of the kind of environment they created in the program.

Despite the temptation to dwell on this more conventionally 'positive' coaching experience, we are going to find another place and time to tell this group's story. The story we will focus on is that of a second group where things played out quite differently. (Since the authors worked individually and were each assigned to different teams, we are going to use the first person in describing the experience one of us had with this second team).

Team number two's beginning was characterized by a series of difficult interpersonal exchanges that never got responded to. The cumulative effect left participants feeling embarrassed, angry and guarded. A dominant mode of interaction became sarcasm, and criticizing others. A 'hit and run' style of engaging emerged (simultaneously aggressive and self-protective), and there were preemptive moves to discredit me as the coach with program and organizational leaders. Meanwhile group members proved unwilling to talk through any of this with me or in team sessions. What proved to be a critical support for me was being able to limit my tendency to personalize these dynamics, which would just allow them to cloud my vision and stop me from being functional. At the same time I needed to acknowledge that coaching this group promised to be an on-going struggle.

Gradually, as I regained my bearings, I was more and more able to assess and work toward the best the situation allowed – to recognize the limits of what was possible with one group member and to maximize the possibilities still available with the others. By working individually offline with members and by coaching and supporting the person who took on the team leadership role – a very difficult challenge under the circumstances (and one that no-one else volunteered for when it became time for others to take their turn practicing as leader) I made some headway. All this took time, but I became increasingly able to see the most challenging member as struggling to support herself and to actually imagine her behavior as a poorly articulated 'reach for support.' (My guess is that the early ruptures triggered a shame reaction which impacted their ability to be available or open in any meaningful way).

The more I grounded myself in how I might understand what was going on from a relational view, the more I was able to work myself out of seeing the hostile behavior as directed 'at me' and see what was going on as an expression of how vulnerable this participant (and others in their own way) might be feeling. I reminded myself not to value certain affective states as 'better' and to appreciate the value in struggle as a necessary part of development. My focus was on how to make whatever we did developmental, to expand their (and my) experiential range. It would have been a lot easier to just let them do what they knew how to do – that is, develop their project and complete their task without attending much to learning, development, or leadership. I found myself continually *sensing into the field* and practicing to gain an empathic grasp of their experience so I could better calibrate what they might find most useful in the moment. As I built a better relationship with the other members in my team, doing a lot of inquiry about their experience in the program, as well as their perspective on their task, I was able to build additional support for myself and for them.

My struggle was to try to sense what was happening for the team, as different from being so preoccupied with what was happening to me due to the particularly difficult and challenging way this one member dealt with me. At the same time, I was able to curb the temptation to make this member or the group 'wrong', both in my own mind and in how I related to this person. While the experience here was very different from that in team number one, what it highlighted was the adaptability and flexibility needed to shape our response to the present situation – always different in detail from all previous situations.

Our biggest challenge as coaches is to realize that wherever we are, however we show up and engage with a client – and whether they are 'for us or against us' – we need to discover what will support better contact between us, and remain open to discover what might be possible that we can do together, even when it is more limited than we might wish.

One of the key reminders we take away from the coaching experiences we have described is that support has to do with what can be used by the other party, not what we *think* they need or, indeed, what suits us best. It has also highlighted for us as practitioners how often we are guided unwittingly by, and settle for, what supports *us*, without recognizing that it may not support *them*. Moreover, support is a two-way street: as coaches we do our best work when we get support from our clients; when they support our compassion, talent, creativity through their responsiveness. How we manage when their current capacity to be supportive is limited, or becomes oppositional, is our ultimate challenge as coaches – calling on our emotional courage and resilience and especially our willingness to hang in when our work is messy, clumsy, or deflating. Our difficult work as coaches requires these crucial forms of self-support.

Making the relational turn as coaches

The Relational Turn draws our attention to the *field* as central, rather than what magic the coach can perform or how the group is behaving (or mis-behaving). It focuses our awareness on the array of contextual influences out of which the group's future possibilities emerge. It replaces a model that imagines that, if I assess a group and figure out where they need to be, I can exercise enough control to get them there. It counters the impulse that says, 'if I just skill-up enough, buy more books on coaching, get certified, I will be able to whip any group into shape.' It cuts across our readiness to blame ourselves or to blame the client if things don't go 'well'. It reminds us that the field is much bigger than we are, that our work is to cultivate the field and encourage shifts that create contexts that support development. It tells us that different fields have different degrees of receptivity, and that this has everything to do with the quality of relationship that is possible, and in turn with our ability to bring influence.

By contrast, the individualistic orientation reinforces that it is the coach's competence that is the key variable. One thing our cases illustrate is that, in fact, how events unfolded had only modestly to do with the person of the coach. One team/coach field in the executive program discovered how to support better contact. In the other, the obstacles dominated. In our experience, relational contexts vary drastically in terms of their receptivity, availability, openness to influence, and a myriad of other factors. Our relational orientation leads us to reject the common view that it is the coach's competence that is the key influence[6].

The heart of the Relational Turn is the commitment to – and the living out of – *being in relationship* (as well as recognizing and accepting that experience is the product of relationships). This means leading groups by example and modeling the relational practices described earlier, which we believe expand the range of permissible contact and assimilation of field support.

We value the emergent nature of development which requires us as practitioners to suspend our judgment as to where our client systems 'should be in the future', allowing us to 'dance' with them in our joint expansion of our experiential range. We value our development as coaches, and we see our clients' development linked to our own. Being available to explore with others what is happening among us and between us, especially at an affective level, reveals aspects of the field itself and the seeds of its becoming[7].

We offer these practitioner insights as a means of support for others to make the relational turn as we continue to discover for ourselves and our clients both the challenge and the wisdom of embodying Relational Gestalt theory in coaching and developing groups as complex, emerging fields.

Notes

[1] It may be helpful to say a few words about ourselves, and our 'lineage' in the Gestalt world, to give context to the views we express here. We have each been group and organizational practitioners for over 25 years. We think of *coaching for development* as how we do what we do – whether

it is facilitating a meeting, developing a strategic plan or influencing change in organizational culture. We are professional colleagues and have partnered often in a variety of group and organizational settings and professional development programs since we first met at the pioneering Organization Systems Development Program at the Gestalt Institute of Cleveland. The faculty of that program – particularly Ed Nevis (1987), John Carter, and Carolyn Lukensmeyer – were our formative influences in Gestalt. We also studied at the Gestalt International Study Center with Sonia Nevis and Joseph Zinker. Some years later we were introduced to what we call '*The Relational Turn*' in programs designed for training clinicians and led by Lynne Jacobs (2001, 2009) and Gary Yontef (1993, 2009). Since that time the core of our work has been exploring how that shift in the therapeutic paradigm 'translates' into coaching with larger human systems (Carlson and Kolodny, 2009a and 2009b). Our key supports in this have been our collaborations with Stan Nabozny (2002), who was one of the earliest to apply a relational approach with groups and organizations, and Mark Fairfield and his colleagues at the Relational Center in Los Angeles (2013). Both of them have supported us in the construction of this article. Gordon Wheeler (2009, 2011) has helped us see the implications of Gestalt theory and practice in a much wider stage. The literature building on a relational perspective in Gestalt is growing, first registering on us in Malcolm Parlett's seminal reminders of the place of field theory in our work (1991, 1997). The literature on the application of a relational framework to groups and organizations remains pretty slim. We find resonances and support for understanding what is required and what it looks like to bring a relational outlook and sensibility to coaching groups and larger systems in Mark Fairfield (2004, 2008, 2010), as well as Sally Denham-Vaughan and Marie-Anne Chidiac, (2009).

[2] This in no way implies neglect or devaluation of the individual. We see it as an enlargement and reframing that incorporates individual agency but gives it less dominance.

[3] Co-creating an emergent developmental field assumes that we are embedded in – that we are 'of' – what is happening around us, not individuals outside observing 'it'; that reality is co-constructed and mutually influenced; that development is a function of the relational field

that we are part of; that access to 'field supports' enables development; that the quality of the relationship enables the development of both the client and the coach.

[4] We see this as the original intention of a Gestalt experiment – to expand what is experientially possible – which contrasts with how experiments are often used, as a way to develop a client's underdeveloped side.

[5] Contrary to the initial discomfort of feeling, 'How can I be doing anything useful if I am just part of the group,' it gradually became clear that the coach was not just a regular member of the group, but was there in a particular role in support of the group, with a different and strategic responsibility. But that this expressed itself in how they showed up – embodying and keeping true to references to relational practices – rather than in asserting themselves in some pre-defined or pre-determined way.

[6] The missed opportunity, in our view, was to engage the leaders in examining the deeper systemic issues contributing to their competitive and individualistic leadership approach and standing in the way of a more collaborative one.

[7] The implicit assumption in our previous model is that you can transcend context. You can come in and 'do the right things' and it will all work out. If the coach is good enough, that is what really matters. We think of this as the 'transcendental' theory of coaching. The alternative is an 'immanent' model, which attends to emergence, process, how we all show up. In our mind it is primarily context and the coach/client field's ability to respond to context that is the final arbiter of what is possible.

References

Carlson, C. & Kolodny, R. (2009a). Have we been missing something fundamental to our work? Ullman, D. & Wheeler, G. (eds.), *CoCreating the Field: Intention and Practice in the Age of Complexity.* Santa Cruz CA: GestaltPress.

Carlson, C. & Kolodny, R. (2009b). Embodying field theory in how we work with groups and organizations. Ullman, D. & Wheeler, G. (eds.), *CoCreating the Field: Intention and Practice in the Age of Complexity.* Santa Cruz CA: GestaltPress.

Carlson, C. and Nabozny, S. (2002). *Field Theory and Its Implications for Organizations,* www.keypartnersconsulting.com

Denham-Vaughan, S. & Chidiac, M. (2009). Relational organizational Gestalt. Jacobs, L. and Hycner, R. (eds.), *Relational Approaches in Gestalt Therapy* (249-296). Santa Cruz CA: GestaltPress.

Fairfield, M. (2013), The relational movement. *British Gestalt Journal,* 22, (1) 22-35.

Fairfield, M. (2010). Dialogue in complex systems. Jacobs, L. and Hycner, R. (eds.), *Relational Approaches in Gestalt Therapy.* Santa Cruz CA: GestaltPress.

Fairfield, M. (2004). Gestalt groups revisited: a phenomenological approach. *Gestalt Review*, 8, (3) 336-357.

Fairfield, M. & O'Shea, L. (2008). Getting 'Beyond Individualism.' *British Gestalt Journal,* 17, (2) 24-38.

Jacobs, L. (2009). Relationality: foundational assumptions. Ullman, D. & Wheeler, G. (eds.), *CoCreating the Field: Intention and Practice in the Age of Complexity.* Santa Cruz, CA: GestaltPress.

Jacobs, L. (2001). Pathways to a relational worldview. Goldfried, M. (ed.), *How Therapists Change.* Washington DC: American Psychological Association.

Nevis, E.C. (1987). *Organization Consulting. A Gestalt Approach,* Cambridge MA: Gestalt Institute of Cleveland Press.

Parlett, M. (1991). Reflections on field theory. *British Gestalt Journal,* 1, (2) 69-80.

Parlett, M. (1997). The unified field in practice. *Gestalt Review,* 1, (1) 16-33.

Perls, F.S., Hefferline, R. & Goodman, P. (1951). *Gestalt Therapy: Excitement and Growth in the Human Personality.* New York: Bantam Books.

Wheeler, G. (2011). Who are we? Lee, R.G. and Harris, N. (eds.), *Relational Child, Relational Brain.* Santa Cruz CA: GestaltPress.

Wheeler, G. (2009). New directions in Gestalt theory and practice: psychology and psychotherapy in the age of complexity. Ullman, D. & Wheeler, G. (eds.), *CoCreating the Field: Intention and Practice in the Age of Complexity.* Santa Cruz CA: GestaltPress.

Yontef, G. (2009). The relational attitude in Gestalt therapy and practice. Jacobs, L. & Hycner, R. (eds.), *Relational Approaches in Gestalt Therapy.* Santa Cruz CA: GestaltPress.

Yontef, G. (1993). *Awareness, Dialogue and Process: Essays on Gestalt Therapy.* Highland NY: Gestalt Journal Publications.

9

•••

The 'Bodying Forth' of the Situation

Georges Wollants

Editors' note: We were privileged to interview Georges Wollants about his work during a training programme he offered in Nottingham, UK, in Summer 2012. The interview draws extensively on both his remarks at the time, combined with our knowledge of his work and writings.

Georges, you are known as a Gestalt psychotherapist, but have also worked with organisations, including coaching for a global corporation in the Netherlands. You describe your role as a 'facilitator of situations'. Can you say more about facilitating situations as a coach?

I believe the task of the coach is to explore the possibilities of the situation. A 'situation' is a person and his or her world, in interaction. 'Situation' always refers to the fact that you are in a kind of particular relationship with your environment. 'The situation' is the configuration of interactions of a person and his environment; we are taking into account how both person and the environment *gestalt* their relationship. When we refer, say, to a man who is distressed in his workplace, the way he is looking at his environment is helping to create his particular situation. You can assist people to look differently at what their environment demands and that's changing 'the situation'. When we look from other angles, then we can see things that we have not seen otherwise.

'The situation' is not limited or reduced to the immediate observable aspects of what the client brings, but includes the broader contexts of their life situation – the past and future, the economic, political, cultural forces, the physical environment, all the circumstances that influence the momentary configuration they are part of.

I believe there is a need to broaden the general perspective of coaching to include ways of dealing with the direct social environment of the client. When someone comes to me for help, something is troubling them. And what is 'in trouble' is not the person himself but his situation. There is something going wrong in the interaction between the person and the immediate environment of this person.

Say this is the first time I have met this client… my exploration goes in the direction of what is happening in this situation, not what is happening inside this man or woman. So I see our task as coaches as being to help, to assist the person and his environment to build a situation that fits enough to be healthy for all the elements, if that is possible. Freedom is doing what the situation requires.

How do you view the coach/client relationship?

Coaching demands an ongoing balance of following and directing the process. There are two conversational models – one where the client talks to the coach, who considers the problem that belongs to the client. I describe this as a technical, medical or expert model. While it is suitable for some things, I do not believe this model is suitable for coaching. In a phenomenological coaching model such as mine, the coach does not see the problem as something apart from the client, nor even as something apart from the client/coach relationship. It is something that is shared and solved together.

For this, the coach has to step into the client's experience to some extent, to see the client's situation from inside and explore how the client's situation is making itself felt. At the same time, the coach does not become confluent with the client's experience but stays aside – so that he can be of greater help to the client.

So the coach has to engage with two paradoxical 'response-abilities': to be a part of the client's world to the extent that the coach is able to understand the client in her experiencing of the situation and the significance she brings to it; and to stand aside from the client's world, so that the coach can be an unprejudiced witness and from that point, carry the coaching process forward.

The client is someone in the organisation who is engaging with the 'givens' of her work situation at the interface of her life in that work situation. We explore the difficulties and discontentment the client is facing. So while this is a problem-focused approach to coaching, we do not objectify the problem but consider it in its totality. It's not the client's problem, it's the problem of the totality. You can help the client look at the situation as though it is not her fault. We never consider the problem in isolation from the client's work *and life* contexts. Furthermore, part of our investigation is into what needs the client has in this situation, as well as the needs of the situation.

I think it is important that the coach has no investment in his or her own ideas about what a 'good solution' looks like. It is the client who defines this, and a coaching process comes to an end when the client and coach together have managed to find a satisfying solution – even if there is no apparent change in the situation.

How can there be a solution without a change in the situation?
Because I look at development *not* in the individual stages of a de-contextualised person, but as a situation that is becoming more and more complex. A person can learn to interact in more complex and differentiated ways. In reality, the developmental task each time is to nurture a greater range of ways and forms of interacting with his environment, with participation in more and more complex situations – and enjoying it! In the end, what we are talking about is that *we have to attend to the situation of someone in order to complete the developmental process that is started.*

A developmental process begins with the arising of a developmental need. What is the developmental need of a CEO of a company in transition? A business team that is not performing to expectations? Or more broadly, of a dying person, or a five-year old child playing football? Most personal difficulties that clients experience result from a rupture of the 'we' in a situation. How do we address the 'we'? Through respectfully sensing into what the person's or group's developmental need might be. For most of the time, the needs of a situation are also developmental needs for the client.

Needs are not to be conceptualised as purely intra-organic states, which have to be satisfied by required elements in the environment. Lewin saw that there is a reciprocal relationship between needs and the demand character of parts of the environment. Or, as Koffka (1935) said, 'Things in our environment appeal to us, they tell us what to do with them', what they can offer us.

Some parts of a situation appeal to me because I am 'appealing on them'. The situation has specific 'appeal values' to me and different ones to you. At a welcome reception I may drink fruit juice while you drink sherry or champagne. The attraction of the juice is different to the attraction of the champagne in that situation… For me, the situation calls for juice.

As coaches, we are not only looking at what the client and the situation needs, but also at what the situation *affords*. We have to accept the situation first, then explore its 'affordances' (Gibson 1979), which are the qualities of the environment that are attractive for me but not necessarily for you. They can appeal to us even without our being aware of them. It is like the way that stairs appeal to a young child, as Lewin says. The child cannot resist. Once a child is able to crawl, the stairs become climbable. They are inviting because they are climbable. When the situation of my developing calls me to climb and part of the environment does not support climbing it becomes an unfinished developmental task. Equally, when the situation of my developing calls me to take on a new responsibility, and part of my work environment does not support me, it becomes an unfinished developmental task.

Needs and the perceived situation are tied up with one another so closely. Needs can be considered as the basic patterns of the types of relationships that a situation calls for.

I think that most coaches would be surprised to learn that you ask almost no questions of a client. How would you describe your core methodology?
It's no use asking questions. Questions have less value than statements. Questions can send people into their heads, close down possibilities and move them away from their present experience. Not asking questions is a way of actively not preferencing where to go in the encounter. Asking a question is like asking for only a small slice of the whole pie. Asking questions can also divide you, the person, and the environment too soon. We need to experience the client as a unity, who is more than a person as she is connected to the world.

So asking a question is like making a judgment about the direction in which you as a coach want to take the conversation. I believe you have to postpone your judgments and not differentiate too soon between the person and the world. Allowing a fuller definition of the problem to emerge without questioning the client requires abstinence. This abstinence makes it possible to include more elements of the situation.

A field theoretical and situational approach has to take into account that whatever you do I am participating in it, I am one of the elements that contributes to what is happening and it makes a great difference. Therefore, don't only postpone your own differentiation between person and environment, but also don't support the client's differentiation into cause-effect thinking – whatever is happening is not the client's fault!

It is not so important to find the cause of the difficulties as it is to stay with how the difficulties manifest for the client. The phenomenological attitude is simply to face the situation as it is

– to let it speak for itself without indulging in what we know – 'to stand above all, with reverence and love'.

We are situated beings and we are situated *par excellence* in the body. It's the body that situates us. Therefore we are 'some-body' and if we are not situated and not embodied we are nothing, we are not visible, we don't exist. The first thing that you can do when some-body appears to us, is to try and collect and describe what we are seeing for ourselves, to get in touch with what is happening here when I see the person as I see her, as she is presenting herself to me. And then, next, what is the direction of this embodying? What intention might there be? How is she 'bodying forth' what the situation is for her, with all of the little elements together forming a kind of significance, a kind of direction. We are exploring the situation by assisting the bodying forth. Your body is embodying the way your situation is felt.

What do you mean by 'bodying forth'?

I mean what a body does without a person knowing. I don't mean 'body language', it is not looking at individual gestures (like a hand movement) but at the totality of the body. The same gesture (like a hand slamming down) can mcan different things according to the totality of the body. Don't seek significance in separate parts – look at the whole, it's less complicated!

The first thing about attending to body process is that I make no one phenomenon more important than another. All that the client is communicating is available. There is his voice, not just his words but the melody of his sentences, what he is saying with his eyes, with his mouth, with his ears and his nose, his hands and his feet – they are all important. Also the way he is looking when he says certain words.

I can think of an example. When a man was pronouncing the first name of his wife, I noticed every time he did the same thing with his eyes. He was closing his eyes each time he said her name. I observed it and provisionally I put it in what I call my 'storage-box' – for safe-keeping until further notice. I put my various observations in the box, without prematurely picking one of them as being more important than another. At the same time I am aware of my own bodily feeling, my sense of what arises for me, what I 'taste' in relation to what he bodily shows. After a while a pattern begins to reveal itself, arising out of the whole collection of observations and impressions, and some elements advance themselves as important, more so than other elements. And we proceed again. I call this the 'rule of gradual approximation'. I am moving step-by-step, moment-by-moment, and looking from different angles at the same thing and letting it all come together in the 'storage box' until some interventions keep coming into my mind – or in my body if you want – and I allow myself to bring them into the dialogue. We can say that the key thread reveals itself.

You have to let yourself be led by the body. The body lets us see what is going well and when things are going wrong. I don't name what I see (for example, 'you're crossing your legs') but I gather the overall images and thoughts and give them a choice as to whether they fit. The client can confirm or deny – then this opens a door into the next loop.

I 'interpret' what the client is bodying forth as a possibility rather than as something definitive. It's an offering based on observation and objective elements – I feel in my body when it is right to intervene, and if a statement arises in my mind several times I know it is right to share it. Yet one is more explicitly interpretative in making a statement. Language clarifies but does not necessarily add anything to the client's situation. Before offering an interpretation, I also have to be aware that giving words to the client's experience can support a subtle form of resistance – if we give a name to something it 'explains' it away. A name can kill something as well as intensify something.

So each person 'bodies forth' his situation. The coach's body is resonant with the client's body and has resonances with the client's body, revealing his situation. You can feel yourself entering the world of the other. This is a kind of intersubjectivity. We learned from a phenomenological standpoint that the client is a subject of our attention, but from an intersubjective approach we feel our own bodies too. There's co-emergence here. Paying this quality of attention to the other invokes and invites the client's bodying forth of their situation.

In paying attention to what the client is bodying forth, we are aiming to get to the pre-reflective aspects of his situation (what his body reveals before and beyond what is included in the client's 'story' or self-description). To do this, we have to tolerate liminal space (which is the transformational space between one known thing and the next) and stay with not-knowing.

What do you believe are the main things to avoid in coaching?
Often we quickly tend to feel responsible for finding a solution, but being too quick to present solutions that are not the client's is risky and fake. The client will not stand by a solution that is not hers.

Nor should we give advice, although when you *really* understand the person and situation, then you can offer possibilities. Advice is generally a hidden judgment that the client is not doing something right. Encouragement and praise are also risky, as they can push the client too far. Praise can also be bribery – as the client is persuaded to like the coach. Praise can also suggest hierarchy.

If you have a fixed idea about how a coaching session should be, you can't know the moments when you can enter in to your client's subjective world. You need to be with the person, not with your model or thoughts. This positively affects the quality of the relationship as the client feels taken seriously, and is not frightened or offended.

How would you sum up your approach?

The most important starting-point is the subjective world of experience of the client in his situation. So ideally the coach should not ask 'what is this problem about?' but rather, 'how does this person experience this situation?'

Focusing on the subjective world of the client has tremendous advantages: the coach has more space to really listen and does not feel responsible for solving the client's problem. The point of coaching is not change, but staying with.

Successful coaching is threatened by two extreme positions: one is when the coach takes over the steering wheel and refuses to take part in the client's world, and judges the client's world from a standpoint that is not the client's – that is alien to the client, or aimed at a certain target or result. The other is when the coach over-identifies with the client's world and converges on it.

So there are two parallel skills – to 'be on the other side with the client', which requires us to have a phenomenological attitude of emptying oneself of prejudices and beliefs; of identifying with the client and his situation, empathically confirming what the client is experiencing, and concentrating on staying there to express understanding. And second, the skill of 'being the instrument' and directing the process while following the client's experience. This requires pointing to and going back to the client's experience especially when it is passed over by the client; and giving words to what is not yet said – which requires that the coach goes directly to the heart of the matter without flinching.

It is helpful to offer interpretations that open rather than close – for example, 'It's difficult for you to remain positive' is better than 'I see you being negative'. It is also important to use non-differentiating language – for example, if a man says, 'My business is a mess' the coach could say 'you are a mess' or 'you and your fellow directors are making a mess' but it is better to say 'the situation is messy'. It is important not to differentiate too soon.

The client has the support to find solutions of his own and his autonomy is encouraged, while deeper feelings related to the problem are encountered and therefore deeper-level solutions are more likely. The client also experiences equality in the relationship.

Finally, I'd like to emphasise that the coach has an educative role – to help the client see that he is not a *person with a problem* but a *person in a situation*. If we looked at what is going on for a person only as conflicts between some internal states, we would be abstracting the person from his environment, which is as much responsible as his internal state in creating the situation. It is the interchange between the two parts, person and environment, that may be in trouble. So in these ways I am a facilitator of what the situation needs, what the situation requires.

References

Gibson, J. (1979). *The Ecological Approach to Visual Perception*. Boston: Houghton Mifflin.

Koffka, K. (1935). *Principles of Gestalt Psychology*. London: Routledge and Kegan Paul.

Wollants, G. (2012). *Gestalt Therapy: Therapy of the Situation*. London: Sage.

10

The Art and Craft of the Field Attuner

Seán Gaffney PhD

I propose here that the *art of field attunement* resides in sensing the 'music' of the coaching session and noticing its echoes and resonances in me as well as checking its echoes and resonances in my client (whether an individual or a group). Speaking from a coach perspective, this is music I 'hear', and sing along to (either as a melody or in harmony or cacophony), or music I move to as in a dance. To risk stretching the musical metaphor: am I experiencing myself as if in a duet – however harmonious or cacophonous – or in a song-and-dance musical?

Field attunement assumes that the content of a coaching session does not reside exclusively in the cognitive detail of the narrative. The valid content is just as much in the physical reactions and resonances, the emotional relationship of the coach and coachee to the cognitive aspects as the coaching narrative unfolds. This includes the dynamics of the coach/coachee relationship, both as embodied selves and as professionals in a contracted relationship.

This assumes an embodied coach/coachee relationship. By this I mean a working relationship grounded in being together as sensate persons who are working together in an agreed professional context of coach/coachee. It assumes further that each person involved is fully present with senses open and not just eyes and ears but also the proprioceptive senses in our muscles and organs.

The craft of field attunement resides partly in my willingness and ability to communicate this approach to the coachee and to engage her in the process of co-creating an emergent, embodied coach/coachee relationship. The craft is then also in my ability to share my awareness of our process not as opinions or even truths, but rather as possible nuances to our music-making; and her ability and willingness to share her awareness with me, equal in value and musicality. So, the art creates the context for the craft, just as the craft then supports the art of further original music-making.

These are the core themes that I wish to explore and explicate in this chapter.

Perspectives on 'Field'

A Gestalt 'field' perspective encompasses a number of approaches to Field Theory. This chapter focuses on Kurt Lewin's social-psychological field theory in its psychological extrapolation of the new physics as an emerging science (Marrow 1969). For Lewin (as much as for Einstein), a 'field' is the totality of influences at any given moment that can make behaviour understandable in its present expression – for Einstein the behaviour of sub-atomic particles, for Lewin the behaviour of people. As such, behaviour is truly situational. It emerges from a social situation and is, at the same time, an expression of that situation in the moment.

We can certainly understand present behaviour with reference to the past – as classical Freudian psychoanalysis would have it – with the distinction for Lewin that the past does not explain the present in a determined, causal sequence. His focus was always on accepting present behaviours as expressions of a current experience of a situation and an attempt to move from present to future, with intention (whether realised or not). The intention of a future outcome occurs in the present, and it is in the present that we can find the *gestalt* of time and space. Finally, Lewin advised that we de-limit our view of any field to that which we can manage, handle, competently deal with – and all with some sense of agency.

Kurt Lewin borrowed freely from modern physics to extrapolate a field theory of human behaviour. Two aspects of physics in particular: the electromagnetic field, undeniably *there* as evidenced by its influence, though invisible; and vectors – energies or forces with an origin, direction and magnitude. Our contemporary analogy for an electromagnetic field is WiFi. We only really *know* it is *there/here* when we open our devices and get a signal – we know it exists through its influence on our devices. We can then assume that it existed before we opened our devices, and after we closed them…though this can only be an assumption.

The same analogy can be used for vectors: the WiFi energy has its nearest relevant origin in a nearby router and is multi- and/or non-directed until we open a receiving device – then the direction is clearly established. And as we know, the signal strength (magnitude) can vary.

As socio-cultural beings, we are living receivers for the signals of our social environment, its history, traditions, norms and expectations of us as members. So a field is both intrinsically intangible – just as WiFi is – and at the same time, just as extremely concrete in its impact on us, and our applications of it.

My focus in this chapter is the application of field theory as a methodology – not only as an established research category but also as a methodological practice in organisational coaching. Lewin's contribution of Action Research as a research methodology is anyway particularly applicable to coaching in both individual and group settings.

A necessary clarification: Lewin uses two terms – *field* and *life-space* – as if they are more interchangeable than they actually came to be. Called 'The Practical Theorist' by his biographer, Marrow (*ibid*), I would like to think Lewin himself would approve of my practice-based extrapolations of his constructs.

As abstractions, *field* and *life-space* are clearly very similar. *Field* is 'the totality of co-existing facts which are conceived of as mutually interdependent' and which influence the behaviour of a person. *Life-space* is that person's *experience* of the field – a part's perspective on the whole of which it is a part, and therefore excluding the person herself as a constituent and observable part of the wholeness of the field. That is, the person has little or no ability to consider herself as the origin of any vector and examine its impact in the totality of the field in the abstract. So, while the 'contents' of a field and a life-space would seem to be identical (person/environment), the first is a description of the totality including the person concerned (field), and the second is the phenomenological experience (life-space) of being that person with a sense of agency in relation to her perceived physical/social environment. We are each *of* a field, and we are each *in* a life-space. And that life-space is always of the moment for the person, the perspectival core embedded in all the richness of possibilities emerging from the wholeness of the field of which she is also an intrinsic part.

Lewin had an attraction for mathematical formulae as bearers of his often complex thinking. I have always liked the elegant simplicity of his formula for human behaviour: B = f (P, E). Behaviour is a function of a *person* and her *environment*, that is, a person and what she experiences as her life-space and to which she is relating and responding in an apparent mix of the proactive and reactive (where even 'proactive' is a response). In other words, behaviour is the emergent behavioural figure of the ground of the person-environment field.

In a coaching relationship, the coach is part of the coachee's social environment at the same time as the coachee is part of the social environment of the coach (O'Neill & Gaffney, 2008). Their experiences are functions of each other's presence and behaviours, these behaviours being thus the emergent creation of the social field of the coaching work itself.

The life-space as the situation of the *inter*personal event of the social field is an important aspect of Lewin's contribution to psychology: it represents a move away from the discrete world of the *intra*personal, unrelated individual of classical psychoanalysis. Lewin's focus increasingly became the interpersonal, social world into which we are born, where we learn to be who we are and in which we behave as we believe is consistent with our sense of who we are in relation to others, and of who we believe they are in relation to us. We are each of us both person and 'environmental other' of the shared field.

Field Attunement

I have coined the term *field attunement* to capture a perspective of, and approach to, organisational coaching which involves working our way through a cognitive understanding of coach/coachee dynamics to a processed, assimilated and fully integrated field perspective, transforming field theory into an embodied, relational methodology and practice. So the issue for coaches is not *what* to do or *how* to do it: rather, the issue is *how we can be* while doing whatever it is we choose to do in our practice of coaching.

What follows is my understanding of what field attunement means. As it is *my* understanding, I will describe it in the first person. This will also support me to own and acknowledge my thinking more immediately. I will now present some vignettes that I hope will serve as illustrative examples of field attunement in my practice before briefly discussing the theoretical and methodological implications of each case presented.

Introduction to the vignettes

In my professional life, I have moved from management trainer and management consultant to Business School Lecturer in International Organisational Behaviour, to training and practising as a Gestalt psychotherapist, then moving back into Gestalt organisational development as a consultant and coach. I still practice as a psychotherapist and clinical supervisor, and am well aware of the similarities and distinctions between personal psychotherapy and professional coaching. I could not possibly claim to work from a field attunement perspective if I did not respect the interplay between therapy and coaching in my practice.

In therapy, the focus is on the personal/interpersonal life of the client. In coaching, the focus is on the professional life of the client, including raising awareness of personal issues, which are impacting the professional behaviour of the coachee. Processing such personal issues is best left to a psychotherapist, whose competence is precisely in such areas.

As a Gestalt therapist, I have no investment in changing the client's behaviour. I am interested in exploring her perception of her life space, fully trusting that any change in her perception will emerge as changes to her life space and, therefore, allow her to make choices about her behaviour which she may not have felt were previously possible. The agency is the client's, as are the choices and the actions. The therapeutic process is the possible catalyst for change. The interactive, relational nature of the coaching process and dynamics are likewise the catalyst for emergent change in coaching.

Vignette one: The Executive Director and the Senior Management Team

I am coaching the Executive Director of a voluntary organisation offering a range of counselling, legal and financial services to families in deprived urban and rural areas. The agency is expanding its services to include education and training and has been asked by its Government funders to also cover a larger geographical area. These changes will mean more staff and a more formal management structure. The director has five senior managers reporting to him, and has decided to form a Senior Management Team, or SMT as he likes to call it. During a session with him, I notice how he uses the phrase 'the SMT', then talks about what 'they' do, naming each one of 'them'. Since I, both theoretically and methodologically, regard any pair or group of three or more as a discrete psychological entity, or whole subgroup of a more complex group-as-a-whole, I spontaneously invite him to experiment with imagining the SMT as a unit, and to talk to me about 'it', rather than 'they'. Part of this experiment is to see how long he can speak about the SMT without naming any of its members. He becomes increasingly excited about what is happening to him with this very small experiment, how his thinking is changing and new possibilities are emerging for him. He reports later how the individuals (the parts) become less figural and the whole (the SMT) becomes a discrete entity and clearly delineated environmental other.

Over the course of the following sessions, he describes how he now meets the SMT as a unit and how 'it' has started scheduling planning meetings of its own in advance of his weekly meetings with 'it' in order to co-ordinate common areas of work, so that as well as each member reporting on the particular area of his/her specific functional responsibility, one member will also report on behalf of the team on any shared team project or task which has been either assigned or self-generated by the SMT as an independent agent.

Discussion

The director is not alone in naming a group of individuals a 'team' and then relating to the members individually. Instead of five separate life spaces, I offered him an opportunity to experiment with the five as one, and to notice what happened. Part of what happened is that the five seemed to respond by becoming capable of behaving as a unit, thus consolidating the change and adding a new dimension to the working relationships. This is not something I set out to do with the SMT. An opportunity for an experiment with the Executive Director emerged, I took it, and as he worked it through, I could understand that I had impacted on the SMT itself – though very much at one remove through my coachee.

In other words, the field of our coaching relationship now included a vector – the origin of which is called 'SMT', which was not only acted upon as previously by the director, but now also proactively was influencing him and through him, me. The well-tuned duet of the manager and me was now joined by a quartet. Whilst I have no sense of us ever having become an integrated sextet, we certainly became a field of influences (vectors self-organising towards equilibrium in Lewinian terms). The coaching dynamics of the director and me were now part of a wider dynamic field of influencing and being influenced.

Seen in retrospect from a field attunement perspective, here are some reflections. The manager and I have an established coaching relationship. He knows that I am generally happy to let him lead (singing the melody) and I follow (contributing to the harmony). He also acknowledges the occasional shift to my taking the melody lead and his listening with me to the music that emerges. There are also our cacophonous moments, when one or the other of us shifts from being harmoniously in tune to taking the lead with our own melody and the other chooses not to follow.

In this instance, the director and I reached such a threshold. He was talking about the 'team' and using both 'they' and individual names. This jarred with me intellectually as a group theorist. It also jarred emotionally – I could feel how my appreciation of him as an organisational leader was being impacted. I was becoming judgmental of him. Energised by this sense of jarring, and supported by my trust in myself and my good intentions as well as my trust in our established relationship, I offered an experiment. Since he was probably well attuned to me in general, and in this case in particular, he went with the experiment – and thus took back the lead voice. We had gone from the threshold of cacophony to a smooth segue into an energised duet.

This vignette also helps to distinguish between *empathy* and *field attunement*. I regard empathy as an essentially interpersonal event – in this case between me and the director, whether explicitly mutual or not. Field attunement in organisational coaching refers to *emergent* themes between me and the coachee, his immediate superiors, colleagues, subordinates, and the organisation of which he is a functional part and representative. So here, there is the SMT and also the organisation acting on me through the director and the SMT. In other words, the whole field was alive to the sound of music – to coin a phrase!

Vignette two: The training and supervision group

I meet a group of consultants/trainers for a three-day residential OD supervision/coaching group, four times a year. We explore various aspects of supervision, consultancy and coaching. For example, I supervise whatever client work they wish to bring. At times, members will consult to or coach each other. In such cases, the consultant/coach can choose to have direct supervision, with me available in the room as they work; or they can choose to work first with me out of the room, and then have supervision with me after their work, and *in plenum*. This latter approach allows for fascinating insights into the whole process for all concerned – consultant/coach, client and onlookers. It is truly a field approach to coaching/supervision/training, allowing us the opportunity to experience and observe a multiplicity of life spaces as we process our work.

At a recent session, Angela requested supervision on a very difficult and challenging piece of training that she was engaged in at a hospital. Her own first training and profession was nursing, and she was engaged by a hospital HR department to support the planned merger of two clinics into one unit. The doctors concerned were in agreement about the change, but there were some doubts about the attitudes of the nursing staff. She had designed a two-day programme for nurses from the two clinics, with a focus on change processes, communication and co-operation.

About halfway into our contracted 45-minute coaching session, I was having difficulties connecting her opening input with where she now seemed to be in her narrative. I asked Angela to describe how she had contracted this work, both with HR, and also with the participants. In asking this question, I might just as well have asked her to explain Einstein's theory of relativity in ten words. She stopped functioning in front of my eyes. She was at a loss for words, her eyes were darting all around me though never at my eyes, she became almost incoherent as she asked me to repeat my question. Realising that my question had evoked such a strong reaction, I back-pedalled and shifted back into asking her to tell me how the programme had gone. She reported that she was very pleased with the first day and very confused by the second. Some participants had not turned up for the second day, and a few of those who did were critical of the content of the first day. I asked how general or specific the criticism was. Again, Angela seemed to shut down. She said she wanted to stop there, and maybe do more work with me later in the weekend.

Coming down the stairs the next morning to enter the work-room, I could sense an idea forming…and as I opened the session, I suggested to Angela that she consider talking the remainder of the supervision group through her process of contracting, planning and running the programme, without me in the room. She very readily agreed. After I had left, she spent over an hour with her fellow participants, and reported later that this session had really been very good for her, and she could feel how her next meeting with the nurses would be important for her in establishing a good working relationship with them.

That evening, at the dinner table, Angela began talking about her cousin, Birgitta, who she feels doesn't like or respect her. In fact, Birgitta likes to call Angela a 'pseudo-psychologist' at family gatherings. Someone asked what Birgitta's profession was. Angela said she was a doctor, and then, with a mixture of disbelief and growing relief – a doctor at the very hospital where Angela was now working as an OD consultant/trainer. Birgitta would be certain to hear of any criticism directed at Angela, which would only confirm her prejudices about her as an OD consultant and trainer – and pseudo-psychologist. Suddenly Angela could see the whole matter in a completely new light. The phrase 'elephant in the room' had gone from a trivial cliché to a living example. It was as if Birgitta had been in every room involved: the training room at the hospital, the coaching room at our residential – and now the dining room there! The following day Angela presented her new design for the next session at the hospital.

My hypothesis here is that Birgitta was the originator of a vector of the Angela–Hospital–Birgitta field. Clearly, she was the origin of a devaluing judgment experienced by Angela as being aimed in her direction, with quite a strong energy – though not acknowledged by Angela other than as a force of the field in her extended family. And yet as she could acknowledge, when I did some teaching about field and life space, criticism as a powerful and impactful force was resonating throughout the whole process of the two-day training and the supervision session. Her confusion at the nurses' criticism, her confusion at my questions (which, she agreed, she had taken to be questioning her competence) – all evoked her sense of being unseen and unheard by Birgitta except as a pseudo-psychologist of little or no competence or consequence. Angela's sudden understanding of Birgitta's presence as a force of the Angela–Hospital–Birgitta field, brought Birgitta into her awareness as an environmental other of the field, previously sensed rather than seen, and now an aware aspect of Angela's life space. She dealt with it quite brilliantly, and brought her work to the following supervision residential.

On her return to the nurses, she had opened by apologising for not having mentioned earlier that she was a trained nurse, and spoke of the hospitals and wards where she had been a Senior Nurse. She addressed her own experience of re-organisations, merging wards and so on, and then how she had completed a four-year training at diploma level in Gestalt in Organisations. So here she was working with nurses from a basis of new competence on top of her competence and experience as a nurse in hospitals such as the one they were now in. Angela had been inspired to establish her competence, on her own terms, with her client group.

She also then addressed with us how important it had been for her to experience her relief at working with her peers in the absence of any authority figures (me, for example) at the previous supervision meeting. My hypothesis here concerns the self-organising and self-regulating of the various fields of which Angela was an energy or force, beginning with the training programme, then continuing in the Friday morning coaching session with me, to Saturday morning (her peer session), to Saturday night at dinner (Birgitta's 'appearance'), to Sunday morning and her resolve to define and take a stand on her own unique competence. Included here is the energy I felt to suggest spontaneously the peer review and to remove myself from the scene.

Discussion

This vignette is a rich source of learning for me, still offering its emergent knowledge and know-how as I draft this chapter. Here are some of the most pertinent issues for me in the context of my theme:

1. Friday Morning

Angela and I were clearly in tune with each other – as long as I was prepared to follow her lead. I found this increasingly difficult to do since her narrative did not form an integrated whole. I had a distinct sense of incompleteness, a physical and cognitive dissonance. My intervention focusing on the contract was spontaneous and instinctive, more an intuitive response than a rational decision. It was what I needed to do in the situation – and 'situation' is a word Lewin often used as a synonym for 'field'.

Part of the situation of my coaching session with Angela was obviously that it was taking place as part of a training programme in the presence of other participants. I had thus a 'double' life space: first, Angela, her client and her work; and second, Angela and her participant colleagues as the training group which had engaged me for a specific purpose – coaching and coach training.

One of the core aspects of that training is presenting, discussing and reaching conclusions about the distinction between what I call the 'business contract' and the 'working contract'. The business contract is with the person engaging my services as a coach – often a HR executive or staff-member with a formal mandate – and is concerned with the time frame, the fees, payment procedures and in some cases, the assigned task of the coaching. I urge my trainees (and remind myself!) to consider carefully not only our competence for the task, but also our willingness to do it – whether humanistically, ethically, ideologically, theoretically or methodologically.

If the coach accepts and finalises the business contract, including the assigned or re-negotiated task, she can then meet the actual client and negotiate the working contract. The working contract begins with checking the assigned task with the very person on whom it is focused – the coachee. Then there are issues around method, values, wishes, expectations: at this point, the coaching has truly begun and a solid foundation is being laid for establishing the parameters of the future work. Part of this contracting is a mutual willingness to re-negotiate the working contract at any time.

In my experience as a coaching trainer and coach supervisor, I have met countless examples of a mismatch between the assigned task and the coachee's expectations and/or needs, or also between the task and the coach. This has usually resulted in such confusion that all parties feel frustrated and un-supported. The 'usual suspect' and scapegoat of choice is often then the coach or even the methodology she represents. Sometimes, the coachee gets the blame as a prelude to some organisational politics.

A natural consequence of what I have described in these recent paragraphs is that my trainees and coaches were 'conditioned' to pay particular attention to their contracting. It has become customary for them to present this at the opening of any working session where they are coachees.

So, to get back to my intervention with Angela: 'double' life-spaces (where two life spaces come together), bring with them complex challenges for field attuners. In this case, I was fortunate in that both dissonances became a harmonious whole: my coachee, Angela, had barely alluded to any contracting at all. My training group had probably noticed this (their conditioning!) and so I was responding to two field influences when I made the intervention – one in the life-space of 'me-Angela-the client', and the other 'me-Angela-the training group'.

From Angela's perspective, I was clearly so out of tune with her narrative and its direction that she seemed to have experienced my intervention and the ensuing cacophony as overpowering and silencing her. (I know from subsequent conversations that the remainder of the participants were anticipating my intervention). Just as in Vignette 1, I trusted the relevance of my energy to intervene, its direction (directly at Angela *and* the training group) and its strength. I also, as always, trusted that the outcome would possibly reveal whatever dynamic need was self-organising the field and that this outcome could be explored subsequently with our collective curiosity and mutual respect.

As always, I allow events to occur around me. If I feel energised to respond to field influences in some way, then I will do so. Otherwise, I will 'bracket' my cognitive processes and thus reach no rational conclusions, nor design a future intervention in what will be a thoroughly unique and new life-space for me, and field for all of us involved. How could anything I plan on a Friday night in such a dynamic situation be assumed to be automatically relevant on Saturday morning? So, in a nutshell, I slept on it.

2. Saturday Morning

The following morning, walking down the stairs in sight of the workroom and moving bodily towards it without a plan in my head, my field attunement antennae came to life and I simply 'knew' that I was responding to field influences. I walked in, greeted the participants and without the usual 'check-in' suggested that Angela talk through her work at the hospital in the company of her colleagues, and without me in the room. Angela herself and all the others readily agreed, which I took as an indication of us all 'singing from the same sheet-music'. I can happily admit to a tingle of joy when shared attunement segues so smoothly into mutual music-making. Truthfully, I even got the tingle as I typed that last sentence!

Seen in the context of the whole of our experience on that training weekend, Angela finding her own voice in the company of her peers on Saturday morning certainly seems to be in tune with her emerging self-confidence and sense of professional identity. And this was clearly on her own terms, and not Birgitta's – or anyone else's, including mine.

The next step in what was becoming a complex field attunement process occurred at dinner with the introduction of Birgitta and her 'quasi psychologist' remarks. And her emergence as 'the elephant' in so many rooms...

3. Sunday Morning

When I move into teaching mode I need to be attuned to the content, to the participants, to my – and their – relationship to the content (including its consequences for us): and to our process as co-creators of the field of our dynamic interactions.

I see one of my responsibilities as a field theorist as being to de-personalise events and to allow the field itself – now come and gone – to be in focus; so that we can all learn from exploring our experience of it. So this session dealt with exploring some hypotheses about such vectors as criticism, competence, professional identity and support, for example.

It was easy to locate Birgitta, myself, Angela herself as well as some of her trainee colleagues as likely origins of the vector criticism of varying strengths, directed at Angela. The energy of competence clearly originated in Angela – as well as some of her colleagues, and me. The same may well apply to professional identity. Support became exciting for us: as an energy, it certainly expressed itself through me, Angela herself, her colleagues and also, perhaps, Birgitta. Without the vector 'criticism' all the rest might never have come together and self-organised in the unique way in which it did.

Biased as I may be, I am convinced that our mutual interest in and openness to field attunement both as a theory and a methodology is a fertile ground from which such complex processes and concrete outcomes can emerge.

Concluding Reflections of a Field Attuner

The field is indeed alive with the sound of music. And *field attunement* supports me to be always tuned in and ready to sing along in harmony or a congruent dissonance, especially with an unknown tune.

And I repeat: field attunement is not a model or technique in its own right; nor is it a replacement for any of the many models and techniques which are readily available and which you, the reader, may already be using. Field attunement is a *way of being* as we work. It is *embodied* in as much as it has been understood, assimilated and integrated into who I am as an embodied self, including my professional knowledge, experience and competence. It is intrinsically *relational* in as much as the client is very much my environmental other, and I hers, in our mutual journey.

For a field attunement stance or approach, mutuality is an essential aspect. Coaching is not something the coach *does to* the coachee, as object for the coach's knowledge, competence and hierarchical position as an engaged and paid 'expert' of some kind. Or even more objectifying, as occasionally still happens, for the organisation's use of the coach as a surrogate manager in the absence of a manager competent enough, able and willing to do what is organisationally necessary.

Field attunement as an approach is intrinsically unpredictable, non-directive and always curious and explorative. The outcome is what actually 'comes out' in and of itself, and *in* and *of* us, the coach and coachee in our happy meanderings within the parameters established by our overall and currently agreed business contract as the professional context for our work-contract.

So being a field attuner is not for the faint-hearted amongst organisational coaches and it is certainly not for executives who see organisations as engineering structures and themselves as engineers. I have a quotation here the source of which I have lost and forgotten: 'Do you regard your organisation as a car, whose engine you can mess about with, adjust and repair, or a coach and six (horses) you learn to handle?' The organisational coach with a focus on field attunement is most at home with the coachman of the coach-and-six and the organisation whose leaders understand and accept this.

And yes, I admit: I have been there, done that and have the attuning-fork! And the attuning fork is me – just as it can be you.

References

Marrow, A.J. (1969). *The Practical Theorist – The Life and Work of Kurt Lewin*. New York: Basic Books.

O'Neill, B. & Gaffney, S. (2008). Field-theoretical strategy. *Handbook for Theory, Research and Practice in Gestalt Therapy*. Brownell, P. (ed.) Newcastle: Cambridge Scholars Publishing.

11

'Living Moments' in the Art of Coaching

Ty Francis PhD

'A dot means everything,' said the Japanese artist, Katsushika Hokusai. For this intensely talented and productive artist, who created over 30,000 woodblock prints, paintings, illustrations, picture-books and manga, each full of astonishing vitality, a dot is not only the point of origin of a work of art; it also distills the essence of the subject, as well as capturing and communicating the relationship between the artist and the art. A dot thus becomes an exquisitely expressive punctuation point in the creative process, although we might be forgiven for overlooking it in our appreciation of the finished work.

I think of coaching as a creative process. Hokusai's statement therefore leads me to wonder if, as coaches, we are paying enough close attention to the 'dots' of our conversations with clients – *those pivotal micro-moments of the change process* that are intrinsic to each client encounter? Coaching is a relational process that spans time – client conversations continue for hours, and extend over weeks, months and sometimes years: and as coaching professionals we can become so concerned with the bigger-picture issues of crafting better questions, so interested in opening up options, so absorbed in forming actionable outcomes, that perhaps we fail to notice that there are particular, fleeting *moments* in the dance of dialogue that matter more than others… This chapter explores my interest in these 'dots' – these experiential 'living moments' (Shotter, 1999) in the art of coaching.

A 'living moment' is experienced as key *while it is happening.* Such a moment is often experienced as having a numinous quality, and is emotionally moving, arresting or 'striking' in some way. Something else seems to come alive in the conversation, and both coach and client may have a felt sense that something deeply significant yet almost inexpressible is occurring… I believe that these moments are pregnant with possibilities, loaded with what Bakhtin (1984) calls 'event potential' – with the freight of novelty, renewal and resources for change. Stern (2004) describes such moments as 'Now' moments. He regards them as moments of heightened connection and improvisation. For Stern, it is these moments, above all others, that allow for new possibilities in the client's range of functioning (I would add, also in the coach's).

If we notice and respond to them while they are happening, these moments can call us, *as coaches*, out of our habitual pursuit of question-sequences and return us to the immediate, living experience of being present with the client – without any manipulatively 'helpful' agenda. These moments can also, *for clients*, shift responses from the automatic and habitual to those that are more novel and tentative – opening unexpected new possibilities for action. For *both coach and client*, 'living moments' can creatively interrupt and usefully disorient our accustomed ways of relating to self and others, and thus offer the possibility of transformational learning and development.

Case Study 1: 'The Blessing'

In many ways, my interest in 'living moments' in coaching has its point of origin in a client conversation approximately ten years ago. I was working with the Chief Executive of an Anglo-Asian company, who was struggling to develop a business strategy for European market penetration. He and his director team had no shortage of ideas. However, it seemed impossible for him to decide on any way forward. In several previous coaching sessions, we had explored dimensions of the same theme – namely, their struggle to decide on a strategic direction. We had explored whether this was a crisis of belief; what his part in the stuckness might have been; what was happening within his team; how the larger commercial context of the company and its relationship to its customers might not yet be supportive of developing a new strategy...

This time, as he bemoaned again the lack of strategic vision and plan, I recalled that the other 50% shareholder in the business was his Chinese partner, who had founded the company and was based at headquarters in China. Intuitively, I asked my client if he believed he had his partner's blessing to expand into Europe? He paused, put down his pen, fixed me in his gaze, and went quiet for some time. I could see his face redden and he exhaled deeply. I felt bewildered, as though I had broken our flow. I had a 'felt sense' of the shift in the climate of our conversation, but at that time, no trust in the alchemy of the moment. Somewhat awkwardly, I collapsed the silence with another question and so returned to what seemed to me to be the 'safe ground' of action possibilities – what he might actually *do* next that would help develop a plan? After picking up his pen to make a short note, my client continued to talk, but I sensed a significant moment had passed and I had a profound sense of having missed something.

In our next coaching session a month later, he began by telling me that straight after our last session he had booked a flight to China and asked his partner for his 'blessing' on the European strategy, after which he found more confidence in the company's intended direction. He shared that my rather poetic word, 'blessing,' was so appropriate that he decided to use it. The word not only seemed to him to be culturally sensitive, but also expressed something important and unspoken about the systemic relationship – the act of asking for his business partner's blessing also respectfully acknowledged a subtle but unspoken hierarchy between them – although they were equal partners in shareholding, the business had originally been founded by the Chinese partner.

Even given my gaucheness at the time – I recognised the living moment but did not know how to work with it – I realised our conversation four weeks earlier had been transformational: it produced a change of 'being' in my client, in his relationship with his business partner and director team, and subsequently in the company's market position. His story of his trip to China was also a transformational moment for me – an 'aha!' experience of epiphany. From this joint experience, I wondered how my own coaching practice could be deepened in ways that might add even more value for my clients: perhaps I could harness more awareness of both the preconditions that give rise to living moments, and also discover more about how to work *within* such moments when I felt the relational field shift between us as client and coach.

I have since learned that – like all creative endeavours – living moments in the coaching relationship cannot be mechanistically planned for. They seem to arrive as friends often do – quite unexpectedly, when we might not feel as prepared as we would like for the visit. Yet over the years of my coaching and supervision practice, I have also come to believe *that it is possible to create the relational conditions through which living moments are more likely to occur*, and also to work with them more skilfully from within the moment, rather than be surprised into silence by them.

FieldSmithing

The practice of co-creating and working within such transformational living moments, I call 'FieldSmithing' (Francis, 1999). In Gestalt, a 'field' (Lewin, 1951) is a metaphor for a *relational environment* that both forms and informs us. FieldSmithing is, therefore, a set of practices that enable us, as coaches, to intentionally influence the relational environment so that clients can access new possibilities at work and in life.

This chapter describes three ways in which I have explored how to 'fieldsmith' living moments in my coaching practice. First, in the case study I have just described, I noted how poetic forms of language can be a threshold to a living moment. It is as though 'new' language can open up new vistas of understanding, and transform the inner landscape of ideas and experience that clients use as orientation-points for exploring their issues. The intervention here is at the level of the *linguistic environment*. Second, I shall build on this insight by sharing how I use aspects of the *physical environment* where the coaching takes place, through a practice account of team coaching; and third, I shall describe how I attend to our embodied experience as coach and client – to our *somatic environment* – through a case study of one-to-one, in-person coaching. I work with all three elements simultaneously, rather than in a linear and sequential way: however, for the purposes of describing my practice in this chapter, I shall focus on each element exclusively and bring the elements together in a later, integrative discussion where I shall explore practice implications for coaches.

Case Study 2: Entering the bat cave

I was invited to coach a project team of six people, comprising laboratory chemists and managers from a global household chemicals manufacturer. They were under pressure from the company's Marketing Department to dramatically shorten the lead-time to produce new products. The team was at a loss to understand how they could re-engineer their product development process.

At my first working session with them (after one-to-one introductory meetings had been conducted), I suggested that we approach the challenge from a *creative*, rather than a scientific starting-point. I suggested that we explore how working in a radically different physical environment than the company's laboratories might help us develop radically different initial ideas. After some consternation and discussion, the team agreed to participate in a one-day, off-site workshop that we framed as a 'creative experiment' in getting ideas. The team brainstormed many unorthodox possibilities and decided to go to a zoo!

I designed a process that would involve the team walking around the zoo as a group of six (but without me), looking at the various animals and conservation work the zoo undertook, while holding the question, "How does this suggest new products for our company?" The walk would be conducted in complete silence and take two hours, before we reconvened for a coaching conversation outside the zoo's coffee shop to explore what had happened.

I explained that while each *individual* should take notes or photograph personally-exciting experiences, they should also notice if, at some point, the whole group was having a *collective* experience that brought people together. Their job was not to manufacture a joint experience, nor to analyse their excitement in the moment, but simply to notice if a 'living moment' occurred, and to pay attention to it – capturing details in their private journals such as where, when, what the subjective impact on them was, and so on. We would subsequently explore both personal and collective experiences when we reconnected for our debrief conversation.

They set off together around the zoo and returned roughly on schedule. As the storytelling about their experiences progressed, one single experience seemed to ignite them all – their visit to the bat cave! The group excitement mounted as we realised that everyone had been most energised by the experience of being in an 800m^2 dark space where over 500 bats flew freely among the visitors! The darkness, humidity, stench, silence and proximity to the swooping bats had aroused fear, fascination, excitement, joy and more, and stood out as being the most significant collective experience of the day at the zoo. The whole group 'lit up' as individuals described their experience!

After this first round of storytelling, we focused on the central question: how could this experience of the bat cave link to their need as scientists to develop ideas for new household products? I posed the question and advised them *not* to give intellectual consideration to this question, while at the same time staying in touch with highly-energised feeling of the group. There was a pregnant silence. People avoided making eye contact with one another and with me. Many fidgeted awkwardly. I said nothing more…

Before too long, one person noted how the bat cave was actually an eco-system in miniature – for example, he speculated how the bats were a part of a miniature natural system in which their excrement fertilised fungus which attracted insects which became the bats' food, in an ongoing cycle. Another person quickly built on this realisation by suggesting that they had never before thought of approaching product development from a *systemic* angle – they had been intent on producing single products, but what if they could creatively adapt learning about eco-systems such as the bat cave and apply it to their new product development process? What would household cleaning products that worked synergistically and inter-dependently look like? For the second time, the group 'lit up' at this possibility. They had experienced a 'living moment'.

A participant wrote a report later about the group's visit to the zoo, emphasising not only the systems insight but also the importance of the sensory experience the group had in originating the insight:

> *Revelations in the bat cave and in conversations at the zoo gave the team a creative hook for the project's work: the insight of ecosystems. This led to a team goal – inspiring innovative oikos-systems... 'Oikos' is the Greek word for 'home' and also the root of the word 'eco'. It speaks of new systems for the home, cleaning products that work synergistically with each other, systems to truly animate the R&D continuum, drawing on webs of relationships, partnerships, products and the environments in which they are used. And we are still mining this insight! ...Throughout this [project], I have emphasised how sensory experience is implicated in the constitution of home and identity. My notion of 'the sensory home' is one that emerged specifically from this project... This recognition of the importance of sensory experience and the prospect of sensory agency opens up new R&D possibilities for us.*

In this case study, I have emphasised how attending to embodied experience in a novel physical environment, while encouraging people to use language that was saturated in feeling, afforded opportunities for a living moment to occur for a *group*. Before I go on to discuss some theoretical perspectives that I drew on as a coach to open and work with this 'living moment,' I would like to offer another case study. This next practice account represents work with an individual, where several 'living moments' occurred over a couple of years of working together.

Case Study 3: The canine coach

The subject of my next case study was a director of an environmental organisation. She came to see me because of difficulties in relationships at work and also in her personal life. It was clear to me from our initial interview that her request for help would involve us enquiring across systemic boundaries – across both my client's organisational and family systems, and we contracted for this broader-than-usual enquiry. Yet because I framed the core issues as having their point of origin more in the *personal* than the professional lifespace, I suggested that we meet at my home for our coaching sessions, rather than in her office. I recognised that there were boundary implications in this, so did not make the suggestion casually. At her invitation, I also visited her once at her workplace and once at her home.

Our relationship as coach and client has now extended over several years, during which time, considerable trust has grown between us and we have been able to work at depth on her personal process and on how our coaching relationship has enabled or sometimes disabled her at work and at home. I have not always 'got things right' or been as helpful as I could have been, and we have had several points of re-focusing our work after my approach has been critiqued by her. This notion of coaching as an extended action enquiry, where the coach's approach is itself open to critically reflexive scrutiny by the client, receives little attention in the coaching literature although I believe it to be an important feature of a Gestalt-informed, dialogic approach.

A recurring motif in our work, from the beginning, has been the variety of heightened bodily symptoms my client has experienced in our sessions – especially coldness and shivering, trembling and hand-wringing. In the early days of our work together, these somatic indicators would often be accompanied by extended periods of silence, and stood in sharp contrast to the often scientific, logical, intellectual nature of my client's approach to what she calls 'fixing herself'. With this client (more than some others) I decided to draw on the Gestalt notion of engaging 'the body as consultant' – to invite her to explore her embodied experience in our sessions, and also to draw more on my own embodied data of being in relationship throughout our enquiries. I will provide examples of what I mean in the following two vignettes.

Cariad and Constellations

First, my dog – a very sociable Great Dane called Cariad, has become an integral part of our coaching work. In one session where we were exploring her various ways of relating to others, my client was asserting vociferously that she could not function in any mode other than as a problem-solving, scientific rationalist. Furthermore, she asserted (and seemed convinced) that this was her *only* way of being. I didn't doubt that this was her dominant self-concept, although my direct experience of her was that she showed more creativity, softness, emotion and range than she seemed to be allowing herself to acknowledge. Rather than disagreeing with her, I wondered how we could explore the limits and limitations of her self-concept experientially. I drew on my knowledge of her work with animals in the environment agency where she worked: I asked if she would be open to having my dog present in the room, as a kind of creative experiment.

When Cariad came in to the room, the dog walked directly over to my client and climbed on to the sofa beside her. Delighted, she stroked the dog affectionately, and I asked her to pay attention to her range of bodily and emotional responses – simply to slow down and be curious. She began to play gently with the dog, and with quiet encouragement from me, followed her impulse to hug Cariad. The dog licked my client's hands, slid onto the floor and rolled on her back, as though inviting my client to play more. As their interaction continued, I asked her to check if she was solving a problem here, or being scientific, and if so how she accounted for her way of being with Cariad? She seemed extremely surprised.

The quality of *this* living moment was different than with the group in the bat cave. This time, she looked 'thrown' and disoriented. She stood up, moved back and away from me a couple of steps, and was quiet for some time. Unlike with my other client who asked for his business partner's blessing, this time I stayed silent. While continuing to look carefully at my client, I paid attention to the phenomenology of my own experience – to my breathing, to my sense of deeply empathic connection, to the impact she was having on me as she rocked gently from side to side. I imagined that she was moving between two extremely important self-concepts, trying them on like clothes – a comfortable old image and a surprising new image of herself. I decided to support the emergent new image, and shared with her my feelings of pleasure and fun at seeing her play so pleasurably with Cariad.

This opened up a deeply important conversation about aspects of her contact style of which she was unaware. In the next coaching session we allowed Cariad in again from the beginning, to work with us as a kind of 'canine consultant' in ways that we would allow to emerge. The dog became an ongoing companion to our coaching enquiry, and has enabled my client not only to explore touch safely, but also to access forms of interaction and associated feelings in ways that would have been impossible between us otherwise, person-to-person.

One way in which we used Cariad was by exploring what, for my client, was an optimal distance for her to feel safe and to function without undue stress in relationships? Drawing on my experience of Organisational Constellations (a process of embodied and systemic enquiry that is currently gaining ground amongst organisational coaches) I asked her in one session to use the dog as a representative for a person she was describing. Telling the dog to sit and stay, I invited my client to move around the room, and to find the distance that suited her most, where she felt still in relationship but where her body relaxed. She was astounded at what she experienced physically and emotionally at different degrees of proximity to the dog.

In my client's written reflection to me, she says this of our work with Cariad and Constellations:

> *The work we started with Cariad and optimal distance – and then using bits of paper on the floor to represent others – has been not only weird but also fascinating/intriguing. Cari has had an important role to me, as a responsive living being that not only allows but actively invites touch. She allows me physical proximity – or indeed distance – when I need them. The main realisation for me was that there was clearly a whole world of stuff going on inside me that I couldn't access through our normal discussion or through thinking – but that couldn't be denied or ignored. Initially I felt confusion,*

> *fear, reluctance coupled with amazement, curiosity, anxiety. I was stunned by my physical responses. The change in my breathing (rate and depth) was most notable and undeniable. It made identifying and accepting the associated feelings permissible. I couldn't pretend that it wasn't real and I was a bit doolally. Something was clearly going on that was outside of my direct consciousness. I still don't have the words to describe it to you. It's a more primal, younger place than the world I usually inhabit. Whenever we do this kind of work now, something important seems to come out of it. I feel it's the most productive tool in our armoury for getting to the heart of the matter.*
>
> *The fact that you (and indeed Cariad) persistently refuse to reject or get angry with me irrespective of what I come out with, has really thrown me! It allows me to re-evaluate my habit of thinking that no-one wants me and that anyone I get close to will ultimately reject me and lead me to feel worthless and harmful/toxic in some way. I think I might gradually be growing some trust in myself.*

A helping hand

Second, in another session I asked my client to become aware of her insistent, sometimes frantic hand-wringing – to continue to do it, in silence for a short while, but to bring more curiosity and awareness to the act. To me, it looked painful – as though one hand was hurting the other. Although self-conscious, she continued to twist the thumb and bend the fingers of the other hand, to prod and poke the palm and back of her hand. Yet she was unable to put in to words her physical or emotional experience.

I felt as though we had hit a brick wall. Neither of us knew what to do next, as my intervention had shifted the frame from her story about work (reflecting on what had already happened) to her embodied experience in the room with me (reflecting in the moment on what was currently happening). The silence between us enabled me to question quickly my assumptions about her experience (that she was hurting herself) and for me to check in with my own embodied experience (I noticed I was holding my breath). It seemed to me as though each of us was holding something back, and I wondered how we could reconnect more simply, without words.

I asked her if, instead of using *her* hand as the one being wrung, she experimented with using *my* hand. My suggestion also represented a real risk (or opportunity for deepening trust) on both sides. Coaches rarely use physical touch with our clients because of the shift in the level of intimacy this represents, and the possibilities for being misunderstood! Yet from what I knew about this particular client's frame of reference, touch was extremely important to her. She seemed interested, and agreed to my suggestion.

I moved to sit beside her. I realised, of course, that I would not have exactly the same experience as she was having; nevertheless, I placed my hand into hers and she continued her actions of bending, twisting, pulling and poking, just as before – but now with *my* hand... I bracketed all attempts to understand the experience and instead focused on simply opening to the physical sensations of my hand being touched. To my surprise, it was utterly different than I had imagined some minutes earlier from my chair on the other side of the room. The quality of touch was incredibly soothing. I shared that I had misunderstood something, and was glad to experience her differently now. We didn't talk further about this at that time, we both simply allowed the moment of connection to be complete in and of itself. Sometimes we don't have to anatomise a living moment!

She later explained that she was not so much hurting herself, but that the movement for her was more like stretching a muscle to relieve a cramp: while some other part of her that she could not connect to through discussion at that time was hurting, the physical movement I had drawn her attention to was a way of soothing herself. I would not have known this without daring to suggest that she substitute my hand for hers. The experience of touch not only shifted something about my sense of her; it also shifted something in her at the time, and between us. Since this experience, occasional touch has become an invaluable part of our work together.

Recently, in her written reflections for this chapter on moments that mattered to her over the years of our coaching enquiry, my client expanded on how important physical touch is for her:

> *Thinking back I have been able to remember every occasion of physical contact with a clarity that eludes me when it comes to what we actually talk about.*
>
> - *Holding my hand when I was going through the hand-wringing and trembling period*
> - *Standing at my back and touching my shoulders when we were talking through how I would face my boss at my appraisal last year*
> - *Holding my hand when I was consumed with grief the other week.*
>
> *What happened afterwards is that I find it easier to ask for physical support from my partner, and trust that he really believes in me and wants to be with me. The physical touch*

> *conveys so much more to me than words. It seems to bypass my usual skepticism/distrust/anxiety about relationships that are important to me. It quietens the constant mental chatter like nothing else and has allowed me to be properly sad/grieve for things that I often can't even name, safe in the knowledge that it won't be coupled with rejection. It's helped me loosen the normal grip I keep myself under...*

In this case study, I have described how working creatively with embodiment can open possibilities for 'living moments' to occur and for the coach and client to draw on the transformational potential of such moments. I believe that it is also significant that these creative experiments arose from the physical context of working in my home: there would undoubtedly be constraints for such work in a more corporate environment. While I have not described how I use language here, my work with this client often features richly metaphoric references, where the metaphors themselves seem to become 'living moments' that we pause at and refer to over time.

Joining the dots: relating theory and practice

In these three case studies – The Blessing; The Bat Cave; and The Canine Coach – I have described a range of different 'living moments' in which a complex mixture of environmental, embodied and verbal influences is revealed. The intricacy of the responsive interplay between client, coach, and context is illuminated in such moments, which are like orientation points within a wider change process – signposts in a landscape of possibilities that call us to be deeply present and connected with each other so that transformation is possible.

Methodologically, I propose that 'fieldsmithing' our encounters with our clients requires more acuity of us as coaches, in working with the physical, somatic and linguistic environments that constitute the relational field of the coaching session. What is the theoretical basis for such an assertion?

Field affordances

Building on an aspect of Lewin's (1951) Field Theory, Gibson's (1977) notion of 'field affordances' suggests that the physical properties of an environment *invite us* to make use of them for our developmental needs. It is in the physicality of a room or natural space that we find opportunities to hide, climb, move, rest, make tools, gain vantage, or (as in the cases cited here) to re-imagine product development possibilities or rethink how we could relate to others differently.

An 'affordance' is, therefore, a perceived or latent possibility for action within an environment, that is specific to a particular individual or group at a specific time – in the way that steps on a staircase are an affordance to a toddler learning to walk and climb, but are not an affordance to a newborn baby. The affordance is not the stair (or the bat cave, or Great Dane, for example) but a property of the environment *relative to us*. Just as the stair invites the toddler to climb but does not afford this opportunity for a newborn child, so for the group of scientists in search of a product breakthrough, the zoo afforded them different opportunities than it did for the tourists and children who were also visiting at the time; for my environment agency client, my dog afforded a quality of self-insight and opened up a way of relating that is not so for dog-walkers we encounter in our local park.

Viewed from this perspective, environments are not just physical backdrops for our activities. They are also deeply relational and ecological, in the sense that we depend on environments for different and quite personally-tailored purposes and action possibilities. Scharmer (2000) makes a similar point when he states that:

> *Knowledge creation and innovation happen in places. Without temporal, spatial and relational context there is just information, not knowledge. Knowledge creation always depends on situated perception, cognition and action, on the 'ba', as Ikujiro Nonaka puts it, using the Japanese word for 'place'. The quality of 'ba' says Nonaka, determines the quality of knowledge creation.*

How often, as coaches, are we choiceful about the physical environments we work in? How often do we make deliberate use of our physical surroundings in ways that respond to our clients' developmental yearnings? Many of us frame the dialogic encounter with our clients as being concerned with presence and conversation: we often do not think to draw on the richness of the more-than-human world that we are situated in as an integral part of our coaching repertoire.

Could it be that the more creative and radical we are in changing and utilising the working environment, the more we can help catalyse breakthrough for our clients? Whether or not this is so remains to be seen. However, breakthrough is not just a function of introducing novelty to the enquiry process by changing and using the physical environment we coach in. It is also enabled by inviting clients to pay sustained attention to their embodied experience in that environment, while holding a developmental challenge – whether that is the need to develop strategy, originate viable ideas for new product development or integrate a more liberating self-concept and associated relationship possibilities. I believe it is important to remember that dialogue is always both an environmentally-situated and embodied activity. Gibson himself notes:

> *The perceiving of these mutual affordances (of behaviour) is enormously complex... and it is based on the pickup of information in touch, sound, odour, taste and ambient light.*

In other words, it is to our situated *embodiment* that we also must turn if we are to make fuller use of living moments.

The informative body

Developing a refined awareness of the body and of how it both reveals and maintains the emotional and psychological patterns that define us, is a hallmark of Gestalt coaching. This is not about 'reading body language' (with its assumption that the body is a *thing*) but about attuning to the ways in which our experience is present in what our bodies express (an assumption that our bodies are living statements of our history and current situation).

Living moments profoundly return us to our bodies. When a conversation becomes tense, or the weight of significance of a realisation bears down upon us, or when a silence is loaded, we feel it first in our bodies. Learning to pay attention to living moments is, in part, learning to pay attention to our visceral experience as coaches as well as encouraging our clients to tap into their heart-stirrings and gut-hunches – into their *embodied experience* as an intelligent and intelligible form of data.

In the example where I asked my client if she would do with *my* hand what I saw her doing with her own, I was not merely reading her body-language in an objectified way and floating a disembodied idea. Rather, I was attuned to my own somatic experience and felt my body begin a process of reaching out. When she kneaded my hand, it not only transformed my perception of her, but also (as I inferred from what she wrote to me later) the experience of touching my hand helped transform her experience of me, herself and some aspects of her relationships. The impulse was not an interpretive response to her state, but a pre-verbal, embodied inclination.

When my dog moved towards her, wagging its tail and rubbing against her legs, she did not have to think about her response: her body naturally gestured back, stroking and caressing and moving in a reciprocally communicative dance that (as she described) bypassed her analytical mode and changed her state into one of playfulness where there was no problem to solve, just a present-centred experience of relationship where she could grasp that there was nothing for her to fix.

When the team of scientists emerged from the bat cave and shared their excitement together outside the zoo's coffee shop, they described how they moved as one inside the cave – how they huddled closer together, how they all screwed up their faces and exclaimed at the stench, how they reached out into the darkness and held on to one another for comfort, how their pace shortened and slowed… In our coaching session on the zoo lawn afterwards, they knew that they were on to something important because they were having an experience of collective excitement that was visibly expressing itself through their bodies – their senses were awakened before their minds were opened. In recounting their shared experience to me, I was not so much paying attention to a cognitively structured story that was verbalised as to what Stern (2004) describes as 'an emotional narrative that is felt… a *lived story*.' As their coach, I was guided by my *feeling of knowing* that their stories about eco-systems and product families was significant and should be attended to – this was an aesthetic judgment rather than an intellectual one.

Paying exquisite attention to embodiment is not the sole province of a Gestalt-informed approach to coaching. For example, the ontological coaching approach of Sieler (2003) and the somatic coaching focus of the Strozzi Institute (2014) are generally well-known among experienced coaches. Constellations work is also becoming well-accepted as a form of coaching (Francis, 2009; Whittington, 2012). What I find different in a Gestalt approach is both how we support the client to stay with not-knowing – to tolerate liminal space while we invite the body to 'speak its mind' (Keleman 1981); and also how (because we view the coach-client-situation as a unified and indivisible whole) we allow for co-emergence of meaning by drawing on our own embodied experience alongside the client.

The evocation of language

Paying attention to our embodied responses as coaches also means paying attention to our language. In one sense, of course, it's axiomatic that experienced coaches pay close attention to language – for example, to noticing particularly 'loaded' words and phrases the client uses, and playing them back or enquiring directly into their significance; or giving preference to open questions and avoiding the use of multiple or loaded questions; to noticing recurring patterns, themes or metaphors that come up as the client speaks; even, for some colleagues who have studied Neuro-Linguistic Programming (Bandler and Grinder, 1990), to using embedded commands and other forms of 'hypnotic' language. Important and effective though these approaches might be sometimes, they nevertheless treat language and speech as abstractions that can be applied instrumentally, irrespective of the coach and client who are uniquely in relationship. What I find my

Gestalt training offers in addition, is the consideration of language *as an embodied action arising from a situation* rather than as a more abstracted and instrumental element of communication.

The body is always implicated in the moment of utterance – most markedly in the process of breathing. Our breath carries our language. The bodily rhythms of breathing and the physicality of bodily shifts between listening, thinking, concentrating, relaxing and talking are intricately intertwined. Letting another's words resonate within us and impact us is the essence of a caring relationship, yet even as we listen, our bodies respond to the other's language – in our facial expression, our posture, our gesturing and our breathing. As we listen, we hold our breath when anxious, we exhale to release tension, we deepen our breathing when we open to feelings, we stop our breathing when we want to block emotion… All of this inter-corporeality takes place in a given environment and can also be seen as a response to our wider life-situation.

Given the embodied and situated nature of speaking and listening, my interest is in how language (both the words we use and the speech-actions that colour and carry our words) can be used to open up and work within a 'living moment'. The phenomenologist Maurice Merleau-Ponty (1962), whose thinking has influenced contemporary Gestalt practice greatly, noted that words are like new senses, opening up new worlds to us. For Merleau-Ponty, a sentence is '*an organism of words, establishing in the writer or the reader as a new sense organ, opening a new field or a new dimension to our experience* (p.182).' When I asked my CEO client if he believed he had his partner's 'blessing' to develop a new European business plan, this word opened a new and previously unconsidered dimension of the systemic relationship between him, his partner and their business. At the moment of utterance, my client's body registered a change – he exhaled, he sat upright, stopped moving, made more direct eye-contact with me… and I think it is significant that he went to China to convey the word *in person* to his business partner. The language itself created new action-possibilities, which were embedded and embodied in our coach-client and client-partner relationships.

Corporate life asks much of us. Executives and Directors are frequently asked to explore issues of purpose, of passion, of belonging and betrayal, of stability and uncertainty and of many other intensely personal and deeply-felt dilemmas. Yet business language is so inadequate when it comes to articulating the intimacy of human experience that often underlies so many client issues. Consequently, I often draw on a more poetic vocabulary that does justice to the depth of our experience as people. I might talk about love, or grace, or hate, or other terms from a lexicon that has more majesty or elegance to it than corporate-speak, so that the possibility for new forms of thought and action are possible. The coach's ability to shift between, or to synthesise poetic and scientific registers, can be transformational of the client's experience.

Re-imagining our practice as coaches

It has been my experience as a coach trainer and supervisor that coaches do not routinely pay refined attention to the 'dots' – the living moments – of the client encounter. Also, the elements of language, embodiment and environment that I have been referring to here seem to be 'the obvious unseens' of coaching. While I do not believe in *recipes* for transformation, too few coaches can articulate a theory of practice for breakthrough. I hope that the elements I've described in this chapter can serve as heuristics, and go some way towards making transformation a less hit-and-miss process in coaching.

Working with living moments invites us as coaches to relate to our clients as if we are artists rather than social scientists. Many clients come to coaching feeling somehow incomplete, with a lack of coherence and connection to themselves, to others and to their emerging futures. As social scientists, we might more often approach this dilemma with some degree of 'objectivity' – for example, by helping our clients to gather data about themselves, and test hypotheses before agreeing on courses of action. However, as artists, we could instead enter into the unknown together and co-create the conditions for change from the novelty of our encounter in the here-and-now. This is the beginning of a dialogic relationship, where we focus on forms of interaction that have the potential for *mutual* insight and *collective* transformation.

Most coaches approach dialogic relating through the conversational process. I want to extend this conception of dialogue to include not only a specific form of language which is more evocative and even poetic, but also to include a focus on how we can work emergently, and in the moment, with embodiment and with environmental affordances. Taken and intentionally engaged with *as a whole*, these elements can support more co-creative forms of interaction, some of which are experienced as breakthroughs.

A 'living moment' is an emergent property of *contact* between coach and client, and is potentially transformational in that it can create and inform new *contexts* for action. A living moment can re-organise our shared understanding and experiencing of each other and of the situation being explored together, and represents a gestalt in its own right, in the sense that the moment is felt to be whole and complete in itself. It can also be the point of origin of what action researchers call 'participatory understanding' – a knowing from within the conversation when two people become an 'us' and something is felt to shift significantly.

I frame this form of coaching as *action enquiry*, which is an ongoing process of transformational learning originated by Gestaltist Kurt Lewin (1951) and described by Bill Torbert (2015) as follows:

> *In principle, anyone in any family or organisation can practice action inquiry. Gradually, they develop first the reliable capacity to make incremental (single-loop) changes to increase timely, effective action. Next (though few people or organisations today progress this far) comes the reliable capacity to make transformational (double-loop) changes; still later, a few humbly face the challenge of ongoing (triple-loop) listening into the dark – into the present moment and into the "Volume of all Possibilities" from which the future emerges.*

Living moments are emergent phenomena, and call forth participatory and relational knowing. As they are emergent, we cannot *plan* for them, though I believe it is possible to *prepare* for such moments and to use ourselves as coaches more skilfully when such moments arise. Preparation is quite different to planning – it has to do with orienting and opening ourselves, being ready, noticing, entering into conversations differently, sensitising ourselves to be more responsive to certain things and using our resources differently.

What I describe here is not merely some technical shift of focus in our approach to coaching. Living moments take us into areas that coaches know are intrinsically significant, though often little discussed: they relate to matters of aesthetics and ethics –

the place of beauty and the place of truth as they arise in our encounters with our clients.

In characterising 'living moments' as aesthetic I am drawing attention to our direct, pre-conceptual experience of them as conveying a felt-sense of qualities such as harmony or cacophony, resonance or dissonance; of weight, texture, fullness, vividness, rawness; of something to be appreciated. I have come to approach them as I might a poem. The essence of a poem is its ability to articulate a quiet contour of our experience, to draw our attention to life and living in ways that awaken connections and create meaning. In regarding living moments as of ethical significance, we are touching on how we conceive of ourselves in relation to others and to the world at large. The 'ethical call' of such moments invites us to 're-view' who we are and how we see the humanity of each other beyond our roles as coach or corporate executive. Simon Critchley (2002) makes clear that for the philosopher Emmanuel Levinas, ethics is simply a calling into question of ourselves as received by another – a view that helps us re-imagine what we are about as coaches by reminding us that we are both responsive to and responsible for one another. These 'pivotal micro-moments of the change process', as I described them at the beginning, are 'spots of time' in our coaching conversations at which aesthetics and ethics often converge: their 'rightness' can be savoured in the moment, and in retrospect.

References

Andersen, T. (1991). *The Reflecting Team: Dialogues and Dialogues About the Dialogues*. New York: Norton.

Bandler, R. & Grinder, J. (1990). *Frogs into Princes. Neuro-Linguistic Programming*. London: Eden Grove Editions.

Bakhtin, M. (1984). *Problems of Dostoevsky's Poetics*. Emerson, C., (ed and trans) Minneapolis: University of Minnesota Press.

Critchley, S. & Bernasconi, R. (2002). *The Cambridge Companion to Levinas*. Cambridge: Cambridge University Press.

Francis, T. (1999). *FieldSmithing*. Unpublished paper presented at a workshop on Field-Relational practices. Boston, December 11-15.

Francis, T. (2009). Upwardly mobile. *Coaching at Work*. April. 4, (3) 28-43.

Gibson, J. (1977). The Theory of Affordances. *Perceiving, Acting & Knowing*. Shaw, R. & Bransford, J. (eds) Hillsdale, NJ: Lawrence Erlbaum Associates.

Katz, A. & Shotter, J. (1999). Social poetics as a relational practice. Paper presented at workshop on *Constructions of Health and Illness*, University of New Hampshire, September 16-19.

Keleman, S. (1981). *Your Body Speaks its Mind*. Berkeley: Centre Press.

Lewin, K. (1951). *Field Theory in Social Science*. New York: Harper & Brothers.

Merleau-Ponty, M. (1962) *Phenomenology of Perception*. Colin Smith (trans). London: Routledge & Kegan-Paul.

Scharmer, O. (2000). Illuminating the blindspot: leadership in the context of emerging worlds. *McKinsey Society for Organisational Learning Project*. www.ottoscharmer.com

Sieler, A. (2003). *Coaching to the Human Soul: Ontological Coaching and Deep Change*. Victoria: Newfield Australia.

Shotter, J. (1999). Living Moments in Dialogical Exchanges. *Human Systems*, 9, 81-93.

Stern, D., (2004). *The Present Moment in Psychotherapy and Everyday Life*. London: Norton.

Strozzi-Heckler, R. (2014). *The Art of Somatic Coaching: Embodying Skillful Action, Wisdom and Compassion*. Berkeley, CA: North Atlantic Books.

Torbert, W. (2015) *Bill Torbert Action Inquiry Leadership Website* http://www.williamtorbert.com/action-inquiry

Whittington, J. (2012). *Systemic Coaching and Constellations: An Introduction to the Principles, Practices and Application*. London: Kogan Page.

The Editors

Ty Francis PhD

Ty is an independent Organisational Development specialist with more than 20 years' experience of working with global corporations, Government Departments and public sector organisations in the UK, Europe and the USA. He is passionate about supporting people in their personal development as a foundation both for deep-impact leadership and for organisational and social transformation.

His work focuses on designing innovative leadership/talent development programmes that have sustainable business impact; on developing and delivering creative approaches to individual/team coaching and supervision; and to providing change management that produces genuine employee engagement. Ty works collaboratively in the design, development and delivery of thoughtful and innovative programmes that help people to learn, to change and to take more effective and purposeful action. He enjoys bringing together photography, video and other visual techniques, with novel approaches to experiential learning (in indoor and outdoor environments) and with deeply-reflective conversational practices that catalyse opportunity and innovation.

Before establishing his own UK-based Organisational Development practice, Meus, Ty worked for major corporations in marketing, communications and brand strategy roles within the IT, pharmaceutical and news industries. Working on a variety of innovation projects within these fast-moving corporate sectors has always been a feature of his in-house work, and has continued to influence his consulting and coaching interests.

He obtained his PhD in 2011 for research into the psychology of breakthrough and transformation. He adopted both a Gestalt Field Theory perspective and worked within the Action Research tradition first established by Kurt Lewin. He teaches on Middlesex University's MSc in Organisational Development at Metanoia Institute in London, and has contributed numerous articles to Gestalt and business journals on the subjects of personal and brand identity; creative leadership; organisational development and innovation; as well as on the emerging methodology of Organisational Constellations – a discipline Ty has studied, applied in his coaching and consulting work, and taught internationally for the last twelve years.

Ty extends his consulting and coaching work into research, and is currently enquiring into three themes: how mindfulness-based approaches can be applied to develop leadership presence; on the place of love in personal, organisational and social transformation; and on the co-creative use of film in Organisational Development.

Email ty.francis@meus.co

Malcolm Parlett PhD

Malcolm obtained a doctorate in psychology from Cambridge and moved into a more applied field of study: working in organisational research. He began at the Massachusetts Institute of Technology (MIT) before being appointed to a lectureship at Edinburgh University (from 1970-76). During this time he pioneered innovative evaluation methods for the study of experimental programmes in the educational and social spheres (also co-producing the influential *Beyond the Numbers Game*, published by Macmillan in 1978).

For many years he worked as an independent consultant, mainly in the fields of education, philanthropy, and overseas aid programmes; during this time he acquired a great deal of practical organisational, consulting and coaching experience. His numerous clients from this period included the Nuffield Foundation, the Lilly Endowment in the USA, UNICEF/World Bank, Program for International Health (University of North Carolina), Tulane University Medical School, and Wellesley College (Massachusetts). He also worked for the National Foundation for Educational Research (part-time) as a principal research officer, and held visiting professorships at MIT, Surrey University, and the Open University (where he took a leading part in restructuring a research and development institute).

From 1985 onwards, his career altered direction to include more engagement with individuals and small groups. In the 1990s and 2000s he was involved in training/consultancy work and in coaching senior executives in commercial organisations (including Prudential, 3i, WHSmith) and was a member of the Bath Associates group of consultants. Having had Gestalt training in the USA, he also became active as a trainer of therapists, coaches, and counsellors in the UK, and also in supervision of other professionals, including executive coaches, clinical psychologists, and organisational consultants. In the course of his career he has co-founded a major psychotherapy and training institute, set up and co-led two successful long-term training programmes, conducted a large coaching and therapy practice, taught for a number of institutes in Europe, supervised numerous Masters and PhD students, and edited the *British Gestalt Journal.*

His long-term interests have included researching key competences for leaders, exploring work/life balance and ways of managing stress, supporting long-term professional and personal development, and engaging with political, ecological, and spiritual issues as they relate to professional and organisational life.

Malcolm Parlett has published many chapters and papers, notably in the field of Gestalt approaches, field theory, illuminative programme evaluation, teaching and learning, and professional behaviour. His book, *Future Sense: Five Explorations of Whole Intelligence for a World That's Waking Up*, was published by Troubador/Matador in 2015.

Email malcolm.parlett@virgin.net

The Contributors

Catherine Carlson MEd

Cathe Carlson MEd is an organization consultant and leadership development coach who brings 25 years of experience working with a broad range of executives in diverse industries in both public and private sectors (many of the later Global 500 and Fortune 100 companies). She brings to her work a synthesis of insight and practical applications from a variety of disciplines: business management, applied behavioral science, and organization development. Cathe is a member of the professional faculty at The Gestalt Institute of Cleveland, an adjunct faculty member at The Relational Center in Los Angeles, a past affiliate of MIT's Center for Organizational Learning and has led conferences and professional development workshops at The Gestalt International Study Center. Her recent work includes co-authoring two articles: one focused on embodying field theory in working with large systems, and another exploring the dynamics of power and shame in organizational coaching.

Email cathecarlson@msn.com

Sue Congram PhD

Living in the UK, Sue has worked in organisational consultancy for over 25 years and was an early adopter of coaching in her work. As a qualified practitioner of Gestalt, she was a co-founder and leader of a Gestalt in Organisations training initiative in the UK, which ran for 9 years. This was followed by teaching in institutes around Europe, which she continues to do today. Sue's consultancy client-base is wide ranging, largely in finance, IT, logistics, internet marketing, and the public sector. As a leadership coach she works with senior managers, leaders and their teams, individually, as well as in team or group coaching. Sue was awarded a PhD in 2013 for her research on hidden dynamics of leadership. As a consequence of her findings, she co-founded two businesses: Leaderful Women, supporting women in senior roles, and Engendering Balance, supporting men and women in achieving their leadership potential. Sue gives talks on new leadership thinking, and has published books, papers and chapters on psychology, people, teams,

diversity, coaching and supervision. She is now writing books and papers on leadership, based on the findings of her research.
Email sue@engenderingbalance.com

Sally Denham-Vaughan DPsych

Sally Denham-Vaughan is a registered clinical psychologist (HCPC); a UK registered psychotherapist; a registered coaching psychologist (BPS); and an Accredited Coach Supervisor (ISCP). In addition she is an organisational consultant, writer and trainer with over 25 years experience in helping individuals, teams and organisations to develop and innovate. She has coached a number of CEOs, Boards and senior clinical/academic staff to develop their values, collective leadership and strategy for the future. She has worked in commercial companies, the public sector, universities and large and small charities and has a passion for developing individuals and teams to be at their best. She has published widely on the topics of leadership presence, coaching and organisational change, and has developed and co-directed a Master's Degree programme covering leadership, coaching, and consulting skills. She is Visiting Fellow in the School of Business, Leadership and Enterprise, (University College Suffolk), International Board Advisor at The Relational Center in Los Angeles and Core Faculty with the International Group developing Organisational Gestalt Practitioners in Europe. She is the co-founder of Relational Change, an international organisation specialising in developing relational approaches in theory and practice.
Email sdv@relationalchange.org

Mark Fairfield

Mark Fairfield, LCSW, BCD (Board Certified Diplomate in Clinical Social Work), is the Founder and Executive Director of The Relational Center. He received a Master of Science in Social Work from Columbia University in 1995. He has been a faculty member of the Pacific Gestalt Institute and continues to consult with training institutes internationally to provide support in leadership development, program and curriculum planning, and the incorporation of a relational grassroots community organizing paradigm in the global Gestalt training community. For six years, he was the Clinical Director of Common Ground – The Westside HIV Community Center in Santa Monica, California. Mark has

twenty years' experience in direct practice, program development and administration in community mental health, community organizing and public education. He also consults with other nonprofit boards and management teams for strategic planning, leadership development, and technical assistance. He continues to publish in books and journals on the subject of confronting individualism in social services and organizes community action projects internationally.
Email mark@therelationalcenter.org

Rob Farrands PhD
Robert consults on how culture, strategy and leadership intersect in practice. He has consulted widely with large commercial organisations in sectors including oil and gas, banking and health care. He is also a highly experienced executive coach and was a founding member of APECS – the Association for Professional Executive Coaching and Supervision. Assignments include working with the leaders of an international joint venture to develop a central Asian gas field; organisation design and leadership development in the National Bank of Canada; establishing a Consortium of US and Canadian Companies for leadership development; and consulting to a healthcare organisation in a culturally diverse inner city area, to resolve a breakdown in child care provision. His work most often arises from complex strategic or operational problems. He uses progressive re-framing of situations to resolve problems and simultaneously illuminate the organisation. This draws him into understanding the culture, attending to stories and myths that surround uncertain situations and responding to the places where problems arise. Rob has worked in senior industrial relations positions in the car industry and took his PhD at the Centre for Action Research in Professional Practice at Bath University. He co-directs Figure Ground Consulting with his life-long partner Bridget.
Email rob@figure-ground.co.uk

Seán Gaffney PhD
Seán is Irish by birth, culture and conviction. He lived in England and Scotland for a combined total of seven years, and has been a resident of Sweden for over thirty-six years. He has a Diploma in Gestalt therapy from the Gestalt Academy of Scandinavia, and a Diploma in Gestalt OD from the Gestalt Institute of Cleveland. He is a full member of

the New York Institute for Gestalt Therapy, the Gestalt International Study Center (Cape Cod) and the European Association for Gestalt Therapy. He was also a senior lecturer in cross-cultural management and international organisational behavior at The Stockholm School of Economics, Sweden; The Business School at Bocconi University, Milan, Italy and the School of Economics, Riga, Latvia. He has published three books.
Email sean@seangaffney.com

Mark Gawlinski
Mark is a Gestalt psychotherapist, supervisor and coach who lives in Cambridge, UK. He is the co-founder of Cambridge Counselling Service, where he is developing a strong interest in the positive potential of improved relationships for individuals, organisations and communities. He has worked as an organisational development practitioner and coach for the BBC, BT, Pfizer and O2, as well as for training and change consultants The Mind Gym and The Storytellers. He has also worked as a senior lecturer for the NHS Leadership Academy in Suffolk and Norfolk, part of University Campus Suffolk (UCS). His early career was in journalism, television and new media. He is a registered member of UKCP – The United Kingdom Council for Psychotherapy. He has a Master's degree in Gestalt psychotherapy from the Metanoia Institute, London, and a Master's degree in organisational consulting from Ashridge International Business School
Email mark@cambridgecounsellingservice.co.uk

Frances Johnston PhD
Over the course of her career, Fran has coached senior leaders and worked with boards, leadership teams, and senior executives across the world from Global 500 companies to governments to non-governmental organisations. Fran consults on leadership, culture and organisational change, and she is noted for her ability to work within a system's complexity and to design elegant solutions. Through Teleos Leadership Institute and the Brookings Institution, Fran applies Gestalt principles to build the skills of today's and tomorrow's coaches. Fran received her PhD from Temple University, where she worked on adult and organisation development. Fran is a long-standing faculty at the Wharton School's Aresty Institute of Executive Education and a senior faculty member

of the Gestalt International Study Center in Cape Cod, Massachusetts, where she teaches their flagship course for senior executives. She also designs and facilitates classes at Brookings Institution Executive Education program in Washington, DC. Fran has taught at Temple University, Philadelphia College of the Sciences, the Community College of Philadelphia, and the Gestalt Institute of Cleveland. Fran is an author of the highly successful *Becoming a Resonant Leader* (Harvard Business School Press), a book used worldwide by coaches and leaders to deepen self-awareness and mindfulness. In her mind's eye, she is a performance artist, dancing and playing with her clients in service of planetary growth and evolution toward greater peace.
Email fjohnstone@teleosleaders.com

Robert Kolodny PhD
Robert Kolodny is a coach to groups and organizations and consults with a wide range of human systems in the US and abroad. He has a particular interest in the development and role of leaders, and in the evolution of Gestalt practice in fuller appreciation of its relational and field-theoretical core. His guiding professional vision is to help build more satisfying and effective workplace communities and to help create more just and democratic relations in civic affairs. Bob teaches at the Gestalt Institute of Cleveland and at the Gestalt International Study Center on Cape Cod. He has been on the faculty at Columbia University and at the New School University in New York City and has taught at a number of educational institutions around the world. Bob is a professional member of NTL, and a consultant with The Relational Center, Los Angeles.
Email rk@kolodnyassoc.com

Maggie Shelton
Maggie Shelton, LCSW, is a social worker who has spent her career working with systems of relationships. They range in size from one person to a community. Whether she is doing leadership coaching, organization development, public dialogue, teaching, workshop leading or psychotherapy, she is taking into account relational/contextual issues as a pivotal factor in problems that are often storied as individual. She is influenced by social constructionist theory and practice in all of these fields. She has a long history of being adjacent to Gestalt theory

and practice. That changed with her work and friendship with Mark Fairfield. His work in Relational Gestalt and that of other leaders in that field has overlapped with and enriched her approach. She is an avid practitioner of Tai Chi as well as a Buddhist. She lives in Los Angeles with her partner and their three dogs.
Email maggie@maggiesheltonlcsw.com

Georges Wollants

Georges Wollants, Lic.Psych.Ped.Sciences, has a background in coaching and training coaches in a multinational corporation. He was director of the Faculty for Man and Society in Belgium for over thirty years and a member of the Training Courses for Gestalt Therapy training faculty (FMS). He is a full member trainer and supervisor with the Dutch and Flemish Association for Gestalttherapie and Theory (NVAGT), a member of the European Association for Gestalt Therapy (EAGT), and a member of the Association for Gestalt Theory and its Applications (GTA). He has been the editor of the Vlaams-Nederlands Tijdschrift voor Gestalttherapie. His book, *Gestalt Therapy: Therapy of the Situation*, was published by Sage Publications Ltd. in 2012, to great critical acclaim from the Gestalt Therapy community.
Email georges.wollants@skynet.be

Selected Titles from GestaltPress

Organizational Consulting: A Gestalt Approach
Edwin C. Nevis

Gestalt Reconsidered: A New Approach to Contact and Resistance
Gordon Wheeler

Gestalt Therapy: Perspectives and Applications
Edwin C. Nevis, editor

The Collective Silence: German Identity and the Legacy of Shame
Barbara Heimannsberg Christopher J. Schmidt

Community and Confluence: Undoing the Clinch of Oppression
Philip Lichtenberg

Encountering Bigotry: Befriending Projecting Persons in Every Day Life
Philip Lichtenberg

On Intimate Ground: A Gestalt Approach to Working With Couples
Gordon Wheeler Stephanie Backman, editors

Body Process: Working With the Body in Psychotherapy
James I. Kepner

Here, Now, Next: Paul Goodman and the Origins of Gestalt Therapy
Taylor Stoehr

Crazy Hope Finite Experience
Paul Goodman, edited by Taylor Stoehr

In Search of Good Form: Gestalt Therapy With Couples and Families
Joseph C. Zinker

The Voice of Shame: Silence and Connection in Psychotherapy
Robert G. Lee & Gordon Wheeler, editors

Healing Tasks: Psychotherapy With Adult Survivors of Childhood Abuse
James I. Kepner

Adolescence: Psychotherapy and the Emergent Self
Mark McConville

Getting Beyond Sobriety: Clinical Approaches to Long-Term Recovery
Michael Craig Clemmens

Back to the Beanstock
Judith R. Brown

Becoming a Stepfamily
Patricia Papernow

The Dreamer and the Dream: Essays and Reflections on Gestalt Therapy
Rainette Eden Fants, edited by Arthur Roberts

A Well-Lived Life: Essays in Gestalt Therapy
Sylvia Fleming Crocker

From the Radical Center: The Heart of Gestalt Therapy
Irving and Miriam Polster

Beyond Individualism: Toward a New Understanding of Self, Relationship, and Experience
Gordon Wheeler

Sketches: An Anthology of Essays, Art Poetry
Joseph C. Zinker

The Heart of Development: Gestalt Approaches to Working With Children, Adolescents, and Their Worlds (2 Volumes)
Mark McConville Gordon Wheeler, editors

Body of Awareness: A Somatic Developmental Approach to Psychotherapy
Ruella Frank

The Values of Connection: A Relational Approach to Ethics
Robert G. Lee, editor

WindowFrames: Learning the Art of Gestalt Play Therapy the Oaklander Way
Peter Mortola

Gestalt Therapy: Living Creatively Today
Gonzague Masquelier

The Secret Language of Intimacy: Releasing the Hidden Power in Couple Relationships
Robert G. Lee

CoCreating the Field: Intention and Practice in the Age of Complexity
Deborah Ullman & Gordon Wheeler, editors

Relational Approaches in Gestalt Therapy
Lynne Jacobs & Rich Hycner, editors

Aggression, Time, and Understanding
Frank-M. Staemmler

Relational Child, Relational Brain: Development and Therapy in Childhood … Adolescence
Robert G. Lee & Neil Harris, editors

Even If It Costs Me My Life: Systemic Constellations and Serious Illness
Stephan Hausner

Mending the World
Joseph Melnick & Edwin C. Nevis, editors

Contact and Context: New Directions in Gestalt Coaching
Ty Francis & Malcolm Parlett, editors